CYCLING TO THE ASHES

CYCLING TO THE ASHES

A Cricketing Odyssey from London to Brisbane

Oli Broom

YELLOW JERSEY PRESS
LONDON

Published by Yellow Jersey Press 2013

2 4 6 8 10 9 7 5 3 1

First published in Great Britain in 2013 by
Yellow Jersey Press
Random House, 20 Vauxhall Bridge Road,
London SW1V 2SA

www.rbooks.co.uk

Addresses for companies within The Random House Group Limited can be
found at: www.randomhouse.co.uk/offices.htm

The Random House Group Limited Reg. No. 954009

A CIP catalogue record for this book
is available from the British Library

ISBN 978 0 22 409188 6

Photograph on final page of plate section courtesy of Philip Brown.
All photographs © Oli Broom except those contributed by
Viv Blewett, Selda Kural and Safdar Rahman.

The Random House Group Limited supports the Forest Stewardship Council®
(FSC®), the leading international forest-certification organisation. Our books
carrying the FSC label are printed on FSC®-certified paper. FSC is the only
forest-certification scheme supported by the leading environmental organisations,
including Greenpeace. Our paper procurement policy can be found at
www.randomhouse.co.uk/environment

Set in Baskerville BT 11.5/14.5pt
Typeset by Palimpsest Book Production Limited, Falkirk, Stirlingshire

Printed and bound in Great Britain by
Clays Ltd, St Ives plc

To Mum, Dad and Annabel . . . and to Peggy

CONTENTS

'Ever bike? Now that's something that makes life worth living!'
– Jack London

'Cricket brings the most opposite characters and the most diverse lives together. Anything that puts very many different kinds of people on a common ground must promote sympathy and kindly feelings'
– Kumar Shri Ranjitsinhji

'The aim of English cricket is, in fact, mainly to beat Australia'
– Jim Laker

LONDON TO BRISBANE

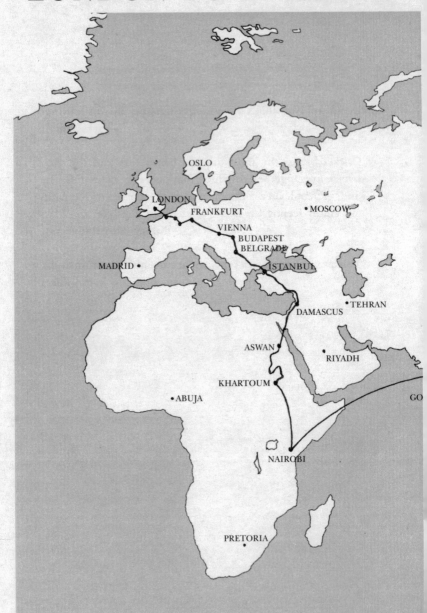

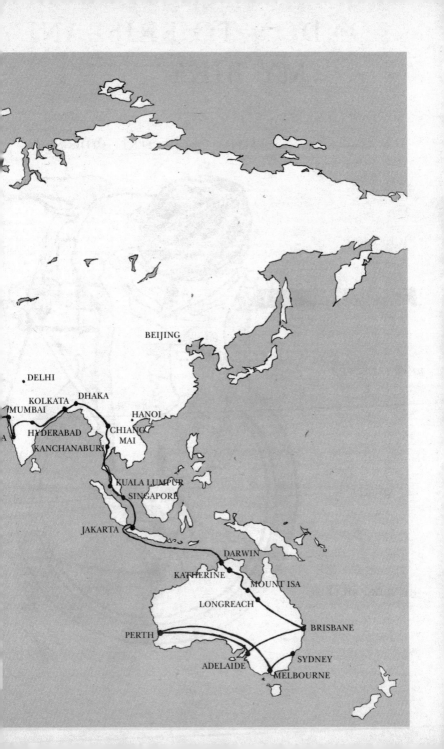

MY BIKE

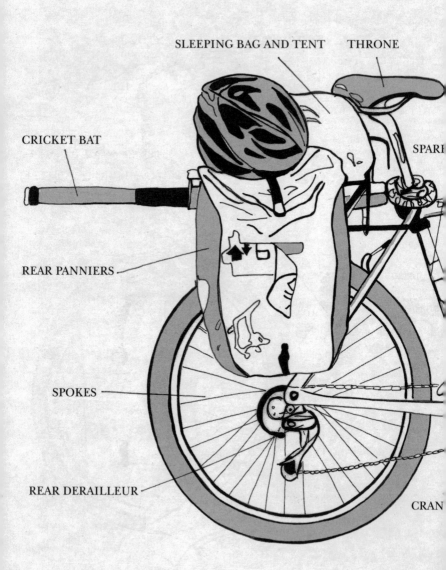

SLEEPING BAG AND TENT   THRONE

CRICKET BAT

SPARI

REAR PANNIERS

SPOKES

REAR DERAILLEUR

CRAN

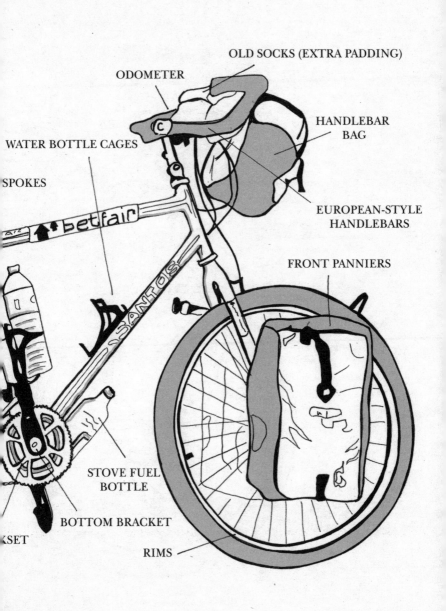

OLD SOCKS (EXTRA PADDING)

ODOMETER

HANDLEBAR BAG

WATER BOTTLE CAGES

SPOKES

EUROPEAN-STYLE HANDLEBARS

FRONT PANNIERS

STOVE FUEL BOTTLE

BOTTOM BRACKET

RIMS

betfair

SANTOS

INTRODUCTION

BREAKBONE – 30 June 2010

My bones ache to their core. I can hold down neither food nor drink. A rash covers my torso. My white blood cell count is perilously low and I am hours away from a blood transfusion. I weigh sixty-seven kilograms – fifteen kilos less than I did last October. From my hospital bed I can see a main road leading south out of town, snaking through uninterrupted jungle before climbing up and over a high ridge, out of sight towards the Burmese border. I should have ridden that road nearly two weeks ago but the past few months have pushed me to mental and physical breaking point. I have finally cracked.

A week ago I was found unconscious in a flower bed. After six days in my room with worsening flu I suffered a blackout trying to find water in my hostel. I fell, first into a large stone Buddha (knocking his head off, apparently), then down a rogue step and head-first into a stone ledge overhanging a cactus-filled flower bed. 'You must go hospital,' the hostel cleaner told me as I came round. Now it is three days until my thirtieth birthday and I am alone in northern Thailand, on an intravenous drip with breakbone, or dengue, fever and a black eye.

Thailand was supposed to be one of the more straightforward legs of my journey. After the cold of Turkey, the heat of Sudan and the ordeal of the Indian subcontinent, I had been looking forward to a fresh start in my nineteenth country; to pedalling hard, eating well, enjoying beautiful jungle and coastline in a country I had never visited before. On the ride into Chiang Mai I got a welcome shock to the system when I noted order and cleanliness on the streets. Drivers used their brains and occasionally their vehicles' brakes and indicators; no one spat in my direction. An Australian expat directed me to a hostel that turned out to have bed-bug-free beds; it even had a small swimming pool. Thailand had promised much.

Now the doctors tell me it will take at least three months to recover. In three months' time I am supposed to be on the boat to Australia to complete the final leg of my journey; a journey that has already provided me with enough ups and downs to last a lifetime, but one that I desperately want to finish.

I am more than two hundred bicycle days and ten thousand miles from home. I have not spoken more than a sentence to another soul in days; not to a friend for weeks. I am lonely. Since leaving London I have often felt strong, occasionally brave; now I am ill, weak and lacking an ounce of motivation. I want to fall into the arms of a loved one and tell them to take me home. Right now, quitting is the only option, which means the road has come to an end, and I have failed.

FIRST INNINGS

ENGLAND

LEAVING HOME – 10 October 2009

My alarm sounds a few minutes before six o'clock but I'm already awake, head throbbing from last night's leaving party. I roll over and hit the snooze button. Five minutes later I do the same, hiding under the duvet, pretending I've woken to just another day.

A knock on the door. Breakfast. Porridge. I peer behind the curtain to see what the weather is doing. It is still dark but I can make out the trees on the village green, swaying in a gusting wind; headwind or tailwind?

I muster the energy to crawl out of bed, find a towel and head for the shower; my last shower. I stand still until the water runs cold, eager to delay the inevitable. The porridge is stuck to the pan by the time I make it downstairs. Burnt. I gulp it down anyway. I'm going to need porridge today, of all days.

I HAD PACKED MY four panniers the night before and now they stood ominously by the front door, ready to be loaded into my dad's car; my tent, sleeping bag and, of course, my bicycle, too. We had all mucked in: Mum, Dad, my sister, Annabel, and me. We soon discovered that everything I would need for the next year fitted comfortably into the confined space at the back of a Volvo estate. Life was about to get a whole lot less cluttered.

I took one last look at the four walls I called home, prayed I would see them again soon and lowered myself into the passenger seat. There were no goodbyes before we pulled on to the B482 and began the half-hour journey to London. They would come later. The sun made a brief appearance in a very English sky shrouded in low-hanging early morning mist, but it quickly disappeared and would remain out of sight for the rest of the day. Pulling away from the traffic lights as we joined the M40, we reached seventy miles per hour within a few seconds and it occurred to me that it might be the fastest I would move for the next fourteen months. I hoped it would be. I had become so used to being mechanically transported to my destination, whether by car, train or aeroplane, that the thought of nothing but my spindly legs propelling me forwards was liberating. It was also, now that my departure loomed, terrifying. So while I could, I enjoyed the effortlessness of car travel until we turned into the car park at Lord's Cricket Ground in north-west London.

The ground is named after Thomas Lord, an eighteenth-century Yorkshireman who was a bowler and general attendant at London's White Conduit Club in the 1780s. In 1786 he was approached by members to find a private cricket ground and in May 1787 got hold of seven acres off Dorset Square in Marylebone.

I watched my first professional cricket match at Lord's in the late 1980s. It is the home of Marylebone Cricket Club and, some say (especially us English), the home of cricket. Like the game itself, Lord's is forever changing to keep up with modern times. The famous pavilion remains but many of the old stands have gone, replaced by flashier models, even since my first visit.

We reached the ground just before seven o'clock, but not the one off Dorset Square. The original lease ended in 1810 so he sought a second ground, which he developed and used until 1813 when again he had to move because the government requisitioned the land to build the Regent's Canal. Lord told his workers to literally pick up the turf and take it with them to a third ground in St John's Wood, on the corner of Wellington Road and St John's Wood Road. It opened in

1814 and is still there, revered by millions of cricket fans around the world.

This was the ground where Dad and I found ourselves. It was a Saturday in mid-October and there was little activity. The stands were empty and the grass was a long, lush green. It seemed sad and unloved; a strange sort of relic in the present. The last time I had been there the ground was full: 28,000 fans enjoying the latest England versus Australia encounter. But now the summer's momentous Ashes series, although less than two months past, was a distant memory. As Dad wheeled my bicycle to the Nursery End and I lugged my kit behind him, we did not see another soul until we found the Sky News cameraman who was to interview me at the start of my journey.

WHERE IT ALL BEGAN

In fact, my journey had really begun way back in 2002 – my third year of university – during a hot and humid summer spent as a hotel gardener in the small Andalucían village of Garrucha.

I had found a rusty old mountain bike collecting dust in the gardeners' shed. Before long I took to setting off each afternoon after work, riding west along the coast, up and down the conical hills that dot that corner of Spain. I rode as hard as I could, well beyond nightfall, returning tired, hungry and eager for more. I was soon as fit as I had ever been and, as the weeks passed, I became excited at the thought of one day continuing west beyond Almería instead of returning to another day manicuring hedges and mowing lawns. While England and India played all summer for a drawn Test series, and Sven-Göran Eriksson led England to another ignominious end to a World Cup campaign in Japan, I spent my evenings scheming a summer of cycling. The urge came out of nowhere and it surprised me as much as those who knew me.

I had flirted with mountain biking during my first two years at university – the odd weekend spent in the Brecon Beacons – but I had not, until then, considered long-distance cycling to be the sort of thing I might take to. Now I bought maps and guidebooks and, lying on the cool floor of my air-conditioned apartment, plotted a route from Garrucha along the south coast to Gibraltar and back across the width of North Africa from Morocco to Cairo, from where I would fly home. It would be an epic desert journey that would take me into a remote and alien world I had always wanted to explore, just not, until now, on my bicycle.

The desert epic never happened, a lack of funds playing a major part in its demise. By late July I was back in England laying bricks and cutting hedges, earning as much as I could to get me through my fourth year at university. I moved to London soon afterwards and five years practising as a chartered surveyor followed. My pedal-powered desert ambitions became a distant memory. I only ever cycled to work and even those sporadic efforts were hindered by the many bicycle thieves that trawl residential London. I had rewarding relationships with nice girls and a degree of financial stability. I was so happy with life in London that I barely even considered the future.

Before I knew it, it was 2008. Five years had passed since I'd left university. Friends were being promoted, getting married, having babies, buying houses. Meanwhile, I could not have been further from doing any of these things and, as my peer group diverged, I was forced to think hard about what I wanted out of life. Was London the be-all and end-all? Was sitting on a train for two hours and at a desk for up to eleven hours each day what I was made for? Where would I find the girl I could see myself with forever? How would I begin to save money for a mortgage? Did I even *want* to get promoted? Did I really love my job that much?

Finding time to think in London is difficult, but eventually it came down to the job. I realised that I had never been really enthusiastic about what I did every day, and that, therefore,

I was wasting my life. I began thinking of possible new career paths but there seemed to be so many to choose from and so many that appealed. It was then, towards the end of 2008, that I began to feel the lure of adventure once again.

BIRTH OF A CONCEPT

17 November 2008
Dear Mum, Dad and Annabel,

Before you see the length of this letter and begin to think that something is wrong, don't worry; there is nothing wrong. What follows is an explanation of my desire to quit my job to have an adventure. The purpose of putting this down on paper is not to obtain your permission (I know I don't need that), but to obtain your support in my efforts. And why write? Well, I know I can explain myself far better on paper than I can in person.

All three of you know that I suffer from a serious malady; a malady known as wanderlust. I want to satisfy this by undertaking a challenge so vast that I don't know if I can complete it. Whilst I have suffered wanderlust for years, and have at times sought to satisfy the symptoms by buggering off to places like India and Morocco, I have always recognised the need to avoid another affliction of many my age, and that is poverty. Through hard work, I have tried to earn enough money to live in London and save for a mortgage. But over the years I've saved so little.

I want to wake up every morning and think: 'I can't wait for today; I wonder what will happen; I wonder who I'll meet.' I don't do this because I don't love my job. I love my friends, I love the three of you, but I don't love what I spend fifty hours a week doing: sitting at a desk trying to make money for myself (which isn't working) and money for other people (which is working rather better).

Perhaps you will think I am running away. But I feel I am

7

running towards something instead. I have always talked about heading off on an adventure and the talk needs to stop. I've got to stop settling, stop being average, stop making excuses, stop worrying about actions and consequences. Life in London has been risk-free for years and the lack of spontaneity and excitement has begun to suffocate me. I want to shape my life, not let the weeks and months and years shape me. I want to forge a new path, away from the well-worn one I am treading in London; to take a step back from the chaos and pace of the city and find space and time and simplicity on a journey that I can pour my soul into. A selfish quest for old-fashioned hardship and endurance needs to begin! Remember that line from Jerry Maguire: *'That's how you get great, man; hang your balls on the line.' Well, I'm not looking for greatness; I'll settle for 'goodness' to begin with and see how I do. That will only happen if I take a risk, if I create opportunities for myself by following my dreams now and in the future.*

So what will this adventure be? Well, I don't quite know yet, but I know it'll be on a bicycle. You know as well as I do that I have not cycled much since my time in Spain. But I loved cycling in those days – battling big hills, getting fit – and have always regretted not setting off across North Africa as I had planned. If I take on the challenge of cycling across a vast land mass and succeed, I think I'll be suitably proud of my achievement. If I don't succeed then at least I will have tried.

I have told a few friends of my plan and they were all supportive. Alex said that if he wasn't married he would come; Tom said he'd come even though he is married. But I want to undertake my journey alone.

Writing this letter has had the unexpected but welcome effect of helping me understand my reasons for wanting such an adventure. At the same time, I hope some of my reasoning has helped you understand too. I am certain that your first reaction has been 'Bloody hell!' but hopefully soon it'll be 'Bloody cool!' If I do this properly and give it my all and use it as a springboard for the rest of my life, then I'm sure you'll support me because that's what you have done my whole life.

And now that you know the basics of what I am planning, I hope we can talk in more detail, and that you'll help me with the next step – deciding where to go, and planning it all.

Love as always
Oli

PS Oh, and I intend to pay for the adventure myself, so you don't have to worry about money. I've started saving already – £500 in the bank (a long way to go!).

In December 2008, about a month after I wrote that life-changing letter to my parents and sister, the idea of travelling to Australia by bicycle first came about. My flatmate Becca was due to move to Sydney. As we wondered aloud on a short tube journey from Oxford Circus to Notting Hill Gate as to when we would next see each other, she casually suggested that if I was to cycle anywhere it should be to visit her, in Australia.

I had been racking my brains for a plan that would turn my vague notion of an adventure into firm reality. Becca's idea appealed and not just because she would be there to greet me when I arrived. I also knew that the next instalment of the Ashes was due to begin in Brisbane at the end of 2010, and that if I was to cycle halfway around the planet, it would help to have a scheduled event to aim for.

As soon as Becca and I got home I began a caffeine-powered all-nighter, plotting various concepts, routes and timetables. I got my atlas out and, with the use of a thumb and index finger (one thumb width was about two hundred miles), I calculated that a route through Europe, the Middle East, Asia and Australia was feasible if I left before the end of 2009. At first light I went out for some fresh air, wandering past the shut-up shops and markets of Portobello Road, chuckling to myself as I imagined explaining to people along the way what I was up to: 'I know it sounds a bit daft, but I'm cycling to a cricket match on the other side of the world. Yes, I could have flown, you're right . . . yes, it would have been a lot cheaper but, well, I wouldn't have met you, would I?'

Cricket has dominated my sporting life for as long as I can remember: on the playing fields at school; representing my county in the summer holidays; and, most of all, following the fluctuating fortunes of the England cricket team each summer. Test cricket has provided a narrative and dramatic spectacle to every summer since I fell in love with the game in 1988, when I was seven. I know it was then because that was the summer I did not speak to my best friend for two weeks because he ran me out in a school match.

In June of the same year in another school match I made the controversial yet noble decision to piss in my box rather than give my wicket away. In hindsight it was a poor decision because I was out in the next over and had to waddle off to the loo to tidy myself up anyway. But yes, I can look back with confidence now and say that the summer of 1988 was the summer I fell in love with cricket. Apart from Boris Becker and Seve Ballesteros, my earliest sporting heroes were all cricketers: Ian Botham, David Gower, Malcolm Marshall, Michael Atherton, Curtly Ambrose, Shane Warne. At secondary school I would try to bat like Gower, mimicking the fluidity of his stroke play to such an extent that for a whole summer, to my delight, my nickname became DG. It did not occur to me until much later that perhaps my team-mates had a greater grasp of irony than I imagined. The following summer I barely scored a run and the nickname disappeared forever.

I decided that having the Ashes – one of the oldest and greatest sporting rivalries – to aim for would provide me with the perfect motivational tool. The Ashes have come to embody the proud cricketing traditions of England and Australia. The series, which takes place every two years, alternating between the two countries, is regarded as the pinnacle for players from both nations. And it is the pinnacle of the sport for millions of fans, including me. I imagined the last few pedal strokes of millions as I rolled up to the Brisbane Cricket Ground (or 'The Gabba' as it is affectionately known) on the morning of the first Test match, ordering a well-earned cold beer as I took my seat. I could not conceive of a finer ending to a long bicycle ride.

By the time I had returned to Becca's flat off the Portobello Road, my mind was made up. Put simply, I would cycle from England to Australia to watch the sixty-sixth edition of the Ashes, which was due to begin in 709 days, in Brisbane, on 25 November 2010. I could not wait, but I had a lot of preparation to do before I could set off.

FOR THE LOVE OF CRICKET

The Ashes story began at The Oval on 29 August 1882, when Australia beat England on English turf for the first time. The next day the *Sporting Times* published a mock obituary of English cricket, joking that its 'body will be cremated and the ashes taken to Australia'. Cricket was at the height of its popularity with followers, thanks to improved and cheaper railway services, able to travel the length and breadth of the country to watch heroes they had previously only read about. The obituary caught the imagination of the general public and the tour to Australia the following winter was one of the most anticipated sporting occasions in English history. The England captain, the Honourable Ivo Bligh, promised to 'beard the kangaroo in his den and try and recover those ashes'. His Australian counterpart, Billy Murdoch, responded somewhat less imaginatively by promising to defend them using the same winning team.

The tour did not begin well for England. On the six-week voyage to Australia the team's vessel, SS *Peshawur*, collided with another ship a couple of hundred miles south of Colombo. Most of the players were fortunate to escape unhurt, although fast bowler Fred Morley wasn't so lucky. He broke two ribs and, despite managing a couple of games while in Australia, his health deteriorated so severely that he died of congestion and dropsy, thought to be a result of his injuries, in 1884.

Still, on the pitch the tour turned out to be a success for the England team. In the first Test, held at the Melbourne Cricket Ground, Murdoch's Australian XI were too good and won easily, by nine wickets. The second Test, also in Melbourne, was equally one-sided, although it was England who emerged triumphant, winning by an innings amid angry debate as to which team's bowlers should have been held responsible for the extreme deterioration of the pitch. Following the controversy, it was agreed that the third and final match of the series would be played on two pitches in Sydney. The English won the match, and with it the series.

It was at a social occasion following the series, near Melbourne on Christmas Eve 1882, that Bligh was given a small terracotta urn to symbolise 'the ashes' he had succeeded in recovering. He met his Australian wife on the same day and the urn stayed on the mantelpiece at the Bligh family home until Ivo's death forty-three years later. It was then bequeathed to Marylebone Cricket Club. These days it rarely leaves a glass cabinet in the Lord's Museum and even the winning captain only gets to hold aloft a replica.

When I began planning my journey, it did not escape my attention that, for the first time in years, England had a decent chance of winning down under. In 2005 the team had succeeded in galvanising the British sporting public and had temporarily replaced football on the nation's back pages. They went toe to toe with, and eventually triumphed over, one of the greatest Australian sides of all time. It was their first victory over the old enemy in an Ashes series since 1987 and, although the status quo was re-established when Australia hammered England 5-0 in 2006-07, England were once again the bookmakers' favourite for the upcoming 2009 series. If they won, they would be favourites to win down under in 2010-11, when I hoped to be there to watch.

In July the 2009 series got under way. During the day I followed its twists and turns via the ball-by-ball commentary from my desk in the office on Baker Street. Meanwhile, in the evenings I was planning my journey, thinking up ways to get the most out of fourteen months on the road. As I pored over maps of Europe, Africa, Asia and Australia, I began to wonder what all of the countries would be like. More specifically, I started to think about where en route I might be able to find the odd game of cricket. My transcontinental bicycle ride from London to Brisbane quickly became a cricketing odyssey.

Full of quirks, nuances and traditions, the game of cricket is said to be the epitome of Englishness. But although its roots are planted firmly in seventeenth-century rural England, the British exported their favourite pastime to all corners of the Empire during the nineteenth and early twentieth centuries. I began to look for obvious locations for potential matches, suspecting they would be the only cricketing outposts on my way to Brisbane. I knew I could find a game on the Mumbai Maidan, where Sachin Tendulkar learned his trade, for example, and hoped to have a hit at any number of Australian outback cricket clubs.

But as I continued my search I discovered that cricket's tentacles had spread further than I had anticipated, far beyond the Commonwealth. Although the sport's governing body, the International Cricket Council (ICC), count only ten countries as Full Members, their website told me there were in fact thirty-six Associate Members and a further fifty-nine Affiliate Members. There were 104 formal cricketing nations, with countries such as Papua New Guinea, Sierra Leone and Rwanda among them. Cricket, a closed, British-owned-and-run shop for hundreds of years, seemed to have survived the turbulent middle years of the twentieth century and since thrived in some incredibly unlikely locations that had little affiliation to Britain. I became hungry to learn more about the game around the world and decided that my expedition would become a journey through which I would attempt to learn more about cricket's own global odyssey. I vowed to play cricket in as many countries as I could along the way.

By the end of August, when Mike Hussey popped a catch up to Alastair Cook to hand England their second home series against Australia in as many attempts, I had quit my job and was free of the shackles of my nine-to-five. Now I was working full time to realise my dream of seeing the next series from the stands of The Gabba, having cycled 14,000 miles to get there.

I set a leaving date of 10 October, giving me less than two months to finalise plans. I needed sponsors. They were hard to come by initially, but after the first one came on board it became easier to persuade people to buy into the concept of my ride. Momentum began to build and I was offered GPS equipment, cameras, solar panels, hats, clothes, sandals, a sleeping bag and a tent. I asked Mongoose Cricket if they would donate bats for me to give to cricket teams as I travelled, and was delighted when their chief executive took a punt and they became a major sponsor.

By mid-September, with three weeks until the start of my trip, I had everything I needed but still not enough financial support. I had saved very little since coming up with the plan – enough to get me to Belgrade perhaps, but certainly not to Brisbane. I had spent hours on the phone begging unsuspecting marketing directors at many of the world's largest firms to sponsor a bloke with a bike and a plan, but to no avail. I began to worry that I might have to delay my departure; cancel even. But then, in the space of a ten-minute phone call, everything changed. The head of sponsorship at Betfair called me up and asked if I still needed a main sponsor. When I told him that, yes, the main expedition sponsor slot was still available he replied, 'Fantastic. We would love to get involved.' If I could have bitten his hand off down the phone I would have. Disaster had been averted and I gratefully accepted his offer.

By the beginning of October I was kit and cash-ready. I had chosen two charities for whom I wanted to raise money – the

Lord's Taverners for the work they do for underprivileged children in the UK, and the British Neurological Research Trust, who are supported by a friend, James, who was paralysed in a freak accident in 2005. I had worked hard to publicise my trip as a way of raising money and my efforts were rewarded with some great media coverage in the lead-up to my departure. Only one thing worried me: it had been more than ten months since I had sat on a bicycle. In January 2009 I had cycled a roundabout route to Paris with a friend, to see if I could manage a few days in the saddle. My perverse belief was that if I could cope for eight days, I could manage more than a year. We made it to Paris, but only just, because my knee gave me so much trouble. Still, I told myself I would find a better bicycle and vowed to rest my knee. Little did I know the next time I would even sit on a bicycle saddle would be at the start of a 14,000-mile journey to the other side of the world.

DEPARTURE

The day of my departure had arrived. As I stood in Lord's Cricket Ground, waiting for my interview with Sky News to start, my head felt ready, but my body felt far from it. So much had happened already but now I had to do what I'd promised.

It had been a hell of a week. Australian fast-bowling legend and purge of the English Jeff Thomson had got me out, caught and bowled, in Green Park; Jonathan Agnew had interviewed me on *Test Match Special*; Steve Bunce, of *Fighting Talk* fame, called to have a chat on BBC London; accompanied by my shiny, as yet unused bicycle, I had met John Edrich, Tom Graveney and Chris Tarrant at the Lord's Taverners England Captains' Dinner at the Park Lane Hilton; I'd spoken to students at Caldicott School about my trip, promising to return in a year and a half when I'd have some stories to tell; and I'd been called a 'cricket tragic' on a couple of Australian radio shows that had somehow heard about my expedition (I expected it wouldn't be the last time I'd be so named).

'Five, four, three, two, one . . . on air!'

The earpiece fell to the floor and I scrabbled around trying to pick it up and stuff it back in. It was a less than ideal start to the world of live television broadcasting.

After the interview, during which I had done my best to sound confident of my ability to succeed, nerves began to kick in, fuelled largely by uncertainty surrounding the strength of my knee. It occurred to me that if I was flying, I would have been confident of my eventual arrival down under. I would have sat in a cramped airline seat, every need attended to by a chirpy, perma-tanned flight attendant. I would have watched in-flight movies, eaten cardboard chicken tikka masala and drunk red wine from an improbably small plastic bottle until I fell asleep or passed out. I would have snored a lot and dribbled a fair bit. After almost a day travelling five hundred miles per hour at 35,000 feet above the earth's surface, my collar would have been wet and it is likely I wouldn't have been friends with the person sitting next to me, but I probably would have touched down on a strip of tarmac 14,000 miles away. In fact, I would have had a 1 in 5.4 million chance of not arriving safely at my destination.

Of course, I wasn't flying. I was cycling and although I had come a long way since conceiving such a notion, I didn't have a clue if I would get close to my destination, let alone make it all the way there. My legs had never taken on such a challenge before. Would they survive? Would I survive? I would be pouring sweat and tears into each pedal stroke, progressing inch by inch with every turn of my wheels. Effort the like of which I had never expended would be required day after day to scale mountains; deserts would bring endless emptiness; people would offer hospitality, but surely danger, too. Off the back of six years at a desk it suddenly all seemed so far-fetched and ridiculous.

Friends and well-wishers began to arrive and although I struggled to ignore the magnitude of what I was attempting, I was soon swept away by their enthusiasm and support. I had invited a few close friends to join me on the ride to Dover and it turned out that I would have seventeen companions; a gentle introduction to cycle touring for all of us. Some were excited, some nervous (for me or for themselves?). A few cried off. One phoned to tell me he didn't feel equipped to cycle for two hours, let alone two days. I wanted to tell him that was how I felt, but decided to keep any lingering doubts about my fitness and preparedness to myself. I would miss all of them, especially my ex-girlfriend, Kate. We had broken up a few months earlier when I'd told her I wanted to cycle to the other side of the world. Unsurprisingly it was not what she was looking for in a boyfriend. There at Lord's, about to set off on the journey I had been dreaming about for so long, it occurred to me, not for the first time, that I was incredibly selfish for risking, and probably throwing away, a great relationship in the name of personal endeavour. I believed I had lost her and it hurt a lot.

I was presented with a replica Ashes urn by Marylebone Cricket Club and promised I would turn up with it in Brisbane in fourteen months' time. And then, before I knew it, I had taken the first pedal strokes of millions, rolling unsteadily towards an avenue of friends and well-wishers inside the Grace Gates. I would see my family again in Dover but, to most, it was goodbye. We set off along St John's Wood Road, Baker Street, past the office I had left two months before, and then the tears came in wave after wave, so that by the time we reached Wigmore Hall I could barely see the road. Excitement, pride, anxiety and fear consumed me, but I knew I had taken a huge step on my way to Australia: my wheels had begun turning. In those few moments I had changed from a slightly overweight Englishman with a dream, into an Englishman who had set out to achieve his dream. I was still overweight, of course, although that would soon change.

Leaving Lord's.

We passed the high ramparts of the Tower of London, crossed the famous old bridge directly to its east and navigated our way safely down the Old Kent Road – where I had made my first unsuccessful bicycle shopping trip months before – and onwards, through south-east London. Before long the endless drone of the city was replaced by silence and we were alone in the Garden of England, heaving ourselves up Kent's hills and flying down them at speed, past oast houses and along secluded, deserted sections of the ancient Pilgrims' Way. I relished the comradeship afforded by friendship on the road.

I was always at the back, the least fit of the group and burdened with the heaviest bicycle, struggling to keep up. While most of my friends climbed the hills as if they weren't there, I attacked them as though they were Himalayan peaks. My knee was already giving me serious pain and feeding my anxieties. At the top of one climb I saw my friends huddled ahead and shouted at them: 'Can I change my mind?' But

I didn't want to really. I knew my task would become easier by the day.

At the end of the first day's ride we collapsed exhausted in the dorm house we had booked for the night. We opened a beer each but not one got finished. Bodies lay strewn on floors and beds and groans of pain came from all corners. We were shattered. More importantly, my knee was in bad shape. I'd wrapped an ice pack around it but by the middle of the night it had flooded the bed. I writhed in agony and became more and more certain that I'd have to delay my departure. I felt pathetic. But in the morning the doctor in our group told me to stop wallowing in self-pity, that 'not all pain is bad', and to get back on my bicycle. With her stern words ringing in my ears I resolved to do exactly that, and continued with a depleted squad of ten towards Dover.

Later that afternoon, near the village of Meopham, I enjoyed the pleasant coincidence of rounding a hedged bend to see a Lord's Taverners minibus parked in a muddy lay-by. It was being used to transport students from the Helen Allison School for children with autism to their homes and served as a timely reminder that the money I was hoping to raise would go to a worthy cause.

By early evening the group was seven and we had made it to Dover. It was time for final goodbyes. My friends rode out of the ferry terminal car park to catch the train that would take them back to their stable lives and careers in London. My family and Kate remained. Saying goodbye to them was the hardest thing I had ever done but rounding the terminal building, pushing my bicycle along the yellow line that guided me to the ferry, I knew that I had made the right decision in setting off on the adventure of a lifetime.

FRANCE, BELGIUM
AND LUXEMBOURG

SOME APPLES AND A ROGUE CABBAGE

I WAS GLAD to escape the brightly carpeted cafeteria confines of the ferry in Dunkerque, but not before I noted in my diary that 'the next time I will need any form of transport other than my two wheels I'll have crossed two continents and reached the Red Sea'. I hoped I was right.

Diary tucked safely inside my handlebar bag, I rode into pitch darkness towards a distant cluster of lights where I thought I might find a bed. I had thirty euros for my first night's accommodation and if the hotel I selected was no more than adequate, in the coming months I would look back on it as a haven of luxury.

I have always liked the French, which made me all the more angry when, upon inspecting my bicycle the following morning, at the start of my first day on mainland Europe, I discovered that my front and rear lights had disappeared from the locked toilet in which I'd been advised to leave my bicycle. The night guard's blatant disregard made me furious but pedalling away from the hotel I managed to calm myself and even chuckled at the luck of being the victim of the world's worst thief. After all, what sort of self-respecting criminal, having broken into a disabled toilet and come face to face with a bicycle of not inconsiderable value, a camera, laptop, sleeping bag and tent, decides to unscrew and wander off with a couple of cheap bicycle lights? It was with dampened spirits, but the knowledge that I had been dealt an early blow and that things could only get better, that I set off for Belgium, my third country in two days.

Things actually got better a lot quicker than I had hoped. Shortly after stopping for my first continental lunch – my legs struggling to ease into their task and my knee throbbing with each pedal stroke – a passing motorist encouraged me to pull over to the side of the road. Without so much as a 'bonjour', the young man delved into his car boot and pulled out a box of apples and a rogue cabbage. He laid the box by my side and, in a heavy accent that I later learned was Flemish, introduced himself: 'Hello, my name is Frank. The garden of my grandmother has so much fruit and vegetables; you must take some.'

I must have stared at Frank with disbelief written across my face but he soon explained the reason behind his generosity. 'I saw the sign on the back of your bicycle!' he said, pointing at the sign my dad had had mocked up by an estate agent in Maidenhead a few days earlier. It read simply LONDON TO BRISBANE – FOR CHARITY and had my website in my own handwriting underneath. 'From here to Brisbane on this bicycle? How long will this take? You are alone? For what are you doing this? Are you crazy fool? What is the Ashes?' Frank asked a lot of questions. But I was in no hurry – the Ashes were not due to start for another 409 days – and I was happy to indulge him for a while. As he sat and listened, I did my best first to explain the game of cricket and then to talk him through the Ashes. Frank did not believe that anyone would do such a foolish thing as to give up a perfectly decent career to cycle to Australia to watch a series of cricket matches. I assured him they would.

At the start of his walk to Constantinople in 1933, Patrick Leigh Fermor found himself in the Dutch town of Dordrecht when he noted, after falling asleep in a waterfront bar and being taken in by the old landlady, that it was 'the first marvellous instance of a kindness and hospitality that was to occur again and again on these travels'. I would look back at the end of my own journey and conjure exactly the same feelings about Frank, but for now he simply got back in his car, wished me good luck and drove off. I would not see him again. I sat on the grass for a while, contemplating my encounter with a kind stranger and his generosity at leaving me with the nutritional contents of his car boot. Then I searched for a home in my panniers for my newly acquired fruit and vegetables and got back on my bicycle, continuing where I had left off, cycling eastwards towards Ypres and, of course, Australia.

MY BICYCLE

When I cycled to Paris in January 2009, I did so on an old, nine-gear, steel-framed Claud Butler mountain bike that I bought on eBay for £15. I loaded the back with two panniers and a tent and set off for the Eiffel Tower. If all went well, I planned to ride the same bike all the way to Australia later in the year.

It was a terrible idea. The bike was a disaster and even to consider taking it on a ride of more than a few days was foolish. Apart from being far too small for me, meaning my back was constantly hunched and my legs never got close to extending, the gearing system was so inefficient that on some gentle inclines I was forced to get off and push. Laura, my companion on that trip, had no problems with her bike and when we returned to England was a picture of health, while my knee gave me so much pain that I could not walk for a week and did not exercise for three months.

When I decided to give cycling to Australia a go I told myself the only reason I had struggled so much in Paris was because of the bike and that, although my budget was seriously limited, I would simply have to find some way of finding a decent bike. I phoned various manufacturers, promising lots of publicity in return for a free bicycle. Most politely informed me that they did not offer sponsorship deals and a couple even laughed down the phone at me. I could not blame them. I was a nobody, and certainly unable to offer any sort of concrete publicity campaign. Would they really benefit to the tune of around £3,000?

One man, who claimed to be the UK agent for Dutch bicycle manufacturer Santos, did not offer an outright refusal straight away and so I hounded him for weeks (daily phone calls, begging emails – I had no shame) and eventually secured a 30 per cent discount for a £2,500 bike. At that point – two months before the start of my trip – I did not have £2,000 for the entire expedition, let alone for the bicycle, but it was all I had so I blindly accepted on the basis that I would find a way of paying for it by the time I left England in October.

In September I went for an ergonomic bike fitting in a shop on the south coast of England. There and then we chose the components for my bicycle and sent the design to Amsterdam. By late September my planned expedition had received a fair bit of press. A few Berkshire and Buckinghamshire newspapers had picked up on the local boy pedalling to watch the Ashes; I had been interviewed on *Test Match Special* and the *Daily Telegraph* had even done a small piece. Importantly, I had arranged to write regular blogs and columns for the *Wisden Cricketer* and the *Royal Over-Seas League* magazine. A bit of exposure was exactly the sort of thing potential sponsors were looking for. I called the England and Wales Cricket Board to ask if there was anything they could do to help and a couple of hours later I heard back that they would be delighted. They bought my bicycle for me, complete with 30 per cent discount.

I picked up my bicycle on 7 October, three days before I left England. It was a sturdy, electric-blue steel machine that, unlike my rusty Claud Butler, certainly looked capable of carrying me all the way to Australia. I fitted 26-inch wheels that I had had made for me before the Paris trip; four hardy Ortleib panniers to front and rear wheel racks; and an odometer, to the handlebars, which would tell me how fast I was going, how far I had gone and my average speed. The handlebars themselves were 'European-style' and offered three different riding positions. Since the bicycle was ergonomically fitted for me, all the riding positions were comfortable and I loved it from the first moment I rode it. I knew that, far from being a solo bicycle expedition as I had advertised, it would be a partnership from the moment I left Lord's.

HISTORY LESSONS: BATTLEFIELDS, BEER AND A BELGIAN GAME CALLED CRICKET

I had never before felt compelled to visit Belgium, but as I rode alongside a canal that cut a geometric path through expansive, open farmland and the occasional sleepy, waterside village, I felt glad to be there. The country that gave the world the saxophone, Tintin, Django Reinhardt, The Smurfs, the waffle and not a lot else also gave a novice cyclist a gentle introduction to European cycle touring. The ride was flat, the weather warm, the people friendly yet pleasantly uninterested and I progressed at my own pace, enjoying the freedom and gentle rhythm afforded by life spent straddling an uncomfortable piece of rubber.

It was late afternoon by the time I found myself bouncing along the narrow, cobbled streets of Ypres, pulling up opposite the town's imposing thirteenth-century Cloth Hall and collapsing on to a wooden bench to rest my weary legs. Forty paltry miles had finished me, sending my right knee into sharp spasm once again – *not all pain is bad – remember that – not all pain is bad. . . .*

Dazed, I watched hordes of tourists wander aimlessly across the Market Square, presumably to and from the town's historical attractions. Busloads of schoolchildren sporting colourful Invicta rucksacks – compulsory kit for any self-respecting Italian teenager – sat around enjoying the early evening sun, sneaking the odd sip of some filthy liquor when their teachers weren't looking. As shop-tenders locked up at the end of their day's trading, outdoor bars filled, mostly with elderly bearded men in cardigans whose eyes flicked from one young female tourist to the next.

I had arranged to stay with local historian Steven Reynaert, a tall, jovial, barrel-chested man with heavy beard, heavy Flemish accent and, as it turned out, heavy alcohol tolerance. I followed him back to the house he shared with his wife, Isabel, and their two children where, over a dinner of fish fingers and chips, we chatted about our respective lives and careers while I was encouraged with increasing insistence to sample most of the contents of Steven's cellar.

Beer. Asking a Belgian man if he would like a beer is a bit like asking a Millwall fan if he'd like a fight: more often than not, the answer is 'Of course!'. Not that I had to do the asking at Steven's place. A series of bottles containing some of the finest nectar on the planet were simply placed in front of me, one after the other, for my swilling pleasure. De Koninck, Kwak, Deus, Orval, Verboden Vrucht: names that meant nothing to me until Steven talked me through the texture, taste and history of each one. He did, however, save his most exalted praise for the last bottle to appear before me: a plain, unlabelled, dark-brown bottle containing, I learned, a beer of legendary status.

Westvleteren ales are rare, world-famous Trappist beers made by Cistercian monks at St Sixtus monastery, not far from Ypres. The monastery was founded in 1831. Seven years later the monks started brewing, initially to feed their thirst – they were allowed two light beers each day – and eventually to feed the upkeep of the monastery.

Production slowed during the First World War, when the monastery was used to look after injured Allied troops, and again during the Second World War. But it never stopped and since 1946 the monks have been maintaining their six hours of prayer a day (first prayer 3.30a.m.) while churning out 60,000 cases of the finest beer in the world each year. The rich, dark-brown Westvleteren Abt 12 I drank with Steven had 10.2 per cent alcohol content and has been named best beer in the world more than once.

I asked Steven where I could buy some. 'Nowhere but the monastery' came the reply. In fact, so in demand are the Westvleteren beers that customers have to phone a special 'beer line' to book a time to visit the monastery to make their purchase. Buyers are limited to very few cases per visit and only one visit every sixty days per person, per phone number and per car number plate. It occurred to me that I prefer my beer a little more widely available, but I did relish each swig and, after slurping the last few molecules from the bottle's base I felt more than ready for a hard-earned kip.

Ypres is renowned for more than its beer. As well as having the dubious honour of being twinned with Hiroshima, it is famous for the atrocities that took place there between 1914 and 1918 when it was the focus of sustained German attention (not a good thing in those days).

I spent the day after my Belgian beer education touring various Commonwealth graves and battlefields with Martin O'Connor, a New Zealander whose interest in nearby battles first brought him to Belgium in 1991, and who has been there ever since. Martin also happened to be the general manager of Cricket Belgium. When the England cricket team visited Ypres a few months before me, it was Martin who showed them the battlefields and graves, including those of many British sportsmen who died while serving their country. Stuart Broad laid a specially made stone cricket ball at the graveside of former England and Kent left-arm spinner Colin Blythe – Ashes hero in Australia in 1901–02 – who, after being one of the first cricketers to sign up for active service in 1914 despite suffering from epilepsy, died in the Battle of Passchendaele three years later. When Martin and I reached the grave there was a weathered, warping mini cricket bat beside it. The headstone read:

49296 Serjeant
C. Blythe
King's Own L. I.
8th November 1917 Age 38
In Loving Memory of
My Dear Husband
The Kent and England Cricketer

The grave of Ashes hero, Colin Blythe, with cricket bat and ball at its base

Later that evening we visited the Menin Gate, the vast arch commemorating those British and Commonwealth soldiers who lost their lives during the Great War and whose resting places are unknown. There are more than 58,000 names on the memorial and, at exactly eight o'clock every evening since 1928 (except during German occupation of France during the Second World War) hundreds of people gather underneath the arch to remember those who died. As members of the local fire brigade played the Last Post before a crowd of more than four hundred, I and a handful of other visitors had the honour of laying wreaths. I laid a wreath on behalf of my two charities but some laid them to commemorate family members whose names were inscribed on the walls surrounding us. Their presence served as a brutal reminder that the horrors had played out less than two generations before.

My feelings during the short time I spent in Ypres tended towards embarrassment at the triviality of what I was attempting. I felt guilty that my life had been such a relative walk in the park, and thinking about the horrors that had occurred at Ypres gave me a very real sense of feeling lucky to have the time and means to head off on a meaningless jaunt to the other side of the world. I was lucky to be alive, and not just alive, but living in a time that allowed such frivolous adventure.

Before I left Belgium I had two more cricket-related stops to make. The first was a pleasant evening spent drinking more beer with Tom van Poucke and a couple of his team-mates from the Arcadians Cricket Club in Ghent. Nestled in the corner of a bar that felt more American Midwest than Western Europe I learned that, six months earlier, new research had claimed that the most English of sports in fact had its roots in Flanders. The research was based on a 1533 poem attributed to the English poet John Skelton in which he referred to Flemish weavers who settled in southern England being the 'kings of crekettes'. Then again the research was conducted by an Australian (upset by England's recent Ashes success?) in cahoots with a German who, in another recent research paper, had claimed that golf, rather than emanating from Scotland, had been invented in Belgium as well.

Whatever the truth, it is clear that Belgian cricket has a distinguished history. The first record of organised cricket there is found in a painting from 1870 which now hangs in the Pavilion at Lord's and shows the opening of the Brussels Cricket Club in 1866. From then on cricket slowly spread so that there are now eight cricket grounds across the country accommodating over twelve hundred players from seventeen clubs.

The second of my cricket-related stops was at the home of Rachel Emerson, a cricket-mad Brit whose son was a pupil at the British School in Brussels and played for the Belgian Under-15 team. At the school I gave my first talk to a class of GCSE students, almost all of whom cared about neither cricket nor my journey (which, let's be honest, had barely started). 'Have you ever played for England?' was the only question that came at the end of my allotted time, and when I gave the answer in the negative the boy in question, having been the only one to display an atom of interest, joined his peers and switched off completely. A far more successful net session with the school first XI boded well for the rest of my journey and the next day, at the start of my eighth since leaving home, I jumped on the bicycle with a sore knee but in a positive frame of mind, heading south-east out of Brussels towards the border.

IN THE ZONE

Diary entry, 17 October 2009, Eghezée

Two more days cycling and I should be in Germany! Managed forty miles from Tervuren to Eghezée today despite flu. Worst moment came when a car pulled up next to me and the clever-dick driver wound down his window to shout 'Hey, you know it's quicker if you drive!' Plenty of good retorts came to mind later but when it happened I just frowned, swore under my breath and rode on. Saw abandoned London black cab as I pulled off the road at the end of the day – that'd make life a bit easier, and my heckler would approve. Jumped barbed-wire fence and now camping next to large pond in some woods. Bit eerie, but I'm not alone – a team of nineteen ducks just wandered over to watch me cook rice and an onion: a thrilling spectacle. They've left now and all I'm left with is bloody French radio. My French used to be average, now it's just shit. I can't under-stand a word. Just recorded the first video message for my blog. Spoke to the camera for ten minutes – it felt like a friend, which was weird. Guess I can't afford to be picky. Wish I had brought a proper video camera with me so I can look back properly when I'm done, even if only for posterity. Ah bugger, just cut my finger on brand new never-used sharp knife. It's deep. Hope those ducks aren't the bloodthirsty carnivore sort. Saturday night so the folks will be watching Strictly Come Dancing. Missing Kate – wonder how long that feeling will last? Until I reach Brisbane?

Map reading in the woods

Reading my diary entry the next morning I sensed negativity as my overriding emotion. In the few days since leaving I had tried to think of cycling as the way I now spent my days rather than a chore that had to be completed. I had struggled to do so, partly because of my terrible lack of fitness – every milestone, however small, felt like a huge achievement – but also because as I inched my way through Western Europe I still had such a ridiculously long way to pedal. There is no doubt that the world is an increasingly small place but it feels pretty big from the saddle of a bicycle. Each fold of a hill is a surmountable but significant hurdle; each settlement a refuge to rest weary legs.

Over the days that followed I made a concerted effort to control my immediate environment, to appreciate the present and to ignore the challenges ahead. As the flat farmland of Flanders was replaced by thick forests covering steep-sided valleys near the Luxembourg border (a false wilderness – I could never be far from civilisation in Belgium), I discovered that if I was to make effective progress and keep myself motivated it helped to set achievable targets. I broke each day down into manageable segments. One morning I allowed myself two songs on my iPod every ten miles and spent the intervening time dreaming up the day's soundtrack. Another afternoon I ate a small handful of Haribo every hour. I felt weak for needing such techniques but, as a way of keeping my mind on the task, it helped.

In Durbuy, the self-proclaimed 'smallest city in the world', I stayed with a local couple who fed me courgette soup, bread and a beer in front of the television while Jensen Button was crowned Formula One world champion in Brazil. It was a reminder that I was still not far from home. On the morning I left I tweeted 'Sports psychologist needed – is it possible to be in the zone when cycle touring? Cos I think I'm in it.' It was quickly becoming easier to enjoy the simplicity and efficiency of my movement. I warmed to the notion that my bicycle was my home, and that my home would transport me across four continents all the way to Brisbane. My knee had improved too. I felt little pain and my legs were warming to their task.

I began to relish the outdoors. I was alone, healthy and happy, exerting myself and feeling with each pedal stroke that I was working off the belly I had cultivated since becoming chained to my desk six years earlier. I forgot all about cricket, the Ashes, the sponsors, the destination and got lost in the simple movement of my wheels through beautiful river valleys. I revelled in the progress that took me from one Haribo to the next, one meal to the next, one sleep to the next. I was energetic and inspired and even wrote in my diary that I had 'fallen deeply in love with cycle touring'. In fact, I was enjoying myself so much that I did not notice I had left Belgium for Luxembourg, and only discovered I had subsequently left Luxembourg when I could no longer understand the road signs. I was in Germany, my fifth country, with only eighteen to go.

CENTRAL EUROPE

FOLLOW THE THIN BLUE LINES

I F YOU'RE EVER on the hunt for an example of German efficiency and planning, look no further than the 30,000-mile network of cycle paths that criss-cross the country with staggering frequency. Meticulously maintained, safe and beautifully scenic, they are a cycle tourist's dream and every river seems to have one. It was some time in the afternoon of my first day in Germany, and my tenth since leaving home, that I vowed to stick to the thin blue lines on my map to save my legs for tough challenges ahead; to savour the natural beauty on offer, even if it meant my route was a rather roundabout one.

The Moselle, a tributary of the Rhine and bordering Luxembourg, came first; then the vineyard-studded valley of its own tributary, the Saar. At a particularly scenic bend of that river I came across a friendly couple from Munich who told me its banks were famous for their red wine. It occurred to me that if my bank account had been healthier I'd have dropped into one of the vineyards for an afternoon of tasting. In fact, it was not just my bank balance that dictated long days riding alongside German rivers: I was discovering that the combination of bicycle travel and deadlines was not always the easiest of relationships to manage. Brisbane in thirteen months was my ultimate cut-off date, but I had arranged various other meetings, the first of which was with friends in the Austrian border town of Passau on 30 October. Another friendly lady warned me against missing out on the ancient city of Trier – the oldest city in Germany and, having been founded in the sixth century BC, older than Rome. But with one week to reach Passau and five hundred miles to cover, I resolved to complete my first sixty-five-mile day into Saarburg instead.

I looked forward to being in the saddle every day now. Generally my tent and panniers were packed up and I was back on my bicycle less than an hour after the alarm sounded. On the morning I was to pedal the Nahe River I was so excited about getting back on the road that I was ready fifteen minutes before sunrise, although I was forced to wait in the cold darkness because, thanks to France (more accurately a French thief, but I enjoyed blaming the whole country), I still had no lights to guide the way. That day turned out to be one I would remember as the finest through Germany, and one of the best through all of Europe: a rare clear blue sky and lush, steep-sided valleys.

Like the other rivers I had pedalled, the Nahe used to be an important trade route for coal, iron and steel, which were later shipped to Rotterdam. Nowadays it sits within a UNESCO World Heritage Site surrounded by vineyards. A proud butcher in Sobernheim told me the grapes of the Nahe Valley would soon be pressed and bottled to become one of the best Rieslings in the world. Although the vines were not yet at their finest, the surrounding deciduous forests were beginning to show their autumnal reds and oranges, and I relished the change that seemed to have come overnight. I could not remember when I had last taken the time to notice the leaves turning.

Since arriving in Germany I had passed occasional villages or small towns where I had ducked into a baker's to grab some bread or a butcher's for a hot sausage roll; but generally I had been far from people, enjoying rivers that flowed serenely down forested valleys. If it had been August I would have been fighting for space with speeding Lycra-clad leisure cyclists, but it was late October and there was no sign of Lycra or even other bicycles. Three or four hours would pass and I would see only a handful of dog-walkers.

From the moment I conceived the idea of riding to Australia I was confident that I would cope with long periods on my own. Even so, it felt great to be putting my confidence to the test, and still so close to home. It was on German cycle paths, with infrequent human contact, that I began to learn that the life of a solo cycle tourist allows for plenty of time for reflection and thought. Most days it was not only my bicycle wheels that meandered. My mind did, too, hour after hour, day after day. Why do so many German pensioners live in run-down caravans? Is the same true in the UK? Why would anyone buy a dog the size of a horse? Why not just buy a horse? Will it be warm enough in the tent tonight to sleep without a hat and gloves? If the first half of Bastian Schweinsteiger's surname means 'pig', what does the second half mean? Surely his name isn't Bastian Pig-Farmer? When will I see another world cyclist on his or her own adventure? What will I do when I get back to the UK? How cool would it have been to be one of The Beach Boys? Will I prefer cycling when it starts to get warm? Why did the moustache go out of fashion in the UK, and yet in Germany it is still worn to such devastating effect? Why do I occasionally scoff at small cultural differences instead of celebrating them? What would I have achieved today if I had been at home? Shall I risk taking what looks on the map like a sneaky short cut? Does the fact that I cycled seventy miles today mean I achieved anything worthwhile?

With a Dictaphone for company I recorded my thoughts. Some I spent an hour on; others drifted in one ear and out the other unanswered. But by the time I reached the somewhat more frenetic Main River there was so much to look at, and so much path traffic to dodge, that I barely had time for quiet reflection. The Main took me from the calm beauty of the German countryside into one of the largest cities in Europe's biggest country.

The cycle path into Frankfurt was not well lit, and I rolled unsteadily down it well after dark and without bicycle lights. I was grateful when another cyclist rode up behind me and lit up my immediate surroundings, improving my chances of avoiding a fully clothed nocturnal swim. 'Cycling to ze ashes? Ah, this iz ze cricket Ashes?'

I turned to find a mountain biker sporting top-to-bottom Lycra – never a pleasant sight on an empty stomach – trying to decipher more of the wording on the sign on my bicycle. He introduced himself as Rasmus and, as we rode side by side hugging the Main's southern bank into Frankfurt, we chatted about his former life as a professional triathlete. He told me he had once raced against Lance Armstrong in Texas, although he admitted using the term 'race' liberally – he and most of the field were left in Armstrong's significant wake from the start. I asked how he knew of 'ze Ashes' and he admitted that, although not a huge fan of cricket ('iz ze most fucking boring game in ze world'), he knew all about them because he'd lived in London in 2005, and experienced the cricketing euphoria of that wonderful summer.

Like most Germans I had met on the trip, Rasmus was friendly and interested in what I was doing, even positive about my eventual arrival in Australia. But he could not get his head around the fact that I had cycled from Dunkerque to Frankfurt without bicycle lights. It is, after all, most un-German to be anything but wholly prepared for all eventualities. When we reached the Friedensbrücke, Rasmus directed me towards a cheap hostel and we bid each other farewell. There was just one bed remaining so I checked it and, despite the unappealing prospect of a night in a twelve-bed dormitory with eleven Chinese *World of Warcraft* addicts, booked in. To save myself from a restless night I drank for most of it with folks I met in the hostel bar: a Spaniard with a bolt through his septum, a Slovakian with a Mohawk, a German man who had once cycled from Tierra del Fuego to Bogotá, and an Austrian girl who, throughout the course of the evening, asked each of us if we would like to sleep with her. None of us was tempted; not even the Slovakian girl with a Mohawk.

I stumbled to bed a few hours before I was due to set off again, checked my emails and found one from a man named Maike:

26 October 2009
Hi Oliver

My good friend Rasmus cycled with you into Frankfurt today.
He (and me also) are just amazed by your adventure. You are
for sure fucking crazy! As a way of saying good luck we want
to give you something. Our gift to you will be deposited on
your way out of Frankfurt, stored in a cycling water bottle
very much close to your route! To find it type into Google
Maps 'hafen 2 offenbach main' and find the café at the place.
The bottle will be right in front of the bar under one of the
tables (after 10am!). So we are both very much curious if this
will work out.

Hope you let us know. Safe travels man, and good
luck!

Maike from Berlin and Rasmus from Frankfurt

The next morning, having managed a restless night's sleep
in Little Beijing, it was with great excitement that I embarked
on the treasure hunt that had been set for me, following the
Main River out of the city towards 'hafen 2 offenbach main',
uncertain what exactly I was looking for. When my GPS told
me I had arrived at my destination the time was 10.14 a.m.
and I could see a café with tables and chairs dotted about a
small, green riverside garden. The café was closed but, sure
enough, under a picnic table standing upright among a clump
of daisies, was a bicycle water bottle. I unscrewed the lid and
inside found front and rear bicycle lights, each with working
batteries. I got my BlackBerry out and sent an email:

Dear Rasmus and Maike,

You have made me a very happy man today. I found the lights
and they'll stay with me all the way to Australia. I can't thank
you enough!

With very best wishes, Oli the Crazy Englishman

Bicycle lights – useful accessories for cycling around the world.
Thank you, Maike and Rasmus!

Surprised, humbled and delighted, I was beaming from ear to ear as I pedalled out of Frankfurt. I wondered if I would have done the same for a foreigner cycling through my city, and came to the sad conclusion that I would not. I never heard from Rasmus or Maike again.

JAMES AND THE GIANT RAINS

With the help of my newly acquired lights I rode well into the night on my first day out of Frankfurt, setting up camp in a field a few metres from the banks of the Tauber River. That and the Altmühl River took me onwards towards Passau. But it was in Ingolstadt, where Mary Shelley's most famous incarnation, Victor Frankenstein, attended university, that for the first time my eyes met another, much larger river.

The Danube is one of Europe's great rivers, rising in the German Black Forest and spilling out into the Black Sea in Romania and Ukraine. It has witnessed everything from early human Neolithic cultures to the Balkan wars and in between was a long-standing frontier of the Roman Empire. When I reached Passau late on 29 October I had already pedalled 130 miles of its length. By the time I said goodbye to it three weeks later it would have provided the backdrop for most of my days cycling in Europe, and spat me out thirteen hundred miles downstream in the heart of the Balkans.

I spent a couple of very pleasant days in Passau, where I had arranged to meet Tali and Jojo – an ex-girlfriend and her German boyfriend, who had driven down to meet me from Berlin – and James, a friend who had flown out for two weeks on the bike. I enjoyed catching up with all three, pouring my efforts into drinking, eating and sharing stories instead of simply cycling. The three-day break was my longest up to that point, but, after an amusing weekend of frivolous behaviour in Fritz Club, James and I were back on the bikes, bound for Budapest.

Memories are all I have to go on from the time James and I pedalled together – I was distracted enough by having company not to bother keeping a detailed diary – and all that happened in the intervening months has rendered those two weeks a series of hazy reminiscences. But I can remember a few things.

I remember the weather, because it made me feel homesick. On our second morning we asked the farmer whose field we had slept in what he thought the day held in store, sun or rain? 'Sun all day, do not worry young men!' came his confident assessment as he peered up at a clear blue sky. And who were we to argue? An hour later the first drops of rain began to fall and, apart from the odd hour here and there, did not cease until we reached Budapest fifteen days later.

On our third day together I received an email from a man in Vienna who had been following my progress online. He warned me that there was two feet of snow on the ground and more was forecast. We never saw snow (it was gone by the time we arrived in Vienna), but it would have been far preferable to what we got instead. James, not unreasonably, had expected to cycle *next* to the Danube, but so flooded was the river in sections that our path tended to merge with it. He had exchanged a miserable English November for a miserable European one; one for which we were both wholly unprepared. Gloves, hats, shoes, trousers, jackets – all were supposed to be waterproof but none was up to the task of protecting us from two weeks of persistent bombardment from the heavens. We were soaking and freezing before we even set off each day, dressed in sodden clothes that had not come close to drying overnight.

Outside the fantastic sounding municipality of Engelhartszell an der Donau an overweight American couple wearing bumbags stopped us and, trying to decipher the sign on the back of my bike, asked: 'Where is this Brisbane place then?' That cheered us up, as did our eventual arrival in Hitler's former hometown, Linz. We were within a stone's throw of the 2009 European Capital of Culture when, to our dismay, the Danube path came to an abrupt end and a sign told us the ferry that would normally have delivered us directly to a warm bed on the southern bank had in fact stopped running the day before for the winter. After anguished groans, a bit of soul-searching and a change of clothes, we did an about-turn and retraced our tracks for two hours until we reached a bridge. Then we cycled back towards Linz for two and a half hours into a worsening headwind. We had ridden roughly eighty miles and it was ten o'clock by the time we pulled up, sodden to our cores, in the centre of Linz. We treated ourselves to a first Austrian Wiener Schnitzel and there began a love affair that would last the width of the country.

It was also while James was with me that I met my first long-distance cycle tourist. He was sitting beside the path, leaning against his bicycle eating bread when we came across him. His name was Kazu and our encounter would have a lasting impression on my ride. Kazu had cycled from Florence to Amsterdam and was now on the long journey home to Japan. He had no money except that which he earned along the way by making leather bags and selling them to people he met. He had never paid for a night's accommodation, yet did not own a tent or sleeping bag; he slept under whatever shelter he could find; football stadia were his nocturnal venues of choice. He ate nothing but bread and the occasional dollop of jam and drank little but water. He said that shampooing his waist-long hair was his only luxury.

Until meeting Kazu I had camped and cooked for myself a bit, but had generally eaten pretty well and stayed in hostels or cheap hotels much more often than I had planned. Apart from anything else, it meant I had spent more than I could afford. As he sped away from us after our first lunch of bread and jam, I told James that the only way I would be able to complete my journey within budget and with my conscience intact was if I became more like Kazu. I did not vow to grow my hair down to my waist, but I did promise to toughen up a little.

THE LUFTWAFFE, THE AMBASSADOR AND A BLACK EYE: CRICKETING ENCOUNTERS IN CENTRAL EUROPE

James and I pedalled through four countries in a little over two weeks and it was during our time together that the 'cricket participation' aspect of my ride really got going. I expect most cricketers – and non-cricketers, too, if they have ever given it an ounce of thought – assume that the game is played in very few countries around the world. It is true that cricket administrators and promoters have a lot of work to do if they hope to compete with football, which over the past fifty years has come to dominate the sporting landscape of almost every country on earth. After all, only ten countries have been granted the status to play cricket at the highest level* and the World Cup has only been won by five nations – Australia, West Indies, India, Pakistan and Sri Lanka.

Before I began looking into it, I expected I would not need

* Test match cricket is the highest level of cricket. Only England, Australia, Sri Lanka, India, Pakistan, South Africa, Bangladesh, West Indies, New Zealand and Zimbabwe are qualified to play this form of the game.

my bat much until I got to India. I assumed that Europe, certainly, would be something of a cricketing desert. After all, countries like Germany, Austria and Hungary have little affiliation to Britain and the Commonwealth, where cricket originated and duly expanded. But once I started to research my route I discovered that if cricket does not dominate the world's sporting landscape, it certainly forms a significant subculture that has spread far beyond the former bastions of Empire. James and I were eager to seek out cricketing experiences – if not necessarily games – wherever we could find them.

Our first challenge was to find cricket in Germany, and to our surprise we found the sport in rude health, and with a rich history. In Passau we arranged to have lunch with a quiet, bearded Yorkshireman called Brian, who we hoped would tell us all about the state of the Germanic game. Brian was a lecturer at the University of Passau and President of the German Cricket Board.

Cricket has been played in Germany since the mid-nineteenth century when some English and Americans got together to form a club in Berlin.* In his weekly Victorian journal, *All The Year Round*, Charles Dickens wrote about the game there in 1865, noting the local population's apathy towards a very confusing and English pursuit: 'After watching the game for a while, impatience began to be manifested. Was this all? Was this the game? Ten men to stand in the hot sun all day, to watch the eleventh throw a hard ball at his friend! Could that be a fit amusement for grown Englishmen? For a whole day, too!'

At Hamburg in the same year, Dickens noted, a 'loudly heralded game was played between France and Germany. That is to say, eleven Englishmen on the side of Germany, found means to induce eleven more Englishmen on the side of France to come from somewhere, or anywhere, and have what they playfully termed an International Match.' Dickens went on to

* Cricket has a rich history in North America, too: the first ever international cricket match was played in New York on 25–27 September 1844 between the United States of America and the British Empire's Canadian Province. The Canadians won by twenty-three runs.

explain that not a single 'native' seemed to take any interest in the sport, preferring instead to sit beyond the boundary and wonder aloud why on earth the man with the piece of wood in his hand did not run away when the ball was hurtled towards him.

Far more surprising than the game's appearance in Germany during the height of British Victorian expansionism is the story of Hitler and his supposed run-in with cricket. In 1930 the *Daily Mirror* published an article entitled 'Adolf Hitler As I Know Him', written by a right-wing MP called Oliver Locker-Lampson. It explained that while the future Führer was recovering from gunshot wounds during the First World War, he came across some British prisoners of war who spent their days playing cricket. He suggested they teach him the basics and in the gentlemanly spirit of the game the prisoners accepted. But when the young Hitler took to the field some time later he found himself to be a terrible practitioner and attempted to change what he considered the thoroughly illogical and confusing rules. It is assumed the team he got together to take on the English lost, because there is no more mention of cricket in the Hitler story. Presumably he felt the gentle pleasures of a game played over twenty-two yards of grass, followed by jam scones and cucumber sandwiches, didn't suit his more aggressive tendencies.

Brian told us that the game has surged in popularity since, but not because of Hitler's dabbling. It has caught on at universities across Germany, especially in the north, so that there are now seventy clubs in the country. There are even occasional cricketing links with the British: Gary Lineker played cricket for MCC against Germany in 1992 and got out cheaply before quipping 'I always score one against Germany'. And of course there are games within Europe: in *Wisden*'s record of the greatest games of cricket in history, one between Germany and France in 1997 comes in at Number 96 – France won off the last ball when a man called David Bordes ran a single despite suffering a fractured skull earlier in the game.

I did not fracture my skull in the game we played at the

University of Passau after lunch with Brian, but I came away with a black eye after an overzealous 'native' called Jan-Ulrich punished me for fielding too close at short leg by smashing the ball into my face. It may have been that I was distracted by the fact that he was batting wearing a Luftwaffe pilot's helmet.

We found cricket in Austria, too, through the unlikely source of an English cycling fanatic. Simon Mitchell had tweeted me when I was in Belgium, suggesting that if I passed through Vienna I should stay with him and his Austrian wife. When I explained to him that I would like to play cricket in his adopted country he told me that although he actively disliked the sport, he would do his best to find us a game. James and I were therefore particularly grateful when, upon meeting us at the doorway to his block of flats, he told us he had arranged a game for us at the Austria Cricket Club the next day. The President of the club, a Sri Lankan by the name of Siva, was apparently eager to host us and had gathered some of the brightest young talent in the country.

The club was in a rough neighbourhood where hooded youths hung about on street corners beneath smashed windows of abandoned warehouses. It was probably lucky James and I were on foot and had nothing worth stealing. The ground itself however, although bordered by an impenetrable, high barbed-wire fence, was immaculate. The grass was smooth and beautifully green and the small wooden pavilion was surrounded by a picture-perfect white picket fence that would not have been out of place in leafy New England. When we arrived, Siva, wearing a tracksuit emblazoned with the words AUSTRIA CRICKET, was desperately attempting to get a barbecue going in a developing rain shower. The scene, in fact, was not far removed from an English summer's day and James and I felt very at home.

From the look of the ground it was clear that Siva had delivered on his promise to get along some young talent for the game. A few prepubescent boys practised their long barriers on the far side of the outfield and a gaggle of young girls, none older than thirteen, were loosening their arms in the middle. But he had gathered some more mature talent, too. A group of greying, middle-aged men stood limbering up self-consciously by the pavilion. One of them introduced himself to me as Simon Smith. He was Her Britannic Majesty's Ambassador to the Republic of Austria and had been chosen to open our innings with me.

I have never been bowled first ball of any match by a nine-year-old girl. And I am proud to say that I still have not. In a clear indication that the Ambassador had underestimated the quality of the infant prodigy's bowling, he failed to take guard and as a result left a ball that struck the middle of middle stump. I played a significantly longer but luckier innings, was dropped four times and eventually out for sixty-three, caught by a dwarf* at square leg to become the seventh victim of the innings for the nine-year-old girl. Still, I was happy with my first – and as it turned out, last – half-century of the tour.

Post-match celebrations were curtailed when our youthful opponents had to go to bed, but James and I were happy as we had an early start the next morning, bound for Slovakia and a meeting with a lady with cricket links in Bratislava. I had not realised how close the Slovakian capital was to the City of Music, but the ride only took us a day, still hugging the banks of the Danube. By evening we were sitting in a bar off a surprisingly regal old square in Bratislava, drinking pints of Guinness with a Mancunian called Janet, who told us the cricket scene in Slovakia was thriving – which made me disappointed that I had not managed to seek out any players. Janet, taught cricket to her class at a local primary school and was hoping we would hang around in the city until Monday to play cricket with the kids and talk to them about our ride. Sadly, we had an engagement to keep in Budapest so we decided to crack on into Hungary, the eighth country of my tour and the one where I met a man who would alter the complexion of my entire journey.

* It may not actually have been a dwarf. It may have been a seven-year-old child.

Wearing the Austria Cricket Club one-day kit before opening the batting with Simon Smith in Vienna.

I had been contacted by a member of the Hungarian Cricket Association Board, an Australian expatriate called Andrew Leckonby who, ten years earlier, had come to Hungary for three days, fallen in love first with a local girl, then with the city, and had never left. Andrew drove out to meet us in the Danube town of Szödliget, about twenty miles north of Budapest, which was soon to be the new stamping ground for Hungarian cricketers; home to the first full-size cricket oval in the country. The land had been bought privately by the cricket association and even on a damp, drizzly November afternoon it was easy to imagine what an idyllic venue it would one day make. To the south of the site was a small stream where I was told wildlife was abundant in the summer months with kingfishers, buzzards, herons, snakes and voles living among the orchids, rushes and laurel. For now, half of the ground was under water and the building that would one day be the pavilion was derelict and unloved. I admired the vision and ambition that Andrew described. The Hungarian Cricket Association was obviously a well-run, professional organisation, something that cannot be said for some of the larger cricket bodies around the world, let alone those inhabiting relatively diminutive outposts of the game.

It is easy to trivialise the efforts of minor sports enthusiasts around the world; to label them as a bizarre and odd collective and to chuckle at their eccentricity: a sprinter in American Samoa; a swimmer in Equatorial Guinea; a bunch of cricketers in Hungary. Cricket is particularly susceptible to such loose stereotyping because its peculiar charms are so challenging to explain to the uninitiated: have you ever tried to spell out the lbw law to someone who is familiar with the basics of the game, let alone a foreigner who is watching it for the first time? Or attempted to explain the theatre of a five-day Test match, or what a googly is, or why the man in the white coat is waving his arms about like a delinquent? I was delighted to discover no sign of eccentricity among the cricket folk of Budapest. Their vision for the future was impressive. The game was taught in schools around the country and the standard, as I witnessed during a cold Saturday night in a sports hall in Buda, on the west bank of the Danube, was high. In fact, I had such a good time playing cricket there that I gave away my first Mongoose of the tour, to Andrew, asking him to pass it on to a particularly deserving young player.

INTRODUCING LÁSZLÓ

Arriving in Budapest felt like a major achievement for James and I, so we spent a long weekend celebrating in the city, playing cricket and drinking. Andrew introduced us to Adrian, another forty-something Australian cricket fan who owned two hostels in the city, one of which was empty with enough room for two cyclists and all their gear. As well as organising our accommodation, Adrian arranged our social lives. Each afternoon during our stay he had people for us to meet and places for us to drink. He sent us off the tourist map, clambering hidden, graffiti-ridden stairwells to apartments that had been turned into speakeasy-style bars and clubs. There we drank with the likes of Erica, the George Harrison lookalike, Stan, the aggressive freestyle skier, and Sergei, the long-haired, stoned drummer. We fell in love with the place just like Adrian and Andrew had.

James and I felt our blowout weekend was well-earned. Besides, I was about to be on my own again and I was not looking forward to it. While a couple of hours with Kazu, the Japanese cyclist, had forged in me a desire to toughen up, pedalling with James for two weeks had taught me that I had a lot of work to do before I became a good cycle tourist. James was always first to emerge from the tent each morning, eager to drag me out into the pre-dawn to get some miles under our belts before the few daylight hours we had ran out; he would wait patiently for me to repack every morning, too, because inevitably I'd have unpacked all four panniers the night before in a rush to find some elusive piece of kit. On the road, mornings tended to go well; I could just about keep up with the mean pace James set. But the afternoons were far tougher: my fitness was inferior and I was often left trailing in his wake. By evening I was usually a physical mess, splayed out inside the tent, shivering and knackered, while James found the energy to get the stove out and begin cooking.

When our cycling partnership came to an end in Budapest, I asked James to sum up a few of his memories of our time together in a guest blog on my website. He wrote:

. . . If sweating during exercise is a sign of an efficient cooler then Oli is one of the most gifted coolers of all time. I should also report back that Oli possesses a horrific ginger beard, that his shoes smell quite repugnant, and that he speaks to his kit when he repacks his panniers each morning (e.g. 'there you go; you sneak in there next to the stove, on top of the fleece . . .')

If I was to work on my weaknesses I was to do so alone. When James left for London I thanked him for being the first to come out and join me on my ride. I had been nervous about sharing two weeks of my adventure, even with a good friend; my selfish gene had told me it was my journey and mine alone. But despite the incessant rain, intense exercise and sharing a small tent, the experience had turned out better than either of us could have hoped. James escaped London for two weeks and I had someone with whom I could share the highs (reaching the end of each day) and lows (getting smashed in the face by a cricket ball) of my particular genre of bicycle travel. I had no time to consider the challenges ahead. I lived in the present.

Just as the nature of my ride had changed when James arrived, so it would when he left. I did not know when I would next have a companion on the road. I was on my own again, slowly making progress towards Istanbul, my first major landmark.

On the morning after James left, I was greeted in the doorway of my hostel by two strange men. I was wearing my boxer shorts and bleary eyed after a night on Hungary's most evil liqueur, Unicum. One of them was holding a rolling video camera. It transpired that Danny and László had heard about my bicycle ride through Adrian and, as keen cyclists and amateur film enthusiasts, had decided they wanted to edit a short film about my adventure and post it on their blog.

László pointed the camera at my less-than-morning-fresh face before he and Danny began bombarding me with the same questions I had been asked over and over since leaving home. Neither had played cricket before, although both were interested in it on account of their friendship with Adrian,

James and Adrian with the Ashes urn.

who had on occasion represented Hungary at the sport. László had even watched the Hungarian national team in action some years before over a few ciders. I lifted the Ashes urn off the floor and showed it to the camera, explaining its history and significance. I then read aloud with pride an email I had just received from David Gower, my boyhood cricketing hero, wishing me good luck for the journey ahead. I had got used to speaking to cameras and now even quite enjoyed it.

Once this questioning was over, it was time to say goodbye to Budapest, and Adrian. He had been generous to James and I during our stay and I hoped we would stay in touch. As I pedalled off through the deserted streets of Buda, László rode alongside me with his camera strapped to his bicycle. I told the camera that I was always emotional leaving places where I had met kind people, but never too sad because I was never in one place long enough. It was an accurate description of how I felt. My sadness was always diluted by a healthy dose of excitement as the next challenge, the next day in the saddle and the next country approached. In three days' time I hoped to be crossing the border into Serbia.

I rather doubted that I was a good subject for László to

film, but he assured me I was. He told me that he was a regular at monthly Critical Mass events in the city, during which thousands of cyclists take to the streets to promote cycling as a healthy, sustainable mode of transport and protest peacefully against the modern enemy: cars. Critical Mass events take place all over the world and Budapest has some of the largest. László was easy to get on with; interested and interesting. He seemed to be one of life's enthusiasts. We formed a good partnership, even if only for the short ride out of Budapest, and I told him he would be welcome to join me onwards towards Belgrade. He seemed sorry to have to say no. He had a wife and a life in Budapest, but he did promise to edit a short film about my departure from his hometown.

We cycled on eastwards until the imperial beauty of central Budapest gave way to ugly residential tower blocks built at a staggering density and then, finally, to open countryside. There, László left me and turned back for the city. We hugged. 'I will film more of this journey Oli,' László said, looking me dead in the eye. 'I will see you very soon.' Later that day, I thought about László's assertion that he would see me again on this journey and realised that I believed him.

Continuing through a flat national park as the sun set, I felt melancholy, partly because I was leaving a city I had grown to love and where I wanted to stay longer, but mostly because I was continuing my journey alone. After two weeks of sharing misery, elation, easy conversation, sociable meal times and a lot of laughter, I was once again riding solo. Decisions were mine and mine alone: where to eat, where to sleep; did the man say left or right to the next town? Shall I ride on into the dark? I questioned again the wisdom of making the journey alone, asking myself if I was cut out for lone travel over such a long distance. In years to come, wouldn't it be fun to share stories from the road with a friend, over a beer? Was fun what I was after?

SERBIA

AN EMOTIONAL RIDE

THE ROAD USERS of Hungary are an incompetent rabble. They wave, they smile, but they are utterly unaware how unpleasant they can make a cyclist's life. The bicycle is not a recognised form of transport in many parts – hence László's involvement in Critical Mass, I suppose – and winding my way through southern Hungary towards my ninth country, Serbia, I was run off the road more than once by passing juggernauts.

I spent my last night in the country nestled in my sleeping bag, in my tent, under a bridge in Szeged city centre, attempting to sleep amid wails of student revelry. The next morning, as I moved smoothly towards the Serbian border, I felt sad to be leaving Hungary. I had made a number of friends I would keep in touch with beyond the life of Cycling to the Ashes; especially László, who had surprised me by showing such interest in making a film about my ride. But, as ever, I had to push on. I had spent too long in Budapest and winter would soon begin to bare its teeth. I had to cross as much of Eastern Europe as I could before the weather turned.

My entry into Serbia was somewhat eventful. Having been advised not to take the motorway across the border, I was soon horribly lost in a network of deserted back roads and eventually, after sneaking through an open gate that appeared to land me safely in Serbian territory, came face to face with a stern employee of the Serbian army. Waving his automatic weapon he pointed back to where I'd come from, into a forest in the direction of the motorway I'd just spent considerable effort trying to avoid. As his movements became more agitated I realised I had in fact entered Serbia illegally and that, if I wished to avoid an even nastier confrontation, I should head to the motorway and take the legal route across the border. I happily obliged.

Motorway and border safely negotiated, for three long days I pedalled through northern Serbia, thick fog my constant companion as I headed south towards the capital, Belgrade. It was a grey and lonely spell that seemed to augur bad news. It soon came, in the form of a phone call from home. My grandmother Peggy's twin sister had died suddenly. I knew that my grandmother would be devastated and I tried to call her later that day, with no luck. I had to be content with emailing her to offer my condolences. I had decided to name my bicycle Peggy, after her, and told her in the email that she had a new namesake. She was touched by the gesture and, if she was following my journey closely before, watched even closer from then on, at least for a few months. I did not know at the time that I would never see her in her right mind again; that her twin sister's death would be the catalyst for the onset of dementia; that when I returned home she would barely recognise me.

I have always cherished the closeness of my family and I sometimes found it hard being so far from them, particularly as I was always moving further from home and especially when they had to deal with such events as illnesses and death. The drama playing out at home made my ride through northern Serbia a particularly emotional one. I felt lonely for the first time in weeks and as a result began to doubt my ability to finish what I had started. During my first few days on the road I had asked myself over and over if what I was doing was selfish and self-indulgent, and I asked myself the same questions again now. I loved my new life as a cycle tourist. I got to see beautiful places roll by under my wheels. I met with kindness that knew no bounds. I slept rough, revelling in the freedom. I cooked when I wanted, rested when I felt like it. If I was afraid I knew I'd get over it and, if I came across danger, I trusted my judgement.

But my parents were far away and – despite the odd email from me saying 'Having a blast!' or 'Bloody cold, beautiful country though!' – could not possibly have known all of this. It occurred to me that adventure into the unknown is fun and easy and exciting when you're living it; I imagine it can be terrifying as hell when you're watching from afar. I promised myself I'd try to give my family no more reasons to worry, but in reality I knew they would be anxious until the day I walked back through the front door of their house.

So it was in a mood of reflection and contemplation that I approached Belgrade. I rarely caught a glimpse of the countryside beyond the fifty metres immediately surrounding me. The land was criss-crossed with an intricate network of rivers and canals and I kept reaching dead ends where I was forced to wait for a vessel – always either a mechanised tugboat or a wooden rowing boat – to appear out of the mist and help me navigate across the water.

Navigating Serbia wasn't always easy.
Thick fog became a familiar companion.

Kind and eccentric people appeared out of the mist, too. At one river I boarded a tugboat and found that, for once, I was not the only passenger. A tractor towered over me and I noticed the driver was wearing a Manchester United shirt. I pointed at it and told him I was English. 'Nemanja Vidić!' he said. 'Yes, yes, Nemanja Vidić,' I said in reply. He smiled, I smiled and then he said, 'Nemanja Vidić' again, and I said, 'Vidić good player', and he looked confused so I pointed my thumbs skywards and said 'Vidić good player' again, giving a little kick of my left foot. He smiled, got into his tractor and drove off. We had reached the other side of the river.

'Nemanja Vidić, good player!'

In the few settlements there were I was welcomed into small cafés and asked by inquisitive locals what on earth I was up to. There was nearly always an English speaker on hand, although in one café I was introduced to an English teacher whose grasp of the English language was marginally worse than my Serbian. I felt sorry for his pupils. In those cafés I discovered not only kind Serbian people who offered unrelenting and generous hospitality, but also burek, a tasty baked or fried pastry filled with layers of stewed minced meat, onions or cheese, that is eaten throughout the former Ottoman Empire. At less than a dollar a time, burek presented a cheap, quick way to refuel.

One afternoon I found myself riding beside field after field of turnips. At a collection of low, derelict buildings I paused for a snack and was approached by a man in a pork pie hat, blue and yellow knitted jumper, stained brown trousers and a pair of wellies. He was called George and he was a seventy-two-year-old turnip farmer with whom I did not share a single word of common language. But we managed to converse with signs and gestures for half an hour before parting with a warm hug (if all I could get was a warm hug from an ageing Serbian farmer I was not about to turn it down) and an exchange of sorts: I took a photo of George holding the Ashes urn and gesturing a 'victory' sign – obviously he was supporting England – and George gave me a couple of turnips for the road (delicious with some rice and half an onion, I found out later that evening).

But as I pedalled away from George I suddenly started crying. I pulled over and sat down on the edge of the road next to a turnip field and the tears just kept on coming, with no sign that they would stop. Eventually I decided I could not afford to waste any more time so I remounted and pedalled on. I must have been a strange sight for passing motorists: big bloke, big bike, big, uncontrollable tears running down his contorted face as he pedalled furiously through foggy fields in the dead of winter.

All sorts of emotions were wrapped up in those tears that had been welling up inside me since I had left my friends and family more than a month earlier. I missed them all, and I was certain that some of the tears were for them. But more than anything I cried because I was happy; perfectly happy. Happy to have put my career on hold in the name of adventure; happy to have begun – and to be enjoying – a journey that I had been dreaming up for years; and above all, happy to be reliant, not on friends I knew I could trust, but on strangers. They might be rare back home, but random acts of generosity and kindness had accompanied me ever since my first day as a long-distance cyclist when I had attached a sign to the back of my bike that said I was pedalling to Australia; endless goodwill and support had followed me. Whether it was the friendly London cabbie who wished me an astonished 'good luck mate!' on my way past St Paul's, Frank, the vegetable donor, on my first day in Europe, Rasmus and Maike in Germany or George, the old turnip farmer, I had been constantly surprised by people I had never met before and each time it happened my faith in humanity soared. I was a stranger everywhere I went; vulnerable – emotionally and physically. Without the help and support of strangers I would have found the past few weeks far more difficult. I now knew that pedalling alone across continents was far from a one-man job and I cried because of people like George, who had given me a few of his precious vegetables and in doing so, shown unconditional kindness to a stranger on a bicycle.

I reached Belgrade long before dusk on 22 November after forty-four days on the road. There I found a city of two very distinct halves. I pedalled in through the twentieth-century architectural horror show that is New Belgrade, where the streets are wide and well-planned – perfect for cycling – yet entirely charmless. The buildings were brutes: cavernous, grey, geometric monsters towering over stark concrete public spaces where boys performed tricks on skateboards and BMXs in the hope of impressing their attendant female fan clubs. The sight of shell-suit-clad youths got me reminiscing about the winters I spent at East Berks Squash Club, Maidenhead, in the late 1980s. Had shell suits really taken that long to make it to Serbia?

I cannot believe that New Belgradians enjoy their environment. I am sure they must dream of better lives across the Danube in Old Belgrade. There my wheels found row after row of eighteenth-century town houses with spectacular views over green parks; ancient, cobbled streets with designer shops and narrow, tree-lined avenues where beautiful people drank coffee imported from exotic locations. New doesn't necessarily mean better, and it necessarily didn't when it came to Belgrade.

I also arrived in Belgrade to a city grieving. Patriarch Pavle, who led the dominant Serbian Christian Orthodox Church through its post-communist revival and the turbulent war years of the 1990s, had died a few days earlier, and the government had declared three days of mourning. His funeral had seen hundreds of thousands take to the streets to pay their respects and the country's President, Boris Tadić, had called his passing an 'irredeemable loss'.

However, Dunya and Bojan, the young Bosnian Serb couple who owned the hostel I was staying in, seemed more concerned that I had arrived just a few hours after the departure of a Scandinavian women's handball team that had stayed with them that week. I spent my evening recovering after the long ride in the hostel which, as luck would have it, was the sort of place a weary traveller dreams of, with clean, crisp linen, a flat screen television, abundant DVD collection, well-stocked kitchen and sofas you could sink into while drifting off and dreaming of Scandinavian women's handball teams.

While I snoozed in front of a comforting episode of *Friends*, Bojan concocted tactical charts that he hoped would secure his own girls' volleyball team a tenth successive league victory the following week. He was a former professional himself and had been forced to turn to coaching on the back of a career-ending injury. His brother, he told me, played for CSK Moscow, too. I was quickly getting a sense that Serbians lived for sport, but when I asked him what he thought of cricket he admitted that the only thing he knew about it was that 'Sean' Warne was a good player. I told Bojan and Dunya what I was doing and invited them to a game I had planned in an extraordinary location the next day. Happily, they agreed to join me.

'HE CYCLED TO SERBIA ARMED WITH A STICK'

The following morning, leaving the mourners to their mourning, we strolled through near-silent cobbled streets to a park on top of a hill where a fort stood overlooking the Danube. Kalemegdan Fort has stood at the confluence of the Sava and Danube rivers for almost two thousand years and for much of that time the city of Belgrade did not exist beyond its walls. The fort *was* the city.

Founded by Celtic tribes in the third century AD, the fortress was conquered by the Romans, who in turn defended it from Goths, Huns, Avars, Slavs, Bulgarians and Hungarians before the Turks came along and ended up occupying it for more than three hundred years until the late nineteenth century. More recently the fortress survived the First and Second World Wars and NATO air strikes on Belgrade in 1999. It has had a hectic, bloody history, but until now had never seen cricket.

I stood in Kalemegdan's north-west corner with Bojan and Dunya. The view, first over the Sava, then the Danube, was striking in the early morning wintry fog. I traced a narrow path that hugged the Danube and disappeared around a bend. That path wound its way back westwards through vineyard-covered valleys, stark industrial towns, past cathedrals, mosques and homeless shelters all the way to goulash, Wiener Schnitzels, Budapest, Passau and beyond – the path I had just cycled. It was easy to understand why, strategically, the fort was the focus of so many conquest attempts over so many centuries. On that day it was majestic and serene, although battles were still being fought up and down the length of the paths that criss-crossed the ancient, ruined ramparts.

Chess. Hundreds of elderly men huddled in tightly packed groups playing or watching chess. Most were dressed in woolly hats and army surplus jackets but some toughed it out in jeans and T-shirts, simultaneously demonstrating disdain for the cold and skin-wrinkled tattoos. Some sipped coffee from paper cups while others chomped on bureks. In the cold their breath created an illusion of smoke, although most were smoking, too.

But I was not there for chess. As I surveyed the scene around me I was keeping watch for a friendly face to emerge from the fog. I did not have to wait long before I saw László, true to his word, walking towards me lugging a rucksack and various other bags full of camera equipment. He had caught the overnight train down from Budapest to film for a couple of days. I had been delighted when I received the email saying he was coming. It read simply: 'it is a fucking waste not to be documenting your journey on film', and so, although he had no idea how he would document the journey beyond Serbia, he was coming to Belgrade. For my part, I was grateful to have found a friendly Central European with a limited interest in cricket who wanted to film my journey anyway.

The four of us waited in the fog for the man we had come here to meet. Before long he appeared, walking towards us with purpose, half smiling, half grimacing at the cold. He was somewhat stout, five foot seven inches perhaps. His hair was dark, clipped around the ears like a military man. I guessed he was in his early thirties. His face was grey. Or maybe it seemed grey. Belgrade was a grey city in late November; even the autumn leaves seemed faded. In good English and with a lilt that I guessed was Serbian, but which sounded perfectly Russian to my untrained ear, the man introduced himself with an outstretched hand: 'Hello, I am Vladimir Ninković, self-appointed General Secretary of Serbian Cricket Federation. It is pleasure to meet you.'

I had a preconception of Serbs as hard-as-nails military types who slept with guns under their pillows, owned night-vision goggles and spied on their neighbours. Some weeks later I would leave Serbia with a fairer judgement, based on actually getting to know some Serbs. Meeting Vladimir was the start of my journey from 'Slavic' ignorant to devoted Slavophile. He was open, enthusiastic and, as befits the self-appointed general secretary of any country's cricketing body, cricket mad. I liked Vladimir immediately.

'Where is the cricket ground?' I asked my new friend.

Vladimir looked taken aback. 'We do not have such luxuries

here in Serbia. We were required to get police permission to play the game today – bureaucracy here is very difficult. We have a lot of enthusiasm though. Come with me, you will see.'

Cricket in this corner of the Balkans is a recent development, and Vladimir wasted no time in telling me the story of its origins as we wandered through the fort. Having returned to Belgrade in 2007 after a compulsory stint as a conscript in the Serbian army, Vladimir contemplated getting back into rugby league, the game he had grown up playing. But he wasn't warm on the prospect of another punishing pre-season training schedule. 'All my free time I was looking for job. I didn't feel motivated to get fit and win my place in the team again.' One of his team-mates, Haris, felt the same. Haris had played rugby with Vladimir since 2000, and neither was getting any younger; they were after something more sedate, less physically demanding. When Haris suggested cricket, which he had come across during time in London, Vladimir was perplexed. 'I had never seen or heard of this game, so I searched online and found many films of men standing in green fields, wearing stupid clothes, doing nothing.'

He was initially indifferent, partly because he thought it looked dull, but also because there did not seem to be a history of cricket in Serbia. Haris checked with the Serbian Ministry of Sports only to be told that no sport called 'cricket' was listed. A little more research led them to a phone number claiming to be the home of cricket in Belgrade but it was out of use, so they gave up and began to direct their efforts towards finding a more exciting, more Serbian sport to play.

The two would-be sporting pioneers did not know at the time, but there had in fact been a few unsuccessful attempts to launch cricket in Belgrade. Red Star Cricket Club was a team founded in 2002 and dominated by expats. They disappeared shortly afterwards. There were also various claims that a former captain of the Yugoslavian cricket team based in Belgrade had been an MI6 secret agent who helped mastermind the arrest of former President Slobodan Milošević. Rumour had it that once his cover as captain of the Serbian cricket team was blown, he was deported.

A few weeks after their brief flirtation with cricket, a friend of Vladimir's returned from India with news that he had been coached the game by a friend called Baba. Baba was due to visit Belgrade in the autumn so Haris and Vladimir arranged to meet him for a drink. They told him of their vague interest in cricket, and it was agreed that the next morning Baba would introduce them to the sport. It was 18 October 2007 when four Serbs and an Indian stood for the first time in the shadow of a third-century Celtic fort armed with a baseball bat, two tennis balls and a bag full of clothes that Baba explained would act as something called 'stumps'.

'After first training session I still thought this cricket was fucking boring game,' Vladimir told me as we began descending the hundreds of ancient cobbled steps that led from the fort's ramparts to the park below. But although not enamoured at first with the slow pace of the game, the Serbs persevered, vowing to train three times a week. At first they practised only fielding, in the perverse belief that if their fielding skills were honed, batting and bowling would come as a sort of natural progression. Within five training sessions the four pioneers of Serbian cricket had become twenty as more disillusioned rugby players were dragged along. Darko, Nenad, Milan, Dragan, Mladen: some loved it, most gave up in search of a more strenuous workout.

'Gradually I started to enjoy it,' Vladimir admitted. 'Unlike rugby, I found I was always learning new skill. There were so many different ways of hitting four or taking wicket. I understood rugby after playing just few times but after two months of cricket I barely knew anything. Not only was my body working hard, but my mind too.'

And so, with no more than a handful of players, the time came for Haris and Vladimir either to give up or invest in the future. Against their better judgement, they invested. In the winter of 2007 Haris caused no small mutiny in his family by acquiring thousands of dollars, worth of cricket equipment online. When the parcels arrived in Serbia, customs officers were suspicious, but eventually came around. Vladimir bought dozens of cricket DVDs (100 Years of Pace Bowling, Brian Lara 400 Not Out, Calypso Summer, Gooch's Indian Summer and more). Bob Woolmer – the former England batsman and Pakistan coach who was found dead in his hotel room shortly after his team's unexpected defeat to Ireland in the 2007 World Cup – became something of a coaching idol in the Balkans in the months following his death. Vladimir would, he explained, invite team-mates round to his parents' twentieth-storey flat in an ex-Soviet tower block in Mirijevo to eat burek, drink rakia and study alien techniques explained by Woolmer. Cricket became a regular topic of conversation among the emerging squad and training sessions became more competitive. 'We started batting and bowling. Some guys had played baseball before so batting came quite naturally, but our bowling was very shit at first. Soon we improved and as you will see today, now we have many good bowlers.'

Vladimir, in Surrey CCC beanie, heading a
posse of Serbian cricketers.

I was about to get my first glimpse of this ramshackle mob. László, Vladimir, Dunya, Bojan and I paused halfway down the giant staircase leading to the fort gardens where we were to play, and saw them for the first time: the indigenous Serbian cricketers. They were a group of twenty or thirty men, some dressed in white trousers, others in white tops, but rarely a full set. As incongruous with their surroundings as any sports team anywhere in the world, most jogged a gentle warm-up to the base of the ramparts and back while a handful chose instead to warm themselves by diving into their substitute breakfast – a bottle of rakia. It was ten o'clock in the morning.

I was told the men below us were the hardcore; the newly diehard cricketers. They'd have to be to come out for a game in such cold and unwelcoming conditions. Throughout 2008 word had begun to spread around the city about a growing throng of men congregating in Kalemegdan Fort dressed in odd white clothing and shouting strange foreign words like 'howzat' and 'no ball' at each other. Newspapers began to take an interest and newspaper journalists would turn up at training with carefully crafted questions disguised as one basic inquisition: 'What the hell are you guys doing?'

Publicity, of course, brought more players. Vladimir was fast becoming the Pied Piper of Belgrade, except rather than luring children from their beds he was guiding ex-rugby players towards a more sedate pastime. The small British, Indian and Pakistani expat communities took notice and lent incredulous but generous support. Vladimir and his band of brothers found themselves suited and booted at formal functions held at embassies around Belgrade. Eventually two clubs were formed in late 2008: Mirijevo and Stari Grad. The Belgrade Cricket Association followed; then more clubs. The International Cricket Council got wind of a cricketing renaissance in Serbia, inviting Vladimir and Haris to go to cricket's spiritual home at Lord's. As we reached the foot of the fort, Vladimir talked keenly, even emotionally, about that specific moment: 'We dreamed of going to Lord's since we saw the pavilion on our DVDs. For two humble men from Serbia it was an incredible moment and made all our efforts worthwhile. It was beautiful.' I had to agree.

After their visit to London, Vladimir and Haris arrived home for the first official cricket match since the formal birth of the sport in Serbia. It was held on 5 June 2009 in the picturesque rural village of Karlovčić. The opposition? Carmel & District Cricket Club, North Wales. Bemused locals and schoolchildren were given the day off school or work to attend. Eight Serbs, an Englishman, an Indian and a Pakistani made up the home team. All the Serbian players had learned the game within the past year and although, inevitably, they lost to the visitors, they put up a surprisingly good fight.

I was intrigued to see for myself the standard of cricket in Serbia. By the time we reached the group they were all either sufficiently warmed up or drunk. It was clear that the day was a celebration of cricket in Serbia rather than a competitive affair. That said, a sullen-faced journalist from *Danas*, one of Serbia's bestselling newspapers, was there to report on my ride and the scene before him. It turned out he had never heard of cricket and cared little about my ride. Vladimir translated his questions and my answers before the disgruntled journalist rushed back to his car and sped off down the path acting as the wicket. The next day there was a long piece on page six of the newspaper, entitled 'HE CYCLED TO SERBIA ARMED WITH A STICK'. It seemed Vladimir and his band of cricketing brothers faced an uphill PR battle in promoting cricket in Serbia.

The indigenous cricket folk were friendlier than the man from *Danas* and, as one might expect, more enthusiastic about their new favourite sport. After introductions, team photographs and a few healthy glugs of rakia, the game began. In the manner of the fort's rich military history, it was a fiercely contested battle; one in which I represented Vladimir's side, Mirijevo, against local rivals Stari Grad.

I have often heard cricket referred to as 'a funny old game' but this, surely, was the game at its funniest. The previous summer I had represented Marylebone Cricket Club, the oldest cricket club in the world, in matches held at grounds all over England. On every occasion players had worn whites, spikes, a helmet when batting and enjoyed luxuries such as umpires, scorers and tea ladies. But mistakes in the field tended to be greeted by little more than a shrug of the shoulders by the bowler and fours were often ignored by the batsmen's team-mates. Now, on a freezing November morning in Eastern Europe, I found myself having a game with the Serbian national team on a path in the ruins of a third-century Celtic fort, wearing the Austria Cricket Club one-day kit, drinking rakia between overs and wearing batting gloves when fielding so as to minimise the risk of frostbite. But such was the emotional investment of my team-mates in the outcome of the game that I was terrified that if I dropped a catch or bowled a wide they would never talk to me again. A funny old game, as I say.

In a city that is no stranger to epic sporting rivalries (think Red Star Belgrade, think Partizan Belgrade, think occasional riot-induced deaths) the Stari Grad versus Mirijevo clash seemed to fit in quite nicely. Mistakes in the field were greeted with severe anger and tongue lashings, normally from up-and-coming batsman Slobodan or beefy middle-order hitter Nicola 'Johnny' Vukelić. It was clear that bragging rights were at stake, a fact helped by a strong Serbian presence in the two teams – apart from me, there were only three foreigners playing.

One of them was an Indian called Rajat who had first visited Belgrade with his Serbian wife a number of years before. 'I stood in the fort, high above the park, and couldn't believe my eyes. I asked my wife "Is this true? Is there cricket here in Belgrade?" and we walked down to see what these guys were up to. I moved to Serbia a few months later and have played cricket here ever since.'

Another expat was Nasser, the eldest son of the Pakistani Ambassador to Serbia. He, Rajat and the various expats who came and went from Belgrade had taken it upon themselves to teach cricket to the Serbs and their coaching had paid off.

Beneath the walls of Kalemegdan Fort with some of the hardcore of
Serbian cricket. Nicola 'Johnny' Vukelić, Rajat and Slobodan are in the
front, left to right.

The relatively small number of expats involved in Serbian
cricket meant that the standard was not as high as I had seen
in Austria or Belgium, but neither was it terrible and it was
clearly improving fast. Although Serbia is officially one of the
tallest nations on the planet, therefore blessed with an abundance of athletic talent just waiting to be turned into a
rampant fast-bowling unit, there is a fair way to go until
cricket can even dream of competing with basketball and
volleyball as a specialist Serbian sport.

The post-match celebration was an equally boisterous, even
jovial affair, held in an empty beer hall where a man and his
mustachioed band-mates played traditional Serbian songs and
drank not a lot less than the Serbian cricket team. Also drinking
a fair bit at the bar were a pair of Frenchmen – Jean-Baptiste
and Jean-Pierre – who, it emerged, were riding a 1936 tandem
from Paris to Istanbul. Swaying as he spoke, Jean-Baptiste
proudly announced that the tandem had been left exactly

as it was seventy years ago, a fact ably demonstrated by forty-seven punctures and seventy-two broken spokes – fifteen in one day – since leaving Paris. I would come across the two adventurous Frenchmen again at the end of their ride, when they would prove themselves spirited cricketers on the paved streets of Istanbul.

Back at our table, Vladimir was in a relaxed and honest mood after Mirijevo's resounding victory. 'When I met you this morning, unshaven and wearing those dirty clothes, I thought you were idle "save the world" hippie. I thought you were probably vegan too. But I was wrong! You like women, cricket, beer and greasy Serbian food. You are just like me – except you don't have belly.'

George, who had been drinking rakia since breakfast – and possibly since the previous evening – dribbled all over the Ashes urn before passing it to Slobodan, who stared at it until I was sure I saw a tear run down his cheek. At the time I remember thinking that perhaps Slobodan, liked cricket more than anyone I had ever met. Certainly more than Johnny, who told me repeatedly that he would give up the game once his Mancunian girlfriend had become his wife. László was still filming, although his camera was hijacked more than once by local cricketers intent on telling me, via the medium of film, that I would 'almost certainly die' on my way to Australia.

Well after closing time, and proudly sporting my newly acquired, beer-drenched Belgrade Cricket Association polo shirt – complete with a logo clearly influenced by that of Leeds United – I stumbled back to Hostelche with Dunya, Bojan and László still in tow, and passed out on the floor next to my bunk. It had been a wonderful and eye-opening introduction to cricket in the Balkans.

When I first heard that cricket was played in Serbia it struck me as both surprising and, frankly, borderline weird. I remember thinking that cricket's journey from seventeenth-century rural England to post-socialist Serbia sounded an

Slobodan, devoted cricketer and avid smoker, kissing the Ashes urn.

improbable one. I asked myself how a game that the British had transported to all corners of their empire had found a home in a country with few historical links to Britain or any of its cricketing relatives.

But well after I had left Belgrade, on long, lonely days in the Sudanese desert or during humid nights on my back under a fly net in the Indian jungle, I thought about the time I spent there. I told anyone who would listen about that cold, foggy corner of the Balkans, and the game I played with Vladimir, Nebojsa, Dragan, Slobodan and the rest. In an interview on *Test Match Special* I told Jonathan Agnew about the cricketing revolution taking place behind the old Iron Curtain; I told Australian cricket-lovers in Syria, players in India and diplomats in Bangladesh.

While I had been pleased to find Hungarian cricket to be almost entirely free of eccentricity, I was equally delighted to find idiosyncrasies in the Serbian game. The story of cricket in Serbia is of course a charmingly odd and eccentric one, but perhaps I should not have been so surprised about its existence; it was born of circumstance, aided by Serbia's emergence from an old regime and subsequent independence, first from Yugoslavia and then from Montenegro as recently as 2006. Links with the West have naturally developed. Vladimir told me that when McDonald's opened its first Central European branch in Belgrade in March 1988 there were street parties the likes of which he had never seen before, and has never witnessed since. McDonald's became the pride of Belgrade; an emblem of the country's emergence and new relationship with the West. At football matches, Belgrade fans taunted teams from neighbouring countries with chants of 'We have McDonald's and you don't!'.

Independence brought with it freedom of labour and technology. Haris travelled to London to study at university. Vladimir went to Spain and became fluent in the language. Serbs can travel more easily, soak up unfamiliar cultures and bring home new ideas ('Let's play cricket!'); more foreigners are visiting Belgrade and the rest of Serbia. Indians in particular, riding the wave of fast-paced development in their own country, have begun to travel more. As I travelled further and played more cricket, I would come to see that wherever these subcontinental cricket junkies settle, the game tends to flourish.

While the circumstances of Serbia's recent past have certainly played their part in the birth of cricket there, I like to think of its emergence as representing huge ambition and enthusiasm on the part of Vladimir, Haris and their friends. As my journey progressed, Vladimir especially became a strange sort of standard-bearer for passion and perseverance, both skills that I was trying to hone and maintain to keep me on the road to Brisbane. I later told Vladimir that meeting him and his cricketing companions in Belgrade had, during difficult times on the road, inspired me to stick with my dream of making the Ashes on my bicycle. In our world of infinite diversity it is comforting to be reminded of the similarities we share with people from far away. Often we are bound by the games we share and Vladimir and I certainly shared a love of cricket. It was good to know that I wasn't the only cricket tragic out there.

Later on my trip I wrote to Vladimir from Asia to thank him again for introducing me to cricket in his country, and to ask him for a few recollections from my time there. He wrote back with his memories of what we got up to:

The day after our cricket match, horribly hungover, I picked Oli up from Hostelche and, in the ice-cold rain, took him to my parents' place in the suburban area of Mirijevo (Serbia is not the richest country in the world, so even the General Secretary of our cricket federation has to live with his parents!). Having eaten much soup and pork, cooked by my mother, we went to my room to watch some of my cricket DVDs. While Oli tried to teach me to bowl underarm leg breaks I checked out his female friends on Facebook. He had many attractive friends – perhaps he will find me an English wife one day!

For the rest of Oli's time in Belgrade we were both working hard – me in my job and Oli preparing for the ride through the rest of Serbia. When he left I said goodbye and watched him ride away from Hostelche towards Požarevac, where Slobodan Milošević is buried and where I was based in the army. The night after he left Belgrade, Oli called me around 8 o'clock. It was dark and he was in his tent. He asked me if there were any wolves in the forests near Belgrade and I told him there were – I was lying, of course.

We kept in touch every day until he crossed the Bulgarian border and we all followed his progress towards the Ashes. He is an Ambassador for Serbian cricket!

GOODBYE BIG RIVER

Sounds and smells from the kitchen woke me on the morning I was to leave Belgrade. Bojan, as he had done every morning since I arrived a stranger a week ago, was cooking a traditional – and free – Serbian breakfast: bacon, a fried egg, cheese and diced, fresh cucumber and tomatoes, all to be washed down with a shot of rakia ('sipped, not gulped – is the way of the peasant farmer!').

Vladimir arrived to say goodbye, to wish me good luck and to warn me about the journey ahead. He was concerned that I was heading east just as winter was beginning to get nasty. There had been freak snow in October that had made road travel impossible and more was on the way. I insisted that I'd cope, although pedalling east out of Old Belgrade it was easy to see the weather shift that had occurred in the week since my arrival. Autumn had become winter. Whereas the streets had been full of hawkers, shoppers, coffee drinkers and people watchers, now chairs and tables were stacked and chained and barely anyone ventured out into the cold. Belgradians peered at me from behind steamy café windows, no doubt grateful it was not them outside, heading for Bulgaria on their bicycle. I stopped at one such café and bought four burek, packed them into the top of my panniers and raced off to try to warm up my limbs.

It is said locally that if Rome has seven hills, Belgrade has seven hundred. I seemed to scale and descend every one of them as my wheels took me from one suburb to the next: Zvezdara, Mali Mokri Lug, Kaludjerica. Towards the edge of the city the neighbourhoods became increasingly rundown; more so than I had expected. Big, ugly socialist-era tower blocks dominated, washing hung from every balcony, drying slowly in the winter sun.

As settlements became less dense nearer the city limits I leapt out of the saddle, pumped my legs furiously up a long, shallow hill, eager to work off the beer and burek of Belgrade. Approaching a forest around a sweeping left-hand bend, I caught a glimpse of a group of racing cyclists in Lycra and, keen as ever to test my fitness, hauled myself out of the saddle to pass them. I gave a cocky 'lovely day for a bike ride' salute and sped past before nipping behind a shed for a pee when they were out of sight. I passed them again twenty minutes later and said the same thing. It amused me, if not them.

At the top of another hill I was ushered to the side of the road by three delightful old ladies; fruit-sellers huddled behind a wall of apples. They were clearly fed up with the lack of passing trade – although surely not surprised considering the distance from any sort of settlement – but, nevertheless, handed me an entire crate of fruit that I made a decent attempt at devouring. I could manage only four or five apples, but as I was leaving they loaded my bike down with even more before refusing payment outright.

The three delightful old fruit-sellers on top of a hill outside Belgrade.

That afternoon I raced through smoggy Smederevo as quickly as possible, stopping only to note in my diary never to return because it was a 'smoggy, industrial hellhole'. By a quarter to four it was getting dark. The area I found myself in was relatively built-up, making wild camping tricky. Just past a sign that told me I was in Vranovo, I found a mud track running away from the river beside five bungalows, each with a burnt-out car or tractor in the front garden.

Smoke climbed out of two gigantic cooling towers adjacent to the bungalows until it met with the low-hanging cloud to form a giant hourglass of condensation.

When cycling the Rhine Valley a few weeks earlier, out of an appreciation for the size, scale and raw beauty of the industry there, I had made up a song I called 'The Majesty of Industry'. I had continued to sing it whenever I saw beautiful examples of industry, although the tune differed depending on my mood: in my low moments it was a melancholic Leonard Cohen-esque dirge that I told myself had every chance of being a cult classic one day; when I felt chipper it turned into a bouncy number that Stevie Wonder might have been proud of. I sang a downbeat version of 'The Majesty of Industry' in front of the cooling towers of Vranovo, and was ruefully aware that I was, even if only a little, beginning to lose my mind.

I reached the bungalows and asked the man shovelling earth in the garden of Bungalow 1 if I could sleep in his garden. He snarled and pointed at Bungalow 2 (I promised myself I would endeavour to learn the Serbian for 'can I sleep in your garden, please?'). The man at Bungalow 2 was marginally less interested than the man at Bungalow 1, but I was happy about that because he had a limp, several scars on his face and was carrying a shotgun, which made the thought of a night sleeping in his garden a slightly less preferable option than drowning in the river that I could make out flowing in the middle distance. No one was home at Bungalows 3 or 4, and when the young girl at Bungalow 5 ran inside screaming as I approached, I set my mind to wild camping.

I spotted a flat, roughly ploughed patch of field beyond Bungalow 5, behind which the land dropped away into a stinking waste pit. A man at Bungalow 5, now on his doorstep holding his daughter's hand and wearing a white string vest and immodest, dirty white underpants, ushered me towards the field. By this time it was pitch dark and below zero so, quickly and with the help of my cricket bat, I flattened some earth in the corner of the field, removed a few loose rocks and began the daily ritual of tent erection.

Just before the tent was up, and just after I lost all feeling in my fingers, an old lady who must have been eighty appeared from the stinking waste pit. Dressed in a long skirt, thick jumper, woolly hat and with more than a suggestion of a wispy, silver beard glinting in the moonlight, she was carrying an impossibly heavy pile of logs over her shoulders. We spent ten minutes conversing in our respective languages, not understanding a word of what the other was saying, but I gathered from her demeanour that the field belonged to her, and that she wanted me off it. Although I felt ashamed for arguing with a bearded female octogenarian carrying many logs, and, of course, for trespassing, I was tired and had no energy to move. I dug my heels in and, eventually, she gave up on me and wandered deep into the woods beside the waste dump. I did not see or hear her again and after a six o'clock bowl of rice, chicken stock and stewed apples, I found myself drifting off to sleep to the distant hum of a tractor's engine.

Four hours later I was woken abruptly by the rather closer roar of a tractor's engine. As the sound began to press uncomfortably upon my eardrums, I unzipped my tent and peeked out wearily into the darkness. A middle-aged man with a beard – more impressive than log-lady's, but less surprising – jumped down from the tractor and walked towards me. My first impression was that he was a committed farmer, and possibly a relative of log-lady, indulging in the remarkably romantic, albeit rarely practised pursuit of moonlight ploughing. I wondered whether he was going to have another go at moving me on, but he did not. Instead he seemed genuinely sorry for waking me up and, somewhat surprisingly, left me to my slumber.

By morning my surroundings were wholly changed. It was light, of course, but visibility was limited to twenty metres by a thick fog. Still, it turned out my imaginings of the night before had been correct and the section of field I could see, except for the small corner which had acted as my bed, was immaculately ploughed; with a little help from my cricket bat, it made a nice breakfast table. Just as I was finishing off a bowl of porridge the nocturnal farmer, up early even after a late night at the tractor's helm, appeared out of the mist and welcomed me like a son who had returned after years in the trenches. After a firm handshake and a slap across the shoulder he handed me a lovely warm mug of tea, watched me drink it, shook my hand and bid me farewell before disappearing into foggy obscurity.

It was lucky there was only one road east out of town, and that I had a compass to find it, because my sense of direction deserted me as I left the field. I always found it strange beginning a new day when I had arrived the previous evening in the dark, but that morning was made even more difficult by the disorientating mist. I did find the road though and, heading eastwards, pedalled for an hour until I reached Požarevac, where I did *not* visit the grave of Slobodan Milošević, but where I *did* stop for a burek and coffee in the Grizzly Café, the walls of which were adorned with a terrifying number of grizzly bear photos. I did a lot of pointing and gesturing, and the owner did a lot of nodding, chuckling and pretending to die.

Out of Požarevac I passed two tanks being tested on an assault course of frozen mud, before rejoining the Danube much later at a place called Veliko Gradište; a name I decided I could say very well in a Serbian accent:

V-y-e-l-i-k-o G-r-r-r-a-d-i-s-t-a-y.

Just south of V-y-e-l-i-k-o G-r-r-r-a-d-i-s-t-a-y the Danube flowed around an island a few miles wide before narrowing between the vertical walls of the Iron Gate Gorge. There it formed the border between Serbia on my side and Romania to the north. Two days later I would be able to see three countries, when I crossed into Bulgaria's north-west corner.

No one in their right mind goes to this part of Serbia in winter, especially not to camp, so when I found a campsite that night near the small settlement of Golubac I was both surprised and delighted; particularly so because it was deserted, closed and, as a result, free. I unloaded my bicycle, hurled her over the eight-foot fence, scaled it myself, and wheeled her down to a wooden pontoon that hung inches above the river. By four o'clock the tent was up and I was cooking rice. It was silent. I was alone. Not a single person on the planet knew where I was. Then I saw a lone fisherman a few hundred metres downstream, near the bank. I escaped his attention for a while as he cast a net the size of a bed blanket into the lake, but during a break in proceedings he noticed me, started his engine and performed the aquatic, slow-motion equivalent of a *Top Gun* fly-by. He neither said anything nor looked like he would say anything and before long he was gone. He was the last person I saw or heard before I got back on the road at first light, sixteen hours later.

November nights are long in Serbia. The sun sets around five o'clock and rises the following morning at eight. The people may have been friendly but the weather was not. Temperatures during the day struggled to rise above freezing and at night dropped much lower. The water in my bottles occasionally froze inside my tent. I wore almost all the clothes I carried: thick socks, long johns, fleeces, woolly hats; one night I even wore a balaclava. In Germany I had taken up the disgusting habit of peeing in a spare water bottle to save having to emerge from my tent in the middle of the night. In Serbia I discovered that the same water bottle became a useful hand- and toe-warming tool for at least ten minutes after the event.

Each morning I struggled to emerge from my sleeping bag, instead letting my alarm go off every five minutes for up to an hour before I mustered the will to start all over again. On the day that brought me my first major hill climb, it was no different.

I hugged the south bank of the Danube until I reached a village called Donji Milanovac, which was notable for two things: one, it was the site of a series of Mesolithic settlements – sadly closed for the winter – dating from 8,000 BC; and two, it was the point at which I left the Danube for the first time for one and a half thousand miles. Until this journey the Danube had simply been a thin blue line on a map and I had known nothing of the myriad characters that inhabited its banks. Since Ingolstadt, when I first pulled up alongside it, Europe's longest river had become a constant companion, a navigator of sorts as I stuck to its path like a limpet. It kept me on the right track to each daily destination and, of course, to Australia. It was no longer just a mark on a map, nor simply an historic trade route that linked medieval villages with the great cities of Central Europe – Vienna, Bratislava, Belgrade. I had explored it, got to know it and made friends along it. I would be sorry to leave it.

My last night camping along the Danube.

I pedalled for most of the afternoon, away from the river until I reached the house of a man called Tihomir Marković. It was beginning to snow when Tihomir saw me fighting with my map. I was unsure which route to take towards the

Bulgarian border, some forty-five miles away. 'You are lost?' came a voice, muffled by the worsening blizzard. I turned to see a man and a woman leaning on a closed gate in front of a small bungalow with smoke rising out of its chimney. A flickering light inside gave the impression of warmth. I nodded. 'Yes, I am lost.'

'Where you want to go?' the man asked. I told him I wanted to get to Negotin before dark. His face dropped and he scoffed. 'Is too far, Negotin. Will take three hours, maybe four, and is very steep road.' He pointed to a mud track leading up and across the cliff face away from the main road in front of him. 'Come inside out of snow. My wife make pumpkin cakes.'

The wooden bungalow was toasty. The fire had been lit some hours earlier. Piled logs decorated one wall. Old wooden chairs were scattered around the main room and an old man, Tihomir's father, lay prone on a steel-framed bed by the front window. He did not notice us at first. Tihomir's wife disappeared into the kitchen to prepare Turkish coffee and cut some pumpkin cake and it was only when she rejoined us that the old man realised he was no longer alone.

Tihomir told me he had come back to live with his father five years ago, when he got sick for the first time. He told me that he, like many young rural Serbs, had worked in Western Europe for years, every month sending back as much as he could afford to his parents. He asked me whether I supported my parents and when I replied that I did not – that, if anything, they supported me – he smiled and shook his head disapprovingly.

He still offered me a bed for the night, but although I was tempted by the thought of a few glasses of wine in good company, a night sleeping in front of a roaring fire and a hearty breakfast to send me on my way up a mountain, I had become obsessed with reaching my daily distance targets as a way of keeping my mind on the final destination. I thanked Tihomir and his wife for the offer and prepared to leave, packing two chunks of pumpkin cake into my handlebar

Tihomir Marković and his pumpkin cake-making wife.

bag and ensuring I was watertight since the snow I had arrived in had been replaced by cold, horizontal rain. I was back on the road an hour before sunset.

Tihomir had told me I would be lucky to make four miles an hour, and before long I was travelling at only three. It was not fun. After seven miles and two hours I stopped to take off my shoes, each one weighed down by a puddle of water within. I tied them to a pannier and replaced them with flip-flops. It was the first – and would be the last – time I had ever worn the unlikely combination of ski trousers, ski jacket and flip-flops. After three hellish hours pedalling in the pitch dark, my face lashed with rain and no bicycle lights – or, more precisely, with no batteries for my bicycle lights – to light my way, I finally rode into Negotin. I raced down the main street whooping with delight. Solitude was beginning to make me do funny things.

Although most of Negotin seemed shut down, I headed for the one building that was dimly lit. At first sight it was the most depressing building I had ever laid eyes on; then it became the most depressing hotel I had ever stayed in, and easily the smelliest. Three of the staff, dressed in matching blue boiler suits, sat smoking and laughing at me from behind a Perspex screen. I had not seen a mirror for days but I knew I looked wet, filthy and ridiculous. I checked in, dragged sixty kilograms of kit up four flights of stairs, kicked off my flip-flops and fell back on the bed.

For the first time in weeks I thought about the journey ahead in entirely positive terms. I knew that days like the ones I had experienced since Belgrade were ones I would cherish when I was back in London, stuck on a crowded commuter train or at a desk in an air-conditioned office. They were tough, but I knew that I could tackle the hardships. I had forced myself to sleep in fields, argue with old ladies and pedal into grim, drizzly darkness. The plains of the various rivers I had cycled had, over the past two days, almost surreptitiously become hills, and they would soon become mountains. No one knew me, but I felt at home in that distant corner of Europe; I felt I belonged because my legs had taken me all the way there. The rain, the cold, the solitude, the long days and longer nights, the effort it had taken to get that far. Whether it was despite all these things or because of them, I did not know. But I *did* know that I had rarely felt more alive.

I fell into a deep sleep, fully clothed in the sodden kit I had been wearing for three days.

BULGARIA

CLIMBING A MOUNTAIN ON A BICYCLE: PART I

The hours pass: one . . . two . . . three . . . four . . . Each corner disguises itself as the summit. I cock my head back, peer upwards and wonder how the road can still be climbing when all I can see are birds circling grey skies. Hairpins, how long will you make me suffer?

NEW COUNTRY, NEW challenge. Before I left home I had taken out comprehensive travel insurance through the Mountaineering Club of Great Britain. It did not occur to me at the time how apt my choice of insurer was. If the ride into Negotin two days earlier was my first big hill climb on a bicycle then the ride into Sofia was my first proper mountain ascent.

I reached the wooded foothills of Stara Planina, or the Balkan Mountains, above the town of Montana at dawn on the morning of 2 December, the meandering valleys of the Danube and its tributaries long forgotten. I paused to take in the scale of what lay ahead. I estimated it would take all morning and most of the afternoon to climb. I guessed I would find it difficult. Almost two thousand vertical metres were decorated with the same hairpin bends Patrick Leigh Fermor described as 'unfurling like a gypsy's ribbon' when he first caught sight of them on his walk to Constantinople in 1933. The Petrohan Pass; back then merely uneven shale and rocks, today covered in newly laid tarmac.

I was grateful for the tarmac if not for the endless hairpins. The air temperature hovered around freezing and the wind-chill made it feel significantly colder. Every few hundred metres I had to pull to the side of the road, breathless and cold. Regulating my body temperature was impossible because my sweat made me shiver to my core. I rearranged my clothing at every self-inflicted pause in an attempt to find a solution, but nothing worked. I resigned myself to my cold and sweaty fate. Lactic acid built up in my legs but I had to carry on because Australia lay over those hills; at least the road that would take me there did. At home I'd have given up a long time ago, but if I wanted to make it to a warm bed I had to keep cycling. My bicycle and that mountain were all I had.

I sang Morrissey songs as I climbed. I had never considered the uplifting qualities of The Smiths, but now they helped me find a rhythm with their punctured bicycles and desolate hillsides. Two hours into the climb I was out of the saddle, pounding the pedals and singing freely to Herman Dune, Josh Ritter, The Band, The View, Fanfarlo. Feel-good tunes for an increasingly feel-good climb. A car passed and I waved and smiled. In return I received the finger and a dollop of phlegm. The revitalising effect of my singalong was gone in an instant. I felt angry and retreated inwards, suddenly all too aware of my vulnerability perched on the side of a mountain in a strange place, so far from home. Since I left I had met with so much kindness, but ignorant abuse had come regularly on the road and it never took much for me to withdraw into my shell. I had no one to laugh it off with, to take it out on, or to share my agony with. The road could be a lonely place.

On the other hand the encouragement of those I met, however fleetingly, always gave me a mental lift that often translated into a physical boost. Here on the mountain, perhaps fuelled by the unlikely sight of a man climbing hair-pins on a laden bicycle in the dead of winter, the majority of drivers slowed as they neared me, shouting words of support before speeding off tooting their horns. They will never know how much they helped me. In that bleak, wintry corner of the Balkans, my fellow road-users were the closest I had to friends and their camaraderie was like a shot of adrenalin that I relied on to propel me onwards.

As I belted out the words to Josh Ritter's 'Golden Age of Radio' my world finally changed and became a far more pleasant place. Anyone who has climbed a mountain on a bicycle will know how I felt at that moment, as my lungs heaved for the last time, the road levelled and I gazed downwards for the first time in hours. Pain in my legs, in my arms, in my lungs dissolved. Sweat on my brow dried into a salty mess and my heart felt like it no longer yearned to escape my chest; like it was content within me. Hours of climbing should have rendered my legs useless, but they felt lighter and younger than when I'd got out of bed that morning. They were fuelled and strengthened by intensity, exercise and achievement. I turned the bicycle, leaned on my handlebars and looked back at the valley floor and Montana, which had become a toy town with toy cars driving toy streets. It didn't matter that snow began to fall as I started my descent because I had scaled my first mountain and nothing else mattered. It felt magical.

AMAZING INCONGRUOUSNESS OF SCENE

The snow fell lightly at first, then heavier as I made my way down the mountain. I rode at a snail's pace to avoid an ice-induced crash and because I did not want the descent to end. I freewheeled for what seemed like hours, past old ladies wrapped up in winter shawls, selling honey at roadside stalls; through villages where the only sign of life was the smoke that tumbled out of every chimney. Most villagers were no doubt thankful to be warm inside but I was grateful to be out on a mountain in the snow, fifty-three days into my bicycle journey and within reach of my next European capital.

By the time I reached the flat expanse below it was pitch dark and raining and I leaned over my handlebars attempting to shield myself for the final two-hour stretch into Sofia. I had found somewhere to stay in the city using Couchsurfing.com, a social networking site for travellers in need of a free bed. I had chosen the home of a half-Russian half-Bulgarian girl called Kristina who, it turned out, lived on the eighteenth floor of a crumbling tower block with her mother. With more than eighty miles and one mountain behind me it was with some dismay that I noted the absence of a functioning lift. With no other option, I lugged my bicycle and gear up the eighteen floors to Kristina's flat.

As I laid out my drenched belongings on a tarpaulin in the immaculate sitting room, I explained with some satisfaction that I was exhausted after a day climbing up and over the Petrohan Pass from Montana. Kristina's response was about to burst my bubble. 'You do not have to take that road from Montana,' she said. 'It is very steep. You can take another road that is completely flat.' Our relationship could have soured after that, but Kristina was kind and chatty and turned out to be a wonderfully generous host. Besides, I was proud of my first mountain ascent and would not have had my arrival in Sofia any other way.

The following evening Kristina and I went for a drink with another couch surfer. Victoria was a scriptwriter for children's television and, well versed in *Blackadder*, *Only Fools and Horses* and *Monty Python*, had an astonishing knack for English word-play. When Kristina left us, we wandered to a candlelit bar where we sat high in the eaves on a balcony overlooking a crowd of well-dressed young Sofians. As they bounced jauntily to the sounds of Western indie bands we drank red wine and I decided that I loved being back in a city. I had already fallen in love with Budapest and Belgrade and although I did not fall for Sofia to the same extent, I did for Victoria. I had spoken no more than a few words to a girl my age since leaving home. But now I was back doing what twenty-nine-year-old single men are supposed to do: meet and fall for beautiful, funny, multi-lingual brunettes from Eastern Europe. By the time we had cracked open our third bottle

Burek at Kristina's Mum's house. It wasn't always so
impressively presented.

of red I had decided to give up cycling to Australia and move
in with Victoria instead. She, however, had decided otherwise
and, thankfully, by morning, when I woke up on the floor
beside her bed, my hangover was such that I agreed with
her. Still, I'd have preferred not to leave her so soon, but I
had to. I had an engagement to stick to.

The Bulgarian National Sports Academy is a typically vast
and offensive architectural monstrosity and throwback to the
sporting ambition of the communist era. There I was greeted
by a man in a black leather jacket who looked tiny beneath
its soaring concrete walls. We had spoken on the phone the
day before when he told me that a representative of the
International Cricket Council had written to him telling him
that if an English cricketing cyclist got in touch, he should
arrange a game to welcome him. The man introduced himself
with a heavy Asian accent. 'My name is Saif Rehman. I am

captain and coach of Bulgarian cricket team and first man in world to study cricket as university degree.'

I had been disappointed to learn that the Bulgarians were under orders from cricket's world governing body because it made me wonder whether they had written to every country on my route, and perhaps that explained all the enthusiasm for winter cricket I had found since leaving England. Still, Saif's passion for the game was apparent and it was impossible not to like him. As he led me into the academy's main building, past shaven-headed gymnasts and barrel-chested weightlifters, he told me that he had been a successful actor and playwright in his native Pakistan.

I had been put in touch with Saif by Angus Bell, an old university friend and cricketing adventurer who had driven his beat-up Skoda from Glasgow to Istanbul and written a bestselling book about his experiences, originally called *Slogging the Slavs*, then reissued as *Batting on the Bosphorus*. As Angus discovered, Saif had always dreamed of spreading the game of cricket to some obscure corner of the world and, after a holiday on the Black Sea coast in 2005, had decided Bulgaria would be the perfect spot. 'I am actor,' he said, 'but my first love was cricket. When I saw that it was only Asians who played cricket in Bulgaria, I thought I should move there and teach it to local people.' I had doubted I would ever again meet anyone who could match Vladimir's fierce passion for the game and I was delighted to have met my next cricket tragic. 'I am so pleased Angus put us in touch,' I said to Saif, and he nodded in agreement.

Cricket had in fact appeared in Bulgaria as early as the 1980s when Indian, Pakistani and Bangladeshi medical students used to play each other in Sofia. But the sport was not recognised by the government until 2001 when the Bulgarian Cricket and Kickboxing Club was formed – the unusual partnership a way of avoiding tricky bureaucracy. By 2005 cricket and kickboxing had sensibly gone their separate ways and Saif, new in the country, approached the National Sports Academy to formalise cricket's recognition at government level. At the academy, modules like Olympism and Olympic Movement, Basic Chemistry, Sporting Intellect, Karate, Greek Folk Dance, Baseball and Weight-lifting were available to students. Saif succeeded in getting cricket added to the curriculum and now a handful of Bulgarians study it as part of their degree, taught by Saif and the established baseball coach, Luci.

Saif led me into a packed, faux-oak-panelled lecture theatre deep in the academy's bowels. Inside, hundreds of men sat in silence. We took two seats in the front row and joined the calm. A suited man wearing spectacles entered and the room rose to its feet in applause. He took to the lectern onstage and began a forty-five-minute monologue in Bulgarian, punctuated by more clapping amid howls of laughter and encouragement.

'What is going on? Who is this man?' I asked Saif.

'He is Bulgarian Minister of Sport. We are celebrating fifty years of Bulgarian rugby and five years of cricket. It is a proud day for sport in this country.'

I did not doubt it. Saif pointed out dozens of Bulgaria's greatest sportsmen and women in the room, most of whom were present in a representational capacity as members of the academy board: an Olympic gold medal-winning weight-lifter here, a high-beam medallist there. A handful of the country's best rugby players were asked to collect medals from the minister. Having slouched increasingly horizontally in my chair I sat bolt upright when I heard my name. Saif jogged my arm and told me that the minister had begun talking about 'an Englishman who is travelling by bicycle all the way to Australia with the aim of promoting Bulgarian cricket'. A round of hearty applause broke out and I was urged to my feet to accept the acclaim. At the drinks reception immediately afterwards I was approached by several of the gathered throng and thanked for cycling such a long way, and all to support Bulgarian cricket. Clearly some of the information had been lost in translation; I was not quite sure whether to admit the mistake or not.

Feeling like something of a fraud, I headed with Saif to an Astroturf hockey pitch within the grounds of the academy, with great views southwards towards the imposing Mount Vitosha. About twenty-five men in whites – more than enough for two teams – waited in the freezing cold. Saif split them into Medical Students (all Indian or Pakistani) and Sports Academy Students (five Bulgarians, a few Pakistanis, an Indian stomach surgeon and me) and encouraged us to get the game going before we froze to death.

Angus and I were not the first Englishmen to play cricket in that part of the world. Not only had Patrick Leigh Fermor preceded me in negotiating the Petrohan Pass into Sofia in 1933, but he had played cricket in the Bulgarian capital, too. Commenting on the game, played with English friends including the British Consul at the time, Boyd Tollinton, he noted, 'I made five. Out middle stump, amazing incongruousness of scene, diversity of nations. Bulgarian onlookers realizing that it is true that the English are not quite right in the head.'

Seventy-six years later I expected the scene still looked fairly incongruous. Certainly the Bulgarians beyond the fence still thought us foreigners not quite right in the head, although now I was the only Englishman in a field of South Asians; and, of course, there were a handful of Bulgarians involved, too.

The Medical Students batted first, posting an above-par 167 off their allotted twenty overs. The Bulgarians on my team, despite having chosen cricket as a module for their degree, seemed utterly indifferent towards the game. Perhaps the cold was to blame, or maybe it was that they had been forced to play to make a visiting cyclist happy; it could even have been down to the fact that they would rather have been practising their Greek Folk Dance moves. But I suspected their lack of interest was a symptom of being left to freeze on the boundary rather than asked to bowl an over or two. Not one of them was given a bowl by the Pakistani captain and I could not help thinking such a tactic was not the best way to encourage local kids to get into cricket.

Still, when it came to our turn to bat I was pleased to see the Indian stomach surgeon and a Bulgarian lad get the innings going. The rest of the Bulgarians huddled together in the bleachers in tracksuits, with woolly hats pulled low over their eyes. They still gave the impression of wanting to be anywhere but playing cricket and I did not really blame them. As far as they were concerned they were about to be on the wrong end of a hiding from a group of Pakistanis who had been raised on a strict diet of cricket.

None of them expected to win, so it was a surprise to them when, in the space of a few overs, the game began to turn our way. After a few fours, the Medical Students started bickering about who should bowl and who should field where. 'He cannot field at fine leg, he is much too fat! Put him short leg, he has good natural protection.' Bickering quickly became infighting and the bowlers lost their way. A few players thought they knew best and shouted unhelpful advice from the boundary: 'Don't bowl a wide! Don't bowl it on his legs, he likes it there!' And the Indian stomach surgeon did like it on his legs as he whipped a succession of fours to the mid-wicket fence. The Bulgarians in the bleachers perked up and hollered support from the sidelines. It was getting dark by the time our Bulgarian number seven hit the winning runs, a nurdled four square of a dawdling fine leg.

Celebrations were short-lived. A verbal spat ensued – something to do with a few poor umpiring decisions – that had not let up when I packed my bags and headed back to Kristina's. When I saw Saif later that evening he laughed and told me the Asians had been so angry about the umpiring that, despite the dim light, they had forced the National Sports Academy team into playing another game and had duly thrashed them.

Unsure what to think of my brief encounter with the cricketers of Bulgaria, I headed to Saif's for a curry that evening and ended up watching recordings of some of his plays in Pakistan. The next morning, after leftover curry (practice, perhaps, for the Indian leg of my journey), I left Sofia and headed into the Bulgarian wilderness.

NOWHERE TOWNS

When I was growing up, Timmy Mallett lived in a house at the bottom of our garden. I am aware that that makes it sound like he lived in a shed; he did not, his house was beyond our fence. Before he moved in, the house had belonged to he of the husky voice, singer-songwriter Chris Rea. So it turned out to be one of the most surprising twists of travel through Bulgaria that every few hours a truck would pass and I would hear 'Driving Home for Christmas' blaring out of its speakers. I found it a very odd and inexplicable experience, but at the same time deeply comforting in the lead-up to the festive period. It flew in the face of everything else in that corner of the world that seemed so alien.

As Serbia had been, Bulgaria was a grey place in winter; even the grass, so green through Europe, had lost its colour and the world around me was monochrome, like an old movie; coats and trousers and hats were dark greys and browns. Only the foreigner, me with a bright blue bike and a red raincoat, lent the landscape any colour at all. Mongrel dogs prowled the streets of down-and-out towns that had probably seen better days, but possibly hadn't. But these dogs were the lucky ones. Some of their brothers and sisters lay on the road, squashed by passing traffic into dog-shaped pancakes.

The only break I got from the back country was in Plovdiv, Bulgaria's second largest city. Victoria grew up there and although she was not able to join me, she introduced me to some of her friends and I spent a couple of nights drinking in fashionable bars with them. Dating as far back as 4000 BC Plovdiv is one of the oldest cities in the world, laid out over seven hills with hundreds of archaeological sites built by its various conquerors: two well-preserved Roman amphitheatres and a forum; medieval walls and towers; Ottoman baths; mosques. It was a welcome distraction from cycling through nondescript towns where gypsies pretending to be cowboys rode horse-drawn carts down dusty main streets. Life for the inhabitants of those nowhere places must have been tough and it occurred to me more than once that perhaps I shouldn't have been brandishing my shiny new bicycle with all its valuable gear through such an impoverished place. People lived off the land and few seemed to have jobs. Gangs of men gathered in one-street towns and I became the focus of every pair of eyes as I rested under shelters or trawled the aisles of greasy supermarkets. For the first time I longed to be somewhere else – Serbia, Hungary, home, anywhere. I felt different from the people I was encountering. I am sure they thought I looked pretty odd and out of place, too.

Outside towns I camped in fields beside the road, hidden behind whatever foliage best protected me from prying eyes. One night I was so tired and the moonlight so weak that a roadside ditch provided ample protection, although the occasional passing juggernaut kept me awake until late. I rode flat roads that followed deep valleys and craned upwards to see snow-capped peaks that, if I had taken a circuitous route towards Turkey, would have offered me the opportunity for a couple of days in a ski resort. But I carried on cycling instead, intent on reaching my second continent before Christmas. Vehicles hurtled by with little thought for little me, until one particularly dumb truck driver ignored me to such an extent that he brushed my pannier as he went by and sent me flying over a railing and down a steep escarpment. I was shaken and seriously angry as I rode cautiously to the next town and holed up in the railway station operations room, where I was plied with endless cups of sweet tea by a Bulgarian fat controller until I had calmed down.

The crash set me on a few days of negativity and it was hard to break the cycle. I was sick of the rain, sick of the cold and the endless traffic. I wondered what cycling in the heat would be like and I came to the conclusion that I would enjoy it far more. I yearned for warmth and to be in places

I had left home to see: Syria, Sudan, India, Indonesia. Europe had felt like a long stretch and the bad weather meant I had not seen the best of her. But I could not let myself dream of sunshine yet. I had been on the road for a little over two months and now I had the Turkish winter to negotiate.

TURKEY

'When you travel, remember that a foreign country is not designed to make you comfortable. It is designed to make its own people comfortable' – Clifton Fadiman

MERHABA, MY FRIENDS

I peer across a shallow valley towards the mosques that tower above Edirne's single-storey skyline. My first view of Turkey. The call to prayer echoes from speakers on minarets to form an exotic orchestra that gives me the sense that I am far from the world I know. My wheels have been turning for sixty-two days but it feels a lot longer.

I HAD LONG considered Istanbul to be the end of the first section of my ride; after all, the waters of the Bosphorus cutting through the heart of the city create the geographic and cultural boundary between Europe and Asia, East and West, meaning that when I pedalled into the historic centre, Sultanahmet, I would have covered the width of an entire continent on my bicycle. This was something I did not dare consider until I was close to achieving it, but perhaps my target should have been Edirne, the old capital of the Ottoman Empire, because it was there beside the Turkish border with Bulgaria that I found my first major cultural shift, as Western Christianity came face to face with Islamism.

Pedalling up a steep hill into Edirne itself I found hustle and bustle and boisterous activity the likes of which I had not seen in Europe. Tradesmen wheeled creaking carts and wheel-barrows, rode rusty motorbikes and drove lurching trucks. Hawkers occupied murky street corners trying to persuade anyone that passed to buy from them. To me, an outsider, it seemed as if I was the only stranger in a world where everyone knew each other; and each other's business. The Turks are renowned as traders and merchants, salesmen of every description; they built an empire on the back of it. When I arrived in Edirne it may have been dark and cold but the streets were jammed and the noise was cacophonous and everyone was busying themselves with some task or another.

Bicycle safely stored in a grubby hotel lobby under the watchful eye of a ten-year-old boy acting as receptionist, I went out for what I intended to be a brief late-evening wander that turned into a mammoth sightseeing and people-watching excursion. There was so much to take in and excitement bubbled away as I thought ahead to all the Turkish and Syrian towns that might offer similar assaults on the senses. I was still officially in Europe and I marvelled at what a diverse continent I lived in. I felt lucky to be seeing and smelling and tasting so much of it first-hand.

In June 2009 I sold a building in Pitfield Street, just north of the City of London. It had a kebab shop on the ground floor and whenever I did a viewing I popped in to chat to the friendly tenants. I told them I was going to cycle through Turkey all the way to Australia. They were convinced of two things: that I would never reach Turkey on a bicycle; and that if I did (presumably by other means), I would fall in love with their home country. I had noted their address and now that I had made it to Edirne I sent them a postcard. 'Merhaba, my friends – I made it. Oli the Cyclist.' I had been sure I would like Turkey too, although I did not realise I would fall in love with it so quickly. In an equivalent kebab shop I ordered a donar and because I looked out of place and had a video camera with me the owner, Mehmet, told me to have a go at making my own, encouraging me behind the counter. I ended up making kebabs for the next ten customers and left the shop to a hearty round of applause and backslapping.

I had never before spent more than a few hours in a predominantly Islamic country and I was enjoying experiencing a completely different way of life. Change – in culture, in landscape, in people – had become my motivator, but standing there it felt like the biggest shift in surroundings yet. It seemed inconceivable that my scrawny legs had transported me so close to such an exotic, faraway place.

But now I had to get to Istanbul, 140 miles away. It was a tough three-day ride. The snow was fierce and getting worse and I ached not only for Istanbul, but for sunshine and warmth. On the first two days I cycled until well after dark on an endlessly undulating road that rolled through farmland as far as the eye could see. The road was mine: it was still under construction and cars could not access it. Engineers and roadworkers shouted at me but it was worth every angry outburst. Europe tested me one last time as rain lashed my back and I shivered and wobbled along the perilous D-100, my final obstacle before Istanbul. The hard shoulder was my friend at times, but at others it disappeared, leaving my safety in the hands of fate as giant juggernauts raced each other eastwards. I was a bundle of nervous energy on the last day, terrified that it would be my last cycling and my last living as a monster lorry-dodging session unfolded. For eight hours I concentrated as rarely before on a road that I knew I would look back on as the worst I had ever cycled.

Finally I emerged in the heart of old Istanbul, completely worn out but equally satisfied. I had seen a little more of Turkey, made it to the heart of its largest city and in doing so crossed my first continent on a bicycle. Overcome with exhaustion and emotion, I slumped on a wooden bench outside the Blue Mosque, the famous sanctuary that has stood for over four hundred years, its towering minarets like periscopes spying on the city. Sitting there contemplating how far I had come and remembering how far I still had to go, I told myself I would have been happy to sit still, like the

Blue Mosque, for four hundred more years. But my road lay ahead of me, and at that moment the scale of the challenge did not bear thinking about. Instead I sat there chuckling, wondering how my bicycle and I had made it across a continent without a single puncture.

On an Istanbul rooftop, with the minarets of Sultanahmet
spying over the city behind me.

SECOND INNINGS

TURKEY CONTINUED

IT IS CRICKET, NOT CRISAY

I was an Englishman with one of the world's great cities laid out before me to explore, so I headed straight for the North Shield Public House to watch Liverpool play Manchester City at Anfield. In fact, football played a significant role in my first couple of days in Istanbul as on my second evening I touched Asian soil for the first time to watch Fenerbahçe defeat a terrible Moldovan side. The quality on display was such that the highlight of the game came after the final whistle when Brazilian legend Roberto Carlos was hoisted on to his team-mates' shoulders for a lap of honour following his last match for Fenerbahçe.

Football aside, arriving in Istanbul was a dream and had the effect of reminding me that despite enjoying an increasingly simple and frugal life when I was in wild places, when I reached a city I welcomed everyday comforts. I had my back slapped in an ancient hammam, stalked equally ancient, arched bazaars in search of kit for the onward journey and became a tourist in a city full of them. I ate a lot and often, too – kebabs, hummus and, best of all, wet burgers (grilled burgers in a bap, put in a humidifier so they turn soggy – I could not get enough of them). My mum even dropped into town for a couple of days to wish me an early Merry Christmas, bringing with her a welcome dose of normality and constancy as well as a Santa hat for me to wear on the big day. By the time she left – after I had promised that the next time I would see her and Dad would be in Brisbane at the start of the Ashes almost a year later – four days had passed since I arrived in Istanbul and it was time to focus on cricket.

I nestled into a deserted corner of the North Shield in front of live action from Centurion Park, where England were taking on South Africa in the first of four Test matches over Christmas. There were twenty-four screens in the North Shield, but I was the only person in front of that particular one.

I considered the progress I had made since leaving Lord's: more than two thousand miles in a little over two months. The England cricket team had made no progress at all, but it was not their fault: they had had no one to play. Their last outing in Test whites had been at The Oval in August, months before my departure in October, and they won that to clinch the Ashes, a victory that sent the Australian team and their supporters home with tails between legs. The game at Centurion represented a chance for back-to-back wins but at the end of Day One things were looking rather too good for South Africa, with Jacques Kallis having stroked a masterful 112.

The start of Day Two saw a couple of Mongooses appear in the North Shield. Sampson Collins, then a journalist at the *Wisden Cricketer*, had flown in to write a piece about my ride, the cricket I was due to play in Istanbul and to rebuild his cricket career on the fields of Istanbul, away from the spotlight of Barnes Cricket Club. Under his arm he held two new Mongoose cricket bats all the way from HQ in London – one for me to use and one to give away to a deserving cricketer en route.

During the tea break Sampson and I sat in the corridor of my hotel while I chatted to Simon Mann on *Test Match Special*. I was not sure if they would have me back a second time so I had written an unashamedly grovelling email, only to be told that of course they'd be catching up with me all the way to Brisbane. I was delighted because it gave me another chance to plug the trip and raise some more funds for charity and, just quietly, I was beginning to quite like being on live radio.

England recovered throughout Day Three but I did not

manage to catch much more of the action; Sampson's arrival had reminded me that I had my own game to organise. An email from László explained that he had trawled the 'Interests' section of Couchsurfing.com and found a film-maker eager to follow my movements in Istanbul. Her name was Serpil and, although she had never heard of cricket, she had an eye for the eccentric so the idea of seeking out a game in Istanbul appealed to her.

With Serpil, who bubbled with artistic enthusiasm and slowly warmed to cricket.

After a day bombarding friends and following up on various contacts, we had one lead: an English guy in his mid-twenties called Rob. He taught at Berlitz University in the heart of the city and claimed links with the Turkish national team, based in Ankara. Although he did not know of any cricketers in Istanbul, he thought his students would be up for something a bit different, so arranged for me to visit the university before classes to give a talk about my journey, show a few photos and encourage any curious souls to join us for a game. I turned up to find the classroom empty but for one seat, the occupant introducing himself to me as Mike, an airline cargo employee from Hemel Hempstead who was on holiday in Istanbul. Completely by chance he had seen Rob's advert for my talk on the university's noticeboard.

It seemed I was a bit late getting to Istanbul. A couple of centuries ago I would not have had much trouble finding cricket enthusiasts. F. S. Ashley-Cooper, a former editor of *Wisden* and collector of eccentric cricket tales from around the world, tells of an active and enthusiastic cricket scene in the second half of the nineteenth century, albeit one dominated, as in so much of the world at that time, by the British. Activity apparently centred around the Candilli Club and in particular the Hansons, a well-known British banking family. Henry Hanson formed the Constantinople Cricket Club in 1857, travelling to matches with his pals in a three-oared caique because the schedules of the Bosphorus steamers did not conform to the hours of play. According to Ashley-Cooper a handful of Turks had taken to the game. One was the Mullah of the Candilli Mosque, another a naval officer and accomplished batsman who was reported to the Turkish authorities for becoming too Anglicised. During a game in 1901 he was arrested by mounted police but refused to surrender until he had finished his innings. When he was bowled, the cavalry carried him off for a lengthy stay in prison.

Despite the game getting big enough for Fenerbahçe Football Club to establish its own cricket branch in 1911, by the 1920s its popularity was on the wane. The father of the newly formed Republic of Turkey, Mustafa Kemal Atatürk, broke ties with Britain, seeking closer relations with continental Europe, and the game of cricket eventually disappeared completely.

The porter at the Orient Express Hotel in Sultanahmet knew nothing of the rise and fall of Turkish cricket, but he listened intently from across the lobby as Serpil and I mulled over our next move. Then he approached us.

'Excuse me, sir, but what is this "crisay" you speak about?'

Like our taxi driver that morning, he struggled with the pronunciation.

I pointed at Serpil who explained that she was Turkish, before recounting our dilemma, later roughly translating it to me as:

'It is "cricket", not "crisay". It's an odd and pretty slow English sport and this man here is making a long journey by bicycle in its name. So far he has played cricket in Brussels, Vienna, Budapest, Belgrade and Sofia. There is an English journalist in Istanbul to write an article on this man's journey, and a game of cricket he is supposed to have arranged in Istanbul. We are looking for somewhere to play – tomorrow. Do you know anyone who can help?'

The porter seemed happy and able to help. 'I do not know this game, but I know some people very important in Istanbul. Maybe I can be of little bit of small tiny help.' This sounded promising, if grammatically confusing. 'My name is Ercan, by the way. Means "person without fear" in Turkish language. Give me few minutes I will be back.'

Ercan made a couple of fearless phone calls. Twenty minutes later Serpil and I were sitting around a low table in the hotel lobby discussing the virtues of cricket over a complimentary Turkish coffee with a high-ranking member of the government of Fatih, a district of old Istanbul.

'So you want play crisay in Istanbul tomorrow . . . hmm, it can be tourist attraction?' The minister looked unimpressed.

'Yes. Yes it can be,' I pleaded with him, uncertain as to whether the game of cricket we were planning would be crowd-friendly in the slightest – so far we had just four participants, one of whom, Serpil, had never played before.

'And we will have many of the Turkish national team playing,' I lied, immediately regretting it.

But his interest was piqued. 'There is Turkish national crisay team?'

'Of course,' I assured him, before launching into all I knew about the history of Turkish cricket. What I failed to touch on was that the nation's cricketers were based seven hundred miles away and that none of them would be present the next day. But he seemed sold on the whole bonkers idea so I kept my mouth shut and, after some reflection and a couple of phone conversations during which the words 'crisay' and 'bicyclet' were mentioned several times, we were given our answer.

'Okay, is agreed. There is pedestrian zone between Blue Mosque and Hagia Sophia. You can play there. I will arrange television and newspapers and bring some government colleagues. You bring only the players.'

With that, the minister bid us farewell, braced himself and rushed out into a freezing Istanbul evening while Serpil and I stared at each other in amazement Ercan, who it occurred to me was the most well-connected hotel porter in the world, was delighted, too. He beamed from ear to ear as he explained that the Fatih government had recently been on the receiving end of severe criticism for their harsh treatment of tourists (harsh in what way I never found out). The minister hoped that our game of cricket would make the national news and reflect well on his proactive approach to encouraging visitors. Of course, it was utterly ridiculous that cricket had become a political pawn and an apparent last-ditch attempt to bring in tourists. If the presence of two of the world's most famous buildings couldn't do the job, what hope would a strange foreign sport have?

In the days of the Hansons and the Candilli Club, matches were held in the Sultan's Valley on pitches prepared by British sailors fresh from the Crimean War and were often delayed because of grazing horses and defecating cattle.* I did not have high expectations for our game but I did hold out in vain hope that we would find enough willing and able players, that the Fatih street sweepers (our replacements for the British

---

* It was not only Turkish cricket that struggled with local cattle. During a knock-up before a local cricket match in Bedfordshire in 1955, a player hit the ball into a field and it was eaten by a cow called Bessie. The game had to be abandoned because the club only had one ball.

sailors) would prepare a satisfactory wicket, and that defeca-
tion would not cause a messy end to our efforts.

The former was still causing us a headache. On the morning
of the game we only had five confirmed cricketers. A few
phone calls to some Turks I had got to know during my stay
met with indifference. Back in the nineteenth century the
genteel pursuit of cricket had won few admirers among local
people, a fact demonstrated when the British Embassy took
on 'the World' and only three players were found to repre-
sent the latter. More than a century later I was facing the
same lack of interest from the inhabitants of Istanbul. Still,
it was with eternal optimism that Rob, Sampson and I
wandered towards the old city completely at odds with our
surroundings, dressed in pressed cricket whites and carrying
a bat each. Surely we should be able to coax at least a couple
of tourists for a game?

The city seemed boisterous. Car horns honked, police sirens
blared, truck engines spluttered, street vendors and groups
of young men shrieked in unknown tongues. We passed a
bazaar that hummed with post-lunch activity: locals picked
up vegetables, tourists shopped for Christmas. Even in the
middle of the Galata Bridge we were surrounded by typically
Turkish enterprise and energy. I was used to seeing lazy
fishermen on fold-out chairs under tarpaulins on the banks
of the Thames; here I had never seen fishermen look so
busy. Buckets and bait by their sides, wrapped up in beanies
and fleeces and black leather jackets, they cast endlessly off
the bridge into the river that flowed eastwards for a mile
before joining the Bosphorus and the waters that divide a
continent. We had turned our backs on Europe now and the
Asian shore lay in front of us, beckoning. It'd have to wait a
few days yet.

Two fishermen stopped us and yanked a cricket bat from
my grip. A terracotta brazier was keeping them warm but
they seemed to be running out of kindling and joked that
they wanted the bat for that purpose. I grabbed it back and
we paced onwards towards Sultanahmet. The Pudding Shop,

a hangout for travellers on the hippie trail in the 1960s and now a Mecca for tourists, marked our arrival and from its porch came a voice.

I tried teaching a forward defensive to the fishermen.
It didn't really work.

'You boys lost I reckon!' Sam and I looked at each other; that rising inflection could mean only only one thing. The Australians were in town.

There were three of them, early twenties I guessed. We met on the pavement and I explained the concept of my ride to the Ashes. 'Bloody waste'a time mate. Your boys are gonna cop a hiding down under,' came the predictable, nasal retort.

I then explained the purpose of our attire, that we were about to play the first game of cricket in Sultanahmet for more than a hundred years. 'Count us in, mate,' came the equally predictable response. Like most Australians, they loved cricket, so not only had we found some cricketers, but we had ourselves an Ashes battle in central, historic Istanbul. What could have been more apt?

We made the short walk from the Pudding Shop, past the

Basilica Cistern to Hagia Sophia, arriving a little before our scheduled three o'clock game. Hundreds of tourists were milling about, heads buried in guidebooks or poring over maps as they dragged themselves from one attraction to another. No television crews or reporters or government representatives were anywhere to be seen but our new Antipodean friends were impressed when Australian radio DJ Adam Spencer called my mobile for a chat – I'd forgotten we had arranged the interview. When it was over we were still alone.

Sam found a couple of large orange bins and wheeled them into the middle of the pedestrian zone, placing them twenty-two yards apart as if it was the most normal thing in the world. When cricket was last played in Sultanahmet, local people watched on until it came time to pray and the followers of the Prophet knelt to face Mecca and went about performing their rituals. There was none of that now, although a group of young Americans did look perplexed as I warned them to move aside because they were standing on a good length.

The bins had been in place for a little over an hour before our friend from the government finally showed his face. He had in tow a small army of reporters, cameramen, photographers and hangers-on, although none seemed too enamoured with the thought of their morning's assignment. A few foreigners in dirty-white clothing arranging some bins into an unfamiliar pattern evidently did not get their juices flowing. But one photographer broke the mould and began putting himself in the line of fire to capture that perfect snap and his peers followed. And what a spectacle it was. The sixth-century Hagia Sophia, for a thousand years the largest cathedral in the world, towering above the offside boundary like a Byzantine version of the Lord's Grandstand. It was a museum now and an unbroken chain of tourists watched us play cricket as they queued to glimpse its riches.

On our other side, the Blue Mosque was a fine sight beyond square leg, and as Serpil and I approached the crowd to seek out willing participants, a familiar threesome rolled unsteadily towards us below its imposing minarets: Jean-Baptiste and

Jean-Pierre were a picture of Gallic satisfaction as they approached on their beautiful old tandem. They had been having such problems with their steed when I met them in Serbia that I was both surprised and delighted to see them make it alive and well to Istanbul, and the end of their road. They were quick to lock her to a lamppost and join our silly knockabout and before long we had an impressively ethnically diverse game of cricket: the two Frenchmen, Americans, English, Indians, Swedes, Irish, Bulgarians, Australians, Canadians, a Jordanian, a German and even a few Turks.

Only one of the Turks who joined us was keen for a bat and although his technique was questionable, he was eager not to depart the crease and had to be forcibly removed by the Australians after being bowled for the sixth time. But it was a man of Pakistani origin who eventually stole the show and sent us home content with our day's play. He showed up in a jacket and tie just as poor light was beginning to make play dangerous, but proved his undoubted ability by hitting a good score, smiting several sixes that threatened the thousand-year-old stained glass of the Hagia Sophia. In 1902, the legendary Australian batsman Victor Trumper broke a window in a shoe factory 150 yards from the ground where he was playing and the factory owners left it as it was as a memorial to the achievement. I was certain the curators of Hagia Sophia would not have reacted in such a romantic manner.

It turned out our show-stealer was Mubashir Khan, a former member of the Turkish national cricket team with the dubious honour of being the man who bowled the ball that cricketing adventurer Angus Bell launched into the Bosphorus at the end of his transcontinental car journey. Mubashir had, I think, just stumbled across our game as he walked home from work. At least I don't remember getting in touch with him.

It was a timely innings, and a reminder that although the history of cricket in Turkey is a very English one, its future is South Asian. It is the cricketing junkies of India and Pakistan who have taken an English and Commonwealth

We gathered a healthy squad for the first ever game of cricket between the Blue Mosque and Hagia Sophia. Samson Collins is far left, holding his hands out as if he has just been asked how much fun he is having.

game and turned it into one played all over the world in the twenty-first century. The sport has been born again in Turkey and today Ankara, although a lone outpost, is the centre of much cricketing activity. Just as in Hungary and Serbia, cricket has grown steadily since the turn of the century. In 2004 a structure for the game's development was set up and in 2005 the country's first domestic cricket competition took place. A year later the game was inducted into the Federation of Developing Sports, the Turkish Cricket Board was formed and in 2008 Turkey was granted Affiliate ICC status.

There is just one difference to cricket in Turkey as found everywhere else in the world: its official name? 'Kriket'.

A FESTIVE TURKEY

I spent my last four days in Istanbul with Clare and Alex, an American couple who had joined us in Sultanahmet for the game. Clare was a designer and Alex a writer and I enjoyed staying with them, living a relatively normal routine even if only for a few days. We ate breakfast at a reasonable hour, lunch and dinner, too. I worked on my blog during the day and in the evenings we ate out or watched movies.

They invited me to stay for Christmas. Alex had a local band and they were hosting a Christmas Eve music night for all their friends. If I wasn't going to be with family over the festive period then this sounded like the next best thing: new friends and live music in their town house overlooking the Bosphorus; far more appealing than the prospect of spending it alone in a small village – or even a field. I thanked them and said I'd love to stay.

Clare and Alex's house, overlooking the Bosphorus,
offered a welcome respite from the hustle and bustle of Istanbul.

Having accepted, I immediately became restless. I knew that I had spent too long in Istanbul already and needed to get back in the saddle; that I was wasting valuable days and that I would regret such a long break. I loaded my iPod with Christmas hits and, with Elvis' immortal lyrics ringing in my ears, decided it would be a lonely Christmas after all. I said goodbye to Clare and Alex, and finally Serpil, who admitted that my cricketing expedition had grown on her and that she hoped to join me for more filming before I left her country. The 6 a.m. Christmas Eve ferry from Istanbul across the Sea of Marmara to Yalova took no time at all and it was there, after a breakfast of two donar kebabs, that I took the first few pedal strokes of millions that would propel me across the vast expanse of Anatolia; my destination the Syrian border post beyond Reyhanlı.

Now I found myself, as I had feared, in a small village where I knew precisely no one and where there was bugger all to do. Iznik, being a small village in a Muslim country, was short on Yuletide spirit. On the way into town I had stopped at a petrol station café to restock on food. 'For me, tomorrow, Christmas!' I had announced in broken English, hoping – but not expecting – the waiters would rush into the kitchen and re-emerge with a steaming turkey adorned with stuffing, Brussels sprouts, cabbage, redcurrant jelly and roast potatoes. I was foolish to dream of such things. Their responses varied from 'You want Iskender kebab?' to 'Where you from, sir, Sweden?' and, most surprisingly of all, 'You need haircut?'

Being offered a hair cut on Christmas Eve was a sad reminder of my seasonal solitude, but I accepted nevertheless and, resigned to celebrating Christmas on my own, checked in at a cheap hotel in town. I was the only guest. The following morning – Christmas morning – I opened the stocking Mum had brought from home: chocolate buttons, AAA batteries, a balaclava, two books and five tangerines. Taking with me my new Santa hat I headed out to see if I could find signs of Christmas; still nothing. There were Roman ruins, though, and I sat among them contemplating my first Christmas away from home. I imagined the scene that would be playing out at my parents' house and wished I were there. But there would be many more Christmases and probably very few opportunities to cycle to Australia. It began to snow so I went back to my room and did not emerge until Boxing Day. At least I had a white Christmas.

I was soon back on the bike, pedalling into the mountains through a series of tunnels that reminded me of the Swiss Alps, though with less snow. I was nearly turned into a statistic by trucks on several occasions, so was delighted when the police stopped me at the entrance to one tunnel and ordered me to dismount. I was less delighted when they gestured for me to jump into their van because I was riding illegally through the tunnels. I pleaded with them to let me ride ahead while their headlights shone a path and eventually, after a stand-off during which I frowned and pleaded a lot, they agreed. With Turkish rock anthems my police-sponsored soundtrack, I was followed at snails' pace for more than two hours before I thanked my escort and ducked down a dirt track, setting up camp next to a narrow stream at the bottom of a steep-sided valley. The following morning I was woken by a chainsaw. Peering out of my tent to check who was providing such an alarm call, I was confronted by a lumberjack who apologised for waking me up. I apologised for sleeping in his back garden.

By the time I reached the remote university town of Eskişehir on the evening of 27 December I was on the edge of the heartland of Turkey: the vast plains and mountains of the Central Anatolian Plateau that would lead me all the way to the Mediterranean close to the Syrian border. Eskişehir's charms delayed me for a few days, though, as I made two good friends in my hosts, local students Deniz and Gozde.

In the coming weeks I would experience the virtue of Islamic hospitality over and over, but Deniz and Gozde were not followers of the Prophet – they were just eager to learn about different cultures, so often stayed in the homes of foreigners when travelling, or had them to stay when in Eskişehir. On my first night we huddled in a quiet corner of Café del Mundo, drinking among hip-looking university students with asymmetric haircuts while Gozde told the story of the first time she couch-surfed on a visit to Amsterdam. She had turned up at her host's flat to be told that he had to fly to London at the last minute so he had given her a front-door key and suggested she post it through the letterbox when she left a week later. Her philosophy in Eskişehir seemed to run along the same trust lines: within two hours of meeting the girls, I was dozing off on a mattress beside Gozde's bed.

Meeting local people in the places I pedalled through was one of the things I enjoyed most about my new life. It made me feel like I belonged, rather than like a foreign intruder. With Gozde and Deniz, mention of my ride came up every now and again, but it did not dominate our conversations and I welcomed the change. Since I had made the decision to cycle to Australia the journey had come to define me and every conversation seemed to centre on how I was coping with the physical challenge, the solitude, whether I missed home and why I had set off in the first place.

Deniz and Gozde did not treat me like a tourist. They just got on with their daily routines and in doing so enabled me to learn a little about them and their city. They worked hard, were ambitious, mainly because they did not trust the Turkish government and yearned to escape, preferably to America or Africa. Gozde dreamed of making films in Hollywood and Deniz of working with animals in a Kenyan game park. We shared a mutual passion for jazz and blues, they wrote a list of some choice phrases for me to use during my time in their country, I introduced them to New Zealand television show *Flight of the Conchords* and they educated me about Turkish film directors, writing another list of films for me to wade through when I got home.

'You eat many kebabs,' Deniz observed every time I tucked into my local delicacy of choice. 'The people of Turkey will love you – you have a Turkish balcony!'

My 'Turkish balcony' caused much hilarity during my stay in Eskişehir. The saying goes that a Turkish house is not a real home unless it has a balcony, and in the same vein a Turkish man is not a real man unless he too has a balcony – a stomach of considerable proportions. The girls found my pot-bellied, but otherwise waifish, appearance amusing and blamed the anomaly on my penchant for Turkish kebabs. I excused my enormous appetite by explaining that when camping I survived on little other than rice and pasta. Besides, the knowledge that the excess weight would eventually drop off if I cycled far enough made me reluctant to sacrifice yet another treat.

After a wild New Year's Eve watching David Attenborough wildlife documentaries and eating kebabs and burek, it was time to get back in the saddle. Forget climbing that mountain in Bulgaria, or cycling across a continent for that matter: saying goodbye to my two new friends on the first day of 2010 was the hardest thing I had done for ages. Deniz said she would fly to Australia to celebrate with me if I made it to The Gabba. Gozde promised to visit me in London when I got home. Though I knew both meant it, I doubted their means to be able to travel at will. As dawn broke on a new year, I pedalled out of Eskişehir into the forbidding steppe of Central Anatolia.

ON TO THE CENTRAL ANATOLIAN PLATEAU

Winding my way south-eastwards in the direction of Syria, I climbed up on to the Central Anatolian Plateau until I was more than a thousand metres above sea level. Camping on the edge of this immense wilderness three times the size of the British Isles, I felt like I was at the start of a new journey, and one I had yearned for since leaving home.

Paul Theroux said: 'I always suspect that the land we are flying over is rich and wonderful and that I am missing it all.' I think the same every time I board an aeroplane. I have flown to New York a handful of times over the years, and on each occasion I make sure I check in early enough to get a window seat. I don't do this so that I can look down on the Thames as it snakes through London's historic landmarks, or even to marvel at Manhattan's famed skyline before we land. I head straight for a window seat because flying over Greenland, the world's largest island, has the effect of firing my imagination and stirring in me a thirst for old-fashioned hardship and adventure. From my seat in the clouds I can trace a seemingly infinite number of winding valleys shaped by chains of snow-capped peaks and inhabited by icy, rushing rivers. Of course, it would be unrealistic to have to traipse across such a vast, impregnable landscape every time I want to visit a mate in New York but, still, what a sin to be missing out on all that wilderness. I imagine being down there, alone in a hinterland that I am utterly unfamiliar with, a remote place untouched by outside influence. I envisage a world that is all too rare in the twenty-first century: air travel, despite its obvious attraction, sucks adventure, exploration and necessary hardship out of billions of journeys every year. From my window seat behind reinforced glass eight miles above the earth's surface, I can look at Greenland but I cannot see it. To see it I must be down there, inhaling the emptiness and feeling the cold wind burning my skin.

Europe was a training ground on which I had learned my trade. There were testing days here and there, but on the whole it was easy pedalling and I was rarely daunted by the challenge it posed. Bulgaria had occasionally hinted at wilderness but signs of life came all too regularly, villages and towns passing under my wheels with fair frequency so that I never felt far from civilisation. But the challenges that now lay ahead were intimidating. I had done little research into a route across Turkey but imagined wilderness on a grand scale.

I wasn't disappointed. Most visitors to Turkey are package holidaymakers who see little more than the chic – or as often tacky – seaside resorts that line the country's fringes. And it's just as well. The Central Anatolian Plateau is not a place for the casual tourist but a vast, inhospitable region of mountains and steppe that stretches inland from the Aegean coast and covers much of central Turkey. Few modern roads penetrate this prodigious back country. Forget tourists – it remains sparsely populated even by its *own* people.

Inching my way across the plateau into headwinds that made progress painful and often impossible, I felt minuscule and utterly insignificant under skies that touched the horizon in every direction. Some days the steppe was so flat that I imagined if I had binoculars I'd be able to see all the way to Australia. I was in a beautiful, beguiling wilderness where chains of extinct volcanoes loomed over multi-coloured fields of grass, sugar cane, wheat, barley, corn, cotton, grapes, roses and tobacco. But I rarely saw farmers. If they had any sense they would be hibernating for winter, avoiding fierce electrical and snow storms and temperatures that drop as low as -30°C, warming their toes next to a roaring *soba**. Mind you, it is little better in summer, when dust storms and swarms of locusts terrorise crop yields.

It meant I had the plateau almost to myself, and I loved it. Huge flocks of sheep were normally my only companions and since I didn't shower for twelve days that was probably a good thing. More than forty million sheep graze the plains and steppe of Turkey, providing vast quantities of wool for one of the country's most famous products, carpets. Outside the towns the only signs of human habitation were abandoned, semi-constructed buildings, the occasional vehicle and the inexplicable presence of a never-ending trail of discarded cassette tape. Endless solitude for day after day meant that I spent a long time wondering why, and could only imagine the drivers of Turkey had recently graduated to CDs, and, in doing so, flung their obsolete cassette tapes out of the window. I saw no evidence of such a practice anywhere else in the world.

---

* 'Soba' is the Turkish word for 'wood-burner'. Sobas form a central part of village life across Anatolia. Most rooms have one and they are used for heating, cooking, drying clothes and making tea.

But, of course, riding through distant lands, while thrilling because of its unfamiliarity, was dangerous for the very same reason. I was a blond misfit in a dark man's world, without an engine and thus vulnerable. Solitude forced me to consider how I would cope, and what I would do, if something went wrong. But I did not dwell on such thoughts. I exercised caution and attempted to control my immediate environment. Still, other people posed the most obvious threat and if someone decided I was a target there would be little I could do to protect myself.

The day out of Muhmadiye started badly. I had been on the bicycle for a little over an hour when a car behind me tooted its horn. Drivers who toot their horns at cyclists, especially in remote places, are nearly always doing so to offer encouragement. But that does not matter to the cyclist. I had learned since leaving home that car horns come in one of two guises: there is the deep, throaty horn that sends the cyclist into an instant rage; and there is the merry, high-pitched horn that puts a smile on the cyclist's face until the next throaty horn comes along. However a throaty horn does not necessarily mean an angry driver and a merry horn not necessarily a friendly one.

The horn outside Muhmadiye was chirpy and, as a result, I smiled and waved as the car passed me. In response, I was pelted with an empty Coke can and an apple core. I wasn't hurt and should have let it go, but I was angry and felt the need to vent my frustration, so I gave the perpetrator a two-fingered salute. The car came to a halt and a huge man in a black leather jacket emerged, pushing me and my bicycle into a roadside ditch before speeding off to leave me nursing a bruised hip that took a few hundred miles to work off. Possibly I deserved harsher treatment, but I certainly learned my lesson and did not swear at another driver for at least twenty-four hours.

My bad day got worse. Several miles east of the farming village of Belpinar I noticed a portly middle-aged man sprinting towards me from the only house for miles around, shouting alien words as he did so. Skidding to a halt beside me he took several seconds to catch his breath before introducing himself as Ali Umay. I told him my name was Ali Brum (I had taken to calling myself Ali Brum in an effort to appear Muslim, although the combination of Muslim name and white-blond hair seemed to confuse rather than enthuse most villagers – still, it made me chuckle). Back at Ali's house, he introduced me to his family as 'Ali Brum' and, sure enough, confusion ruled as they wondered where on earth I had come from.

Ali's wife gasped and rushed off, covering her face with her veil and returning ten minutes later with a tray full of bread, jam and a close-to-inedible bowl of soup. As I did my best to conceal the fact that I was on the verge of vomiting I could not help but notice a sinister feeling in the room, in particular the presence of a heavily moustached man with swollen knuckles, who for the duration of my stay sat on his haunches staring straight at me and my belongings. Nor did it escape my attention that a shotgun hung on the wall above his head. Still, it was the first home I had been welcomed into since starting out from Eskişehir, so I assumed that was how people lived out here: guns within easy reach of children; strangers welcomed with a meal and terrifying stares.

It was when he started mumbling the word 'laptop' that I started to worry; a feeling that matured into a touch of fear as he reached for the shotgun and proceeded to mime the action of a machine gun letting off bullets in my direction. Ali Umay seemed not to approve of his friend's behaviour because animated words were exchanged, both men rising to their feet. I gathered my belongings, including my laptop, which was still inside one of my front panniers, and ventured back out into the cold. As I was reattaching my kit, out of the corner of my eye I saw the mustachioed man take my video camera from the handlebar bag and slip it into his inside jacket pocket. I continued packing, waiting to see if he would give it back. I pedalled off, waving as I did so, but no admission came so I swung round, pulled up beside him and reached into his pocket to reacquaint myself with my most cherished possession. Ali Umay, upon witnessing the evidence of his friend's criminality, pounced on him. As I rode frantically towards the main road, aware that I was riding one of the all-time worst getaway vehicles, a tumbling cartoon brawl developed, with each man slapping and scratching the other as shouts of 'laptop, laptop!' receded into the distance. Within a minute I was alone again, riding the serene wilderness that was the plateau.

Ali Umay with his wife and son.
(The mustachioed thief on the left plots his crime.)

It came as a surprise to me that my first two negative experiences in the wild were caused by other people, but perhaps it should not have. Since leaving affluent Europe for the developing world – a line I considered to be the Austro-Slovak border outside Bratislava – I had become increasingly aware, despite the fact that I was travelling frugally, of my perceived status as a rich Westerner. My bicycle was still relatively shiny and remained an expensive piece of kit. I carried a video camera and two other cameras, a laptop, tent, solar-charging equipment, goose-down sleeping bag, a stove, pots, pans and much more. Many of the towns and villages I rode through were poor, with people either living off their land or unemployed. My amazement at being welcomed so openly by strangers was therefore matched by my understanding of why not everyone greeted me with limitless generosity and warmth.

Of course, it was not only people who posed a danger. As darkness fell after a long day of more than eighty miles out of Beyören I found myself amidst an uncharacteristically hilly section of forested road. A car emblazoned with the words JANDARMA TRAFİK pulled up next to me and two police-men emerged. The irony of a traffic patrol in the area did not escape me: I had not seen a car for three hours.

'Are you okay?' the stockier one asked in what appeared to be an American accent.

'Yes, thank you,' I replied, grateful for his interest. 'Do you know how far the next town is? I think it is called Yunak.'

'Yes, Yunak is the next town. It is only a fifteen-minute drive, but it's very steep.' The stocky man peered ahead, into the darkness. He was clearly the only one of the two able to speak English but was not American and had probably just watched too many episodes of *Friends*. I groaned as I began my calcula-tions: a fifteen-minute drive on the flat would take me around an hour on my bicycle, but a hill climb could take much more.

'Okay, I think I'll camp in the woods and attack the climb tomorrow,' I told the policemen, beginning to cast about for a spot to pitch my tent.

The stocky man looked horrified. 'You must not camp here. It is too dangerous. There are many . . . *BAK*. I do not know the word in English.' And then he lurched back-wards and howled the unmistakable howl of a wolf, before simulating with unnerving accuracy its gnashing jaws.

'Shit,' I replied.

The policemen seemed serious and I seemed to have a

decision to make. If I stayed I would probably be fine, but I would not get much sleep; if I pedalled onwards I would exhaust myself; and I definitely was not taking them up on their offer of a lift to Yunak. All three options were unattractive, but after much deliberation I decided that one was less unattractive than the others.

As I took a swig of water and prepared for the ride to Yunak the policemen exchanged words and the taller one passed me a huge bag of sweets. I obviously looked as tired as I felt and in need of sugar-coated energy. With a thank you, a goodbye and a heave of effort I got back on my bicycle and pedalled uphill into the darkness. But as if the threat from people and wolves were not enough, I was soon to discover that the Central Anatolian Plateau had one more unwelcome surprise up its sleeve.

SHAPES IN THE HALF-LIGHT

There are six of them, moving towards me in a fan formation, spread out over two hundred metres across the steppe. It is getting dark. I can feel a rush of adrenalin and turn to pedal furiously down the dirt track back on to the main road. But my pursuers hold their formation and gain on me fast. A small incline lies ahead and I don't know what the other side hides. A village, I hope. Five minutes at top speed, ten minutes. At the end of an eighty-mile day I have little left in my legs and turn to see my pursuers are within twenty metres of my bicycle and still closing.

Two evenings earlier, after what turned out to be just a one and a half hour climb, I had made it to the 'don't bother ever going there' town of Yunak. To my surprise the ascent was followed by three miles of downhill and I had arrived in high spirits, perhaps helped by the fact that I had not been savaged by wolves. Yunak was exactly as I had expected: one deserted street, one drab hotel, fifteen kebab shops. Hotel

Yilnak was overpriced at eight Turkish Lira, or £3.50, but it had sheets and pillows as standard and several portraits of Mustafa Kemal Atatürk as an added bonus. One particularly damp, pungent, carpeted portrait hung above my bathroom sink in place of a mirror, which made brushing my teeth a novel experience.

For obvious reasons, I only intended to stay one night in Yunak, but on my first morning I woke to the sight of snow being shovelled to the side of the road by hordes of fag-puffing spade-wielders. It would have been foolish to set off in such treacherous conditions so I spent the day eating kebabs and catching up with news from home. When I did leave the following day the snow had cleared but roads were icy and several times I felt my wheels slide underneath me. I was lucky to keep my bicycle upright but before long my snow and ice worries had melted and the sun shone once again on another glorious day in central Turkey.

But on the edge of a cluster of five or six houses amid fields of sheep, I came to a grinding halt. I turned to see what had caused me to stop and soon realised I was being attacked by not one, but four wild dogs. They were huge, each about the size of a St Bernard but far stronger and, of course, wild. The first frightened the crap out of me, coming from nowhere to sink its teeth into my back tyre. The second, equally thick-necked and angry, stood in my way barking a full-throated roar as encouragement to a further two companions.

It wasn't lost on me that a dog had given me my first puncture since leaving home and hatred of the canine beast stirred in me. By the time the other two dogs arrived I had my cricket bat out and was wielding it like the 2005 version of Kevin Pietersen: no inhibition. It did not work. I tried to walk my bicycle along the road, away from the houses, but the puncture made it hard work and the dogs followed, growling incessantly. I spotted a shepherd marching towards me from among his flock in a distant corner of a grazing field. It was ten minutes before he reached me, breaking into a seventy-year-old's version of a jog and raising his staff above his head to ward off my attackers. They obviously recognised him because eventually they left me alone. The old man reached down and picked up several small, sharp stones, placing them in my eight available pockets. By the time he had finished I was five kilograms heavier, but at least I had protection.

I had been warned about Turkey's aggressive wild dogs before leaving home. Other cyclists had come up against them and survived unscathed, but I had seen them first hand now and was nervous about my next encounter. There are various breeds that inhabit the wilds of Asiatic Turkey and my attackers were Kangals, aggressive killers bred centuries ago to protect the region's vast and lucrative sheep population from predators like wolves, jackals, bears and eagles. To this day, the skins of wolves and jackals hang from market stalls all over Anatolia as prizes captured by these huge beasts. Many Kangals are still chained to their masters' properties but most roam wild on the edges of towns and villages, sniffing out lonely British cyclists to terrify.

As a particularly colourful sunset was drawing to a close later that day, I spied smoke rising from the chimney of a building about two miles to my left, on top of a small escarpment. I had not seen any signs of life for hours and, keen to avoid sleeping outside in the cold again, veered off the main road and on to a dirt track that I hoped would take me to a warm bed. That is when I noticed the shapes in the half-light and, faced with the distinct possibility of a nocturnal face-off with six huge wild Kangals, I quickly turned back towards the main road and the dogs gave chase. I knew I should have halted when I first saw them in the distance but it was too late to stop pedalling now. They got to within ten metres of my back wheel and thoughts of my demise in the wilds of Turkey filled my head. But then, at the top of the hill, a strange thing happened. I craned my neck to check on my pursuers, expecting them to be nipping at my heels, but instead they stood together, tightly huddled in the middle of the road. I did not stop to see what they would do next;

I did not dare. I continued up and over the crest, freewheeling away from the pack and towards safety.

Or so I thought. I could see lights straight ahead, at the bottom of a shallow valley. The moon was high and full and before my adrenalin had a chance to subside I saw three more shapes emerging from its shadow, running directly towards me. I realised my initial pursuers had stopped because they knew there was another pack outside the next settlement; they had reached the boundary of their territory.

My new friends were within fifty metres when I made the decision to jump off my bicycle and reach for my cricket bat again. One came for me, tearing a hole in a rear pannier, an act that I would be reminded of for the rest of my journey, whenever it rained and I was left with soaking clothes.

I walked on, ensuring the dogs were kept at bay by a flailing cricket bat. Without warning, on the perimeter of the village the dogs backed away into the darkness. I could not believe my luck at being left alone to find a warm place to sleep. I was shivering with sweat but not yet tired – adrenalin had seen to that. I had rarely been happier to arrive anywhere.

ADIL THE IMAM AND FRIENDSHIP IN ANATOLIA

The sun dictates village life in much of Anatolia, so although sunset was less than an hour gone, there was little sign of life in the village. The few dozen buildings there seemed to have been shut up for hours, if not decades.

I found a patch of dirt, with splodges of snow, doing an impression of a village green and began putting up my tent. Until that moment I considered my cricketing experiences in Belgrade, Sofia and Istanbul to be the most incongruous scenes of the journey so far but the suited man in bow tie and trilby who approached me now was a far more surprising sight. There was little chance of me finding out much about him. He spoke no English and although my Turkish had improved since my time in Eskişehir, I had not mastered 'I've been chased by huge wild dogs all day and I'd really love to sleep anywhere but in a tent', let alone, 'Who are you?'

I found some maps and showed them to him, attempting to explain where I had come from and where I was heading. He pointed at the patches of snow on the ground and pretended to shiver. I nodded and made a shivery noise with my lips. I tried to imitate my wild dog chase using hand gestures and facial contortions and, to my surprise, he seemed to understand. I showed him my pockets full of stones and he laughed before waggling his finger, imitating a gun. Like the traffic police outside Yunak, he was more concerned about wolves. It seemed I had been lucky to avoid them.

The man gestured for me to follow him and I packed up my bags. He took me through narrow streets bordered by single-storey buildings with small wooden windows, frames painted uniformly black. Gas lamps guided us to the most imposing building in the village: the mosque. He knocked three times on a wooden door at its rear. No answer. I waited when he disappeared and by the time he came back he had with him a stout man wearing taqiyah and thobe: the Imam.

The suited man disappeared without saying goodbye and I asked the Imam his name. 'Adil, Adil,' he said, turning wide-eyed to look at me. 'Benim adim Oli,' I replied. This made Adil happy; a Turkish speaker with blond hair! He launched into a monologue and I had to explain that I knew very few words in his language, at which he looked disappointed. Nevertheless, he unlocked the wooden door, behind which was a small, stone-floored room inhabited by a rafter of about thirty turkeys. They gobbled disapprovingly as he chased them into the cold night air and ushered me inside. I felt sorry for the turkeys, having to move on because of an unexpected guest, but not sorry enough to refuse a room for the night, even if it was littered with feathers and stank of turkey droppings.

My luck was about to get even better, however. Adil led me into a second, much darker room where he lit a candle and placed it on a window ledge. There before me was a most pleasing sight. Although the ceiling was low enough that I had to stoop, the room was double the size of the turkey room. A Turkish carpet covered the floor and two mattress-covered wide stone benches ran the length of two of the walls. In the middle of the room was a soba and next to the door was a six-foot pile of blankets. I peered out of the small, solitary window and was so, so grateful not to be sleeping on the dirt outside. If Adil had not been an Imam I would certainly have given him a very firm hug.

The following morning in the mosque.

Adil's was the sort of warm welcome that became a feature of my ride, not only across the Central Anatolian Plateau, but the whole of Turkey. Much of my route took in the Turkish–Islamic equivalent of the Midwest Bible Belt, a religiously conservative area with the ancient city of Konya at its heart. In Islamic tradition, people believe that if they refuse to offer hospitality they will incur divine wrath.

Hospitality, particularly towards strangers, is therefore wide-spread across the Islamic world: a three-way relationship between host, stranger and God, with the duty to supply hospitality in the form of sustenance considered a duty to God, not to the stranger.

In the West the traditional virtue of unconditional hospitality directed towards strangers has been largely lost. We tend to see receiving guests as part of creating relationships that will last. We invest in such hospitality because we know personal gain is likely to come of it. I enjoyed the Islamic way and benefited from it often on my way across Turkey and the Middle East.

'Thank you, thank you,' I told Adil. 'I am very, very grateful.' He seemed to comprehend my gratitude, if not my words. Then he disappeared and returned a few minutes later laden with logs for the soba. Silently, while I made my bed, he got the fire going before bidding me farewell with a wave of his hand. Then I was alone, for my first night spent in a mosque.

I had no television, no company; I left my computer and various books in my bags. I felt alive most days on the bike, but on that day especially so. Since waking up thirteen hours earlier I had seen and faced so much and I had still achieved about seventy miles. Adrenalin soon diminished and exhaustion kicked in. Covering myself in blankets and closing my eyes, I considered that there was nothing that could have made me happier. I felt utter contentment in the knowledge that I had got through it. It was a day I would look back on as one of the most satisfying of the whole journey. Pedalling beneath a beautiful blue sky, taking in the enormous, snow-filled views and breathing in the fresh air at its start was great fun; my encounters with wild dogs, less so. Given the choice I would have opted for a wild-dog-free day. But I did not have the choice, and I had been forced to cope. It made me realise that enjoyment was not guaranteed on my journey, but that if I stuck to my plan, satisfaction certainly was.

*

Storms came regularly on the plateau. One minute I would be pedalling happily in shorts and a fleece, the next I would be desperately reaching for ski trousers, jacket and balaclava as another fierce blizzard rolled in. Normally I found myself far from civilisation at such times and had to be content with hunkering beside my bicycle, under a tarpaulin that I kept at the ready. On one such occasion I hid for two hours while an electrical storm raged and I prayed that it would finish by nightfall. It did and, as the clouds parted, there appeared a perfect, cone-shaped mountain straight ahead of me in the direction I was heading. I pitched my tent there and watched the changing colours of the snow-capped peak from the other side of my fly net. The next day I pedalled towards the mountain and the day after, away from it. That evening it finally disappeared after two days on my horizon, its imposing scale and perfect symmetry a reminder of the transient nature of my visit to that corner of the world.

The plateau was dotted with abandoned buildings and I would occasionally take cover in them. Nearing Cihanbeyli a typically blue-sky morning became a blanket of grey and I holed up in one such building, a remote, out-of-place, modern hall with huge glass windows, most of which had been shattered by the wind long before I arrived. By dusk the storm was still raging so I put my tent up and spent a sleepless night praying I would not be found, listening to rats darting about and glass smashing on the bare concrete floor.

Sometimes I was lucky enough to find myself in a small settlement when the next rumble of thunder arrived. The roads I pedalled tended to be old caravan routes that dated as far back as the Middle Ages. Back then, caravans covered about sixty miles each day and thriving settlements developed at the intervals. The settlements have little to sustain them nowadays and they have become sleepy villages that locals yearn to escape from.

I, on the other hand, welcomed any opportunity to escape the cold. Remote petrol stations or roadside cafés were great places to while away an hour or two, not least because I usually arrived rain-soaked and they always had a soba burning away. As I entered, eyes tended to fix upon me, the intruder, and I'd remember a couple of phrases Gozde and Deniz had taught me: 'Naber hatunlar, yağmur, güzel!' or 'What's up, girls? Rain is beautiful!' Of course there were never any girls and so raucous laughter generally ensued. When it had died down I was always welcomed inside to warm up. I found tables full of men playing cards or backgammon. Tea was served, payment was refused and by the time I was dry and warm my maps were being pored over by groups of men trying to understand what I was up to. Before I arrived in Turkey, if anyone had asked me if I wanted it to rain most days until I reached Syria I would have said no. But rain made me stop and gave me the opportunity to chat and joke with hundreds of local characters who lent personality to the places I would have just pedalled past if it had been dry.

In Gölyazı a man ran towards me shouting, 'What country? What country?'

'England, England,' I replied, and he applauded as he ran, dragging me into his modest house for a cup of sweet tea. His wife was the only woman I spoke to directly in the whole of Central Anatolia. She was studying English via a CD course but had never met an actual English person, so was delighted at my unexpected appearance. 'My dream is to live in very beautiful city of Birmingham,' she said, smiling. 'You can do better than that, my friend; better to aim high!' I thought, but did not say.

The following day, as a particularly ferocious electrical storm developed, luck dictated that I found myself in a small farming community called Demircidamı Mevkii, and I took shelter in an abandoned drystone chicken coop. I lit my fuel stove and began boiling water for drinking.

Before long an old man was by my side. He wore a filthy grey suit and a torn T-shirt and leaned heavily on a wooden walking stick while inspecting the strange blond man he had come across. Insisting that I follow, he led me to another drystone structure that turned out to be a modest house and, without a word, I was ushered into a small, carpeted room with a roaring soba to find another man and his son, sitting in silence. The old man was the second man's father: Ercan, Izmet and Muhammed were the male members of the Cimen family. Ercan was the only one who spoke any English, and he spoke it surprisingly well. 'Why you cycle here in winter? Is too cold!' I had to agree with Ercan on that one.

While I undressed, hanging my soaking clothes around the soba, Izmet played with a toy soldier that looked like it had come straight from Windsor Castle and Ercan explained that he was a cow- and sheep-milker in the winter, while in summer he worked in a bakery in Aksaray. He told me he used to live in Mainz, an industrial city on the banks of the Rhine. I had pedalled through Mainz on my way through Germany. When Izmet turned seven he would go to school there, living with his aunt. I often met people from small villages who dreamed of moving abroad to find opportunity and a better way of life. I wondered how many would eventually make it, and whether they would enjoy it if they did. I wondered what it felt like to yearn to leave your homeland. I felt lucky that I suffered no such desire, at least on a permanent basis. Mainz had not turned out to be Ercan's dream. New Jersey was where he wanted to end up. More than twenty of his friends from the village had already moved there. Judging by Demircidamı Mevkii's size, I assumed the Cimen family were the only ones left.

Ercan's wife arrived, dressed in a burkha and carrying a tray full of food: bean soup, jam, chocolate spread, bread, cheese. By the time the storm had abated my clothes were dry and I had the energy to plough onwards. I was grateful, particularly in light of my experience at the home of Ali Umay, for the Cimen family's kindness towards a stranger. I thanked them and gave Izmet two AAA batteries for his toy soldier. He'd clearly never seen the soldier fully functional before and looked on, terrified, as it marched the length of the room before tripping over the family dog's paw.

Ercan Cimen with Izmet, his wife, and her sister.

A NOSTALGIC RIDE

It is dark and wet and I have not seen another person in hours. I am freewheeling towards Tarsus, my gateway to the Mediterranean; twenty miles to go. Then a sharp, piercing sound: SNAP! I peer beneath my feet to see what has made such a noise. I slam on the brakes in horror, skidding to a halt.

Five days earlier, after a rare detour into tourist territory exploring the magical rock formations of Cappadocia, I pedalled south through occasional snow towards the Mediterranean. Reaching the sea had been on my mind since I last saw it in Istanbul and I knew that arriving there would feel like a significant landmark. Towns came increasingly thick and fast as I approached the coast. High in the Taurus Mountains I rode through the bustling, rural town of Nigde, famous for its apples and potatoes and featuring some of the most beautiful mosques in the country. Ciftehan was a plain one-street town of deserted hardware and kebab shops that was more typical of rural Turkey, yet was deep in a bowl-shaped valley and dwarfed by towering snow-capped peaks amidst thick pine forests. It was a contrast to the desolate, vast country I had been riding through since Eskişehir and another sign that I was making progress towards the sea.

A narrow, vertical gorge guided me out of Ciftehan and the road clung to its western wall, meandering through aban-doned villages and dense forest. Occasionally I was offered a glimpse of the valley floor far below in the distance. I was grateful, once again, to be on a bicycle and to have the time to enjoy my surroundings as I freewheeled for hours to the town of Pozantı where I tweeted: 'Can't feel my fingers I've been freewheeling for so long but map suggests my climbing days in Turkey are over!' The following day, of course, the climb to Güzel was steep, and I soon regretted the previous day's tweet. Rodney and Del Boy accompanied me skywards, though, the theme tune to *Only Fools and Horses* stuck in my head as I pumped my legs furiously all the way into the clouds and up to the summit. I contemplated a sequel: Only Fools, Horses and Englishmen on Bikes.

Tarsus was in my sights when the rain began; thirty miles to go. The road rolled so that some sections were uphill and some down, but generally I was descending towards sea level. Unless there happened to be a particularly beautiful sunset I never liked the last fifteen or twenty miles of any day – I have never been good at finishing anything off, whether school essays or long bike rides – and when it rained, I liked it even less.

With twenty miles to go came the noise that halted me dead in my tracks. My rear rack had snapped off the frame, taking a couple of chunks of the bike with it. Both my front and rear luggage racks were insured against damage but insurance was no good one thousand metres up a mountain in rural Turkey. My two rear panniers, tent and sleeping bag lay strewn across the road. My cricket bat found a home in the roadside ditch.

There was no chance of finding a welder, at least not until I reached Tarsus. My head-torch came in useful and I dug out a handful of cable ties, wrenching them around the bike and rack. An old sock stopped the two rubbing and potentially damaging each other. I was, just quietly, impressed with my resourcefulness. The panniers, once back on, were far from sturdy but as I rode off they did hold. The descent was not much fun after that, with half an eye on the road and half on my makeshift rack. It was midnight when I finally rolled into Tarsus and treated myself to a shabby hotel. I had been on the road for sixteen hours, but even the thought of having to do it all over again the next day did not stop me nodding off as soon as my head hit the pillow.

Legs rested, bicycle welded, I continued pedalling eastwards and it was after two more days that I got my first view of the Mediterranean; majestically calm, wide as the horizon and bathed in an orange evening glow. As I pitched my tent on a patch of grass next to a chicken-wire fence, I shed a tear. I had loved Turkey, but my arrival at the coast heralded the end of my Anatolian adventure; or perhaps not quite. My tent was up and campfire roaring when two men in military garb appeared and asked me to follow them to what I guessed were their headquarters. (I later learned the whole area was under military observation because it was the home of Botaş, the state-owned crude oil and natural gas company.) My passport and wallet were taken from me and half an hour of questioning in a dark office with a military officer followed. Apparently they wanted to check that I wasn't some sort of James Bond character (the name 'James Bond' even came up!). A lamp lit my face so I could barely see the officer. He spoke no English so a man stood behind me and translated. He was wearing flip-flops and boxer shorts, which seemed odd. In the end I guess I satisfied their enquiries because my passport and wallet were returned and I was led to a naval commander's house where I pitched my tent in his garden. When I woke up the next morning, I was surprised, and a little terrified, to find a man sitting on a chair facing the entrance to my tent. Abdullah told me he used to be called Stephen, and was from England – Bath, to be precise. He had moved to the area to work for Botaş a number of years ago and ended up converting to Islam, changing his name and marrying a local girl, Fatimah.

The Turkish military officers with the Ashes urn.

It was in Iskenderun that I spent my last night in Turkey. I remember feeling terribly depressed about the prospect of leaving, but my sadness was lessened by the fact that Serpil had caught the overnight train from Istanbul and would be joining me until Damascus, with a view to sending footage back to László when she was done. When I arrived in Iskenderun, fresh from ten hours pedalling in the pouring rain, Serpil was chatting with a man in a baclava shop about a man he knew who knew another man who once had a car. A few phone calls back and forth and the man – who still owned a car – had cancelled his plans and agreed to drive her to the border town of Reyhanlı, about sixty miles south. One snag: the driver would be following me, travelling at an average of about thirteen miles per hour. I hoped he was a patient man; or a very slow driver.

Abdullah, from Bath, with his Turkish wife.

At the beginning of my final day in Turkey, I tucked into a breakfast of tomatoes, cucumber, feta cheese and my old friend, burek. I will miss you, burek. I packed my panniers and readied myself to head back into the unrelenting rain.

Serpil and her driver were ready and waiting in the car, heaters firing warm air towards their toes, radio tuned for their pleasure. My thoughts turned to the warm bed I had emerged from less than an hour earlier and the possibility of a day doing nothing. They were the sort of thoughts that I had whenever the outdoors looked unappealing but I knew that I just had to go for it. I resigned myself to another day shivering under torrential skies.

I was on the road out of Iskenderun, hugging a narrow ridge so that my views were either of the road that climbed steeply or of the magnificent Mediterranean far below. Although I was due to follow its curve over the next few weeks, pedalling south into Syria, Jordan and eventually Egypt, it was the last time I saw it, my route taking me inland rather than along its coast.

I had been lashed by rain for months so another soaking didn't do any harm on the climb out of Iskenderun.

I climbed for eight miles until I reached the clouds and the views disappeared. I could see less than five metres ahead and it was significantly colder at altitude. At the start of the descent every car and every bend in the road came as a surprise but before long a cultivated valley on the other side of the ridge began to emerge and I wondered if the rocky outcrops in the distance were in Turkish or Syrian territory. For twenty minutes I descended, reaching the fastest speed of my entire journey, a terrifying – especially in the wet – forty-four miles per hour.

Upon reaching the emerald-green valley floor, an armoured convoy overtook us and ten machine-gun-toting military police performed a perfect display of paranoia, surrounding me, my bicycle and Serpil's support vehicle. Not even in my worst nightmares had I ever dreamed I would have ten machine guns pointing at my head but if I *had* dreamed about it I would have been terrified. In the event I surprised myself by remaining relatively calm and it seemed to have the desired effect because, by the time Serpil and I had shown our passports and visas and proved our innocence, guns were pointing at the floor and we were being wished a pleasant onward journey. 'Be careful in Syria,' one of the soldiers said in a hushed voice into my ear, 'they are a nation of thieves and criminals.' I reflected on how sad it was that neighbouring countries never trusted each other.

Such unexpected encounters are a feature of long-distance bicycle travel and I laughed to myself at the strange two-wheeled world I inhabited. But my laughter quickly turned to tears. In a strange way I was pleased that tears were becoming a feature of my ride. Of course, a little part of me felt somewhat feeble for letting myself get choked so easily; but on the whole I enjoyed sobbing quietly to myself because the tears were never born of a negative experience; and they were a reminder of how alive I felt.

From very early on in my ride I began to think that the way I handled my emotions would determine whether I succeeded or failed in my attempt to get to Brisbane for the Ashes. Riding sixty miles each day became routine; my legs learned how to do it. The struggle was lived between my ears and crying was a reminder that my mind was healthy. The tears I cried on a windswept, grassy plain close to Syria were mostly for a country that had seduced me over the past six weeks, for the friends I had made there and for the villagers who had added colour to my ride through Anatolia. I could remember the exact details of every day since Istanbul; I could not remember ever having that feeling before. My bicycle had felt like the perfect vehicle on which to explore a vast country, and feel the wind, rain, snow and thunder that typified my ride across it.

But some of the tears were even more personal. Achievement against the odds has always made me sob, especially in sport. I get it from my mum. Neither of us can watch the Olympics in a public space, it is just too embarrassing. Whereas I have never cried so readily where my own achievements are concerned, I did at the end of my time in Turkey because, quite simply, I had not expected to make it as far as I had. That made me proud and gave me hope and confidence for the road ahead.

The lush, fertile Turkish side of the border with Syria.

SYRIA AND JORDAN

THE NO-MAN'S-LAND BETWEEN Turkish and Syrian customs posts inhabited a narrow, rocky valley that was so long I thought I might have taken a wrong turn; but there was little chance of that. The road was punctuated by stern-looking armed guards and shouldered on both sides by an eighteen-foot barbed-wire fence.

After fifteen minutes pedalling in neither Turkey nor Syria, I reached a huge white, black and red flag, swarms of truck drivers and hundreds of stationary vehicles that marked my arrival at the Syrian border post. I was put through a surprisingly gentle line of questioning before being welcomed warmly into my twelfth country by a salute from a uniformed military officer. Armed with a healthy dollop of apprehension to accompany my excitement, I was free to continue into Syrian territory.

Although borders were always reminders of the necessary segmentation of our planet, from the saddle of a bicycle they rarely seemed to bring huge change to my two-wheeled world. One country tended to merge into the next. With the odd exception, such as the border that separated Bulgaria from Turkey, they seemed to bring little but a new, colourful stamp in my passport. It was a symptom of my slow pace of travel; the gradual movement from one country to its neighbour. Change came with time, as I rode deeper into a new culture.

My arrival in Syria was a little different. A customs post is presumably so called because it marks a line between the customs of one country and the next, although the two changes I noticed upon my arrival in Syria were neither cultural nor religious. The first was in the landscape. Whereas

The rocky scene across the border in Syria.

the Turkish side of the border had been a flat, fertile, emerald-green plain, the Syrian side was how I imagined a biblical landscape to be, with undulating rocky outcrops and abundant olive trees. It was obvious why it had been chosen as the location for the border.

The second was my direction of travel. Since leaving home I had largely been pedalling south-east in the vague direction of Australia. But I had decided against tackling Pakistan and Afghanistan and so, with my arrival in Syria, came an eighth of a compass point shift that sent me directly southwards for the first time. I hoped I would continue on that path until I reached the Kenyan coast at Mombasa.

I relished these small changes, which somehow seemed significant in the little world I had created for myself. Although each country and each day brought with it new faces and new challenges, there was an inevitable monotony to my days that came with turning my legs while straddling a bicycle saddle. I clung to any hint of variety, which tended to send me onwards in a positive frame of mind.

Variety was certainly provided in the first restaurant I stopped at after crossing into Syria. I had just been served the chicken shawarma I had ordered when a small flatbed truck pulled up outside the open-fronted restaurant. A man in overalls jumped on to the back, picked up a plucked, unwrapped chicken and hurled it in my direction. It sat resting against my foot for a few seconds until the man reached me, picked it up, offered a raised hand in apology and chucked the chicken towards the closed kitchen door. For the next ten minutes several paying guests and I dodged a hail of poultry that ended up in a huge pile at the back of the restaurant. What is more, I was the only person who seemed to think this was slightly out of the ordinary. I left half of my shawarma, paid up and pedalled on.

Back on the road the sun came out and I considered it the sign of a fresh start. I felt certain that after four months of persistent cold, rain and snow, my luck was about to improve. The further south I travelled, the warmer I would become. At the time I did not bother to think that warmth and heat were two very different things.

For now, although sunny, it was still cold and I pedalled in woolly hat and gloves as sunset approached. Serpil phoned to tell me she was still stuck at the border trying to persuade a taxi driver to bring her south to meet me. The plan was to camp our way towards Damascus over the coming week; I did not know how I felt about the fact that I would be sharing my tent for the first time since James left. But for now I was on my own, waving at groups of kids sitting on the grass by the side of the road or knocking a football about, and keeping my eyes peeled for a safe place to spend the night. Before long, a pick-up truck screeched to a halt in front of me and two men in black trench coats emerged. They did not wave or acknowledge me, they simply walked with purpose in my direction.

'What are you doing here?' the taller of the two asked. He had a thick, black beard to match his black trench coat and spoke firmly. The second man was stockier, clean shaven and kept his distance while his friend did the talking. 'You are a blond man very far from home.'

I will confess to being a little nervous at the arrival of my new acquaintances, but I told the man what I was doing and admitted that I was indeed a bloody long way from home.

'You are staying with me tonight; put your bicycle in back of truck.' They were not the words I had expected to hear next, but he was smiling now and seemed trustworthy; I liked to trust people. I bundled my bicycle and bags into the pick-up and jumped in with them.

During the two-mile drive back into Maarrat al-Nu'man, I called Serpil to let her know that I had secured us a place to sleep and to tell her where to meet me. Musab, the taller of the two men, was a civil engineer just returned from ten years working in Mecca. A devout Muslim, he was the patriarchal figure of a huge extended family living in an empty shop and adjoining flat in the heart of the town. When Serpil arrived shortly after dark she ate olives, hummus and sweet pastries filled with cheese and played cards upstairs with the female members of the family (one of whom apparently had fifteen children under the age of twenty-five). I hunkered next to a gas fire and did the same on the shop floor with twenty or thirty men: 'We love the British, even though we hate Tony Blair,' I was told over and over again as friends and relatives came and went, all taking a photo of the strange blond intruder and saving it as their phone screensaver. Musab said none of his family could understand the reason for my journey, but that he did because he had travelled abroad and knew that us Westerners had too much time and money. I told him that I was travelling on about $10 a day, but that piece of information did not make him change his mind. I asked him where he would like to travel to next. 'Nowhere,' was his answer. 'I came back to be with my family because I missed them so much. I will not leave Syria again.'

I must have nodded off at some point because when I woke at around midnight I was alone, a mattress and blankets by my side, and a note that read 'SLEEP WELL MR OLI – I HOPE YOU ENJOY OUR HOSPITALITY. AND I HOPE YOU RECEIVE MORE SYRIAN HOSPITALITY DURING YOUR TIME HERE. MUSAB'

During my search for sponsors before I left home I had arrogantly advertised the expedition as 'solo and unsupported'. In fact, nothing could have been further from the truth. Each time I was welcomed into a home or provided for in some way, it helped me understand that it was the friends I made on my way around the world, whose lives touched mine, however fleetingly, that would ensure my safe passage to Brisbane.

It was not until June 2011 that I finally sent an email to Musab, thanking him again for his kindness, and wishing him and his family well in the face of the mounting Arab Spring rebellions. Maarrat al-Nu'man was one of the first cities seized by rebel fighters. I received no reply to my email. As the civil war developed the town became the focus of sustained attacks from Syrian government forces because of its strategic position next to the M5 highway which links the country's two largest cities, Aleppo and Damascus. It is the route I cycled through Syria. The Battle of Maarrat al-Nu'man began in October 2012 and continues as I write. I have written to Musab several times, but I have not heard back.

As I pedalled onwards through Syria, I noticed signs of a nation ruled with an iron fist although at the time, of course, I had no clue of the troubles to come. Various social networking websites were banned by the government and in every town I stayed I was required to report to a government official to register my presence. Nobody spoke politics, and I got plenty of searching questions from apparently humble workers whenever I stopped for some food in a café, or in a hostel overnight. There always seemed to be someone watching or listening. I had heard that one in three Syrians either worked, or informed, for the government. Although I never found out the truth of that statistic, it came as no surprise to hear it.

Certainly many Syrians were keen to show their allegiance to the President, Bashar Al-Assad, if not to talk about him. On about one in three cars the entire back windscreen was taken up by a sticky poster of his face. In every town and city were statues of him in all sorts of faintly ridiculous poses.

He had become President in 2000, when his father, Hafez Al-Assad, who had ruled Syria for thirty years before him, died of a heart attack while on the telephone to the Lebanese Prime Minister. Bashar was never meant to be President. His elder brother, Bassel, had been groomed for the role from a young age, but he was killed in a car crash in 1994. Only after his brother's death did Bashar become the President-in-waiting. I could only assume that he spent the six intervening years scouring the world for the worst sculptor he could find.

Although I had hoped for better weather, the rain returned on the road towards Damascus. Each day Serpil travelled ahead, found a free or cheap place for us to stay and filmed me when I arrived soaked through. I think she was surprised by my mood swings. She saw a relaxed, calm person most mornings and a knackered, impatient and occasionally short-tempered one most evenings. It was not just that I was pushing myself hard to get miles done in the hope of catching up on lost time. I had also been filming my journey with a small handheld camera since Belgrade but, with Serpil travelling with me, I found it hard being the focus of a camera lens held by someone else. Mornings and evenings were no longer mine and I was often too tired for small talk, or even idle banter. Still, I appreciated her being there, and I would have to get used to company anyway. Back in Budapest, László was working hard to put together a team of film-makers and enthusiasts from all the countries on my route.

On the way into Homs, as the rain lashed down, I veered into a roadside ditch attempting to avoid falling under the wheels of a passing truck. I did not know at the time if it was the crash that did it, or persistent wear and tear, but inspecting my bicycle later that night I noticed the crankset was bent out of shape and the bottom bracket loose (I later found out it was wear and tear). Serpil and I scoured the city in search of a bicycle shop. We found nothing but a hardware store and an old guy in a vest, covered in grease and filth, who owned a hammer. One hefty whack of a chisel wedged beside the crankset was enough to persuade me to get on the phone to Santos, the manufacturer of my bicycle, and ask them to send a new bottom bracket and crankset. I called the Sheraton Hotel in Damascus and they agreed to take delivery of the package. I was told it would take a week to arrive.

So it was by train that Serpil and I arrived in Damascus. I had pedalled on for a couple of days after Homs, lugging 130 kilograms using only two gears. Just north of Damascus the bottom bracket gave up on me completely and my pedals would not turn. Part of me was sad as I stared at the ruin of my bicycle; after all, my tyre tracks had been broken for the first time since Dunkerque more than four months earlier. But another part of me was proud that I had cycled far enough to have achieved something very rare indeed: wearing out the bottom bracket of a bicycle.

While I waited for the package in Damascus, I spent two days exploring every inch of the city in search of a bicycle shop that might sell a replacement in-country. No luck. After four days, there was still no sign of the package. Eventually I discovered I would have to wait another week before it arrived. Frustrated with the interruption to my progress south, I took off to the eastern desert on a local bus with an Australian backpacker called Ross. We spent a day at the four-thousand-year-old Roman city of Palmyra, an oasis in the desert which we had almost to ourselves. We scaled the wrought-iron gates of an ancient city dating from 300 BC at Dura Europos while the security guard was on his lunch break and sat on the edge of an escarpment one hundred metres above the Euphrates River, staring out at mosque minarets and listening to the distant echoes of the call to prayer. Before we headed back to Damascus we decided we were too close to the Iraqi border not to visit it. A minibus took us there and we celebrated our adventurousness at almost setting foot in one of the world's most dangerous countries with a freshly squeezed orange juice. We were quite the intrepid pair.

The minibus journey back to Damascus later that afternoon

We had the four-thoursand-year-old city of Palmyra almost to ourselves.

offered respite from an increasingly intense sun. Ross translated the Arabic sign above the driver's head: THIS BUS IS LICENSED TO CARRY A MAXIMUM OF 10 PEOPLE. I counted heads; there were sixteen, most of them under either a black and white, or red and white checked kefiyeh, the Arab headdress made so famous by Yasser Arafat. For four hours we bounced along a rutted, potholed tarmac road, vehicle horns providing an enduring soundtrack to the journey. Whereas in England if someone cuts you up you might – or might not – hoot to inform the guilty driver of your mild displeasure, it seemed that in Syria such an offence was not a necessary precursor. I imagined a scene at a Syrian car mechanic's:

Car owner: 'Hi mate, listen, my car's got a few problems. The steering is shot, the brakes don't work, the engine blew up yesterday, I need four new lightbulbs and the horn doesn't make a sound. Don't worry about the steering, brakes, engine or lights for now; just make sure the horn works, okay?'

Mechanic: 'Of course; what else would I do?'

I noticed that whenever our minibus driver saw a pedestrian in the road ahead he smiled, accelerated and hooted his horn simultaneously, so I was delighted when we arrived back in Damascus safely. I was even more delighted when the crankset and bottom bracket finally arrived the following morning. I fixed them ready for my departure but before I left there was something else I had to do.

I gathered a group of travellers I had got to know during my time in Damascus and led them through the souks of the old city and out the other side, into an area where tall residential towers dominated. There, in a rubbish dump, we played what must rank as one of the most multi-cultural games of cricket the world has ever seen: an Englishman, two Australians, an American, a Turk, a Canadian who played club cricket in Vancouver, three Syrians, a Palestinian refugee working at the rubbish dump and three of his colleagues – one Kurdish and two Iraqi refugees. After a couple of hours a decent crowd had formed and the Kurd was teaching the Iraqis how to hold the bat, with the 'V' pointing down the splice. The game ended when the Palestinian refugee got a little too militant with Ross when he refused to sign his refugee papers. Still, I was pleased to have managed a game in the oldest continually inhabited city in the world.

New country; new start. On the roof terrace of my hostel that evening I took some nail scissors to the thick ginger beard that had kept me warm through the Turkish and Middle Eastern winter. But I guessed that the worst of the weather was past and I felt like getting some sun on a face that turned out to be far thinner than it had been when I'd last seen it, in Istanbul.

Bad timing. Having been nudging 25°C for the past week, it snowed persistently on the morning I left Damascus. Still, I said goodbye to my newest group of friends, and to a city that, despite an extended time off the bike, I felt I had not really got to know. I was off again, bound for Jordan. The call to prayer rang out from the city's mosques as I hid deep within my red winter jacket, longing to feel the sun's warm glow on my pale skin. I had been outside for most of the past four months, and cold for most of that time.

On my first night out of Damascus I camped far from anywhere, between two rows of olive trees. Around lunchtime

'Do it like this!' The Kurdish refugee teaching me how to teach cricket.

on the second day I made a very easy border crossing into the Kingdom of Jordan, my thirteenth country. Compared with its northern neighbour, Jordan seemed liberal and wealthy. I spent my first night there in the university town of Irbid, where the main street had a strip of neon lights that rivalled the most Anglicised of Greek islands. Young female students wore jeans, not hijabs or niqabs. I ate in a sterile burger joint and marvelled at the cleanliness of the place; cleanliness and hygiene had come to mean so much in the past few months. I uploaded videos on to YouTube, something the Syrian government's ban on social networking had not enabled me to do. I may have been just twenty-five miles from the Sea of Galilee, forty from Nazareth and sixty from Bethlehem, but Jordan was positively modern.

As I descended a hairpin road that led me from dense housing to green pastures far below, I waved at shepherds and groups of young kids alike. The shepherds waved back but the kids just threw stones at my wheels. I had heard about stone-throwing kids from other cyclists, but had not expected them until Ethiopia. They did not dampen my spirits, though; it would take more than a bunch of kids to do that.

The following morning I was riding the lowest road on earth, the Dead Sea Highway, at four hundred metres below sea level, and enjoying a miraculous temperature of 32°C. The snow of two days earlier, and the cold of my entire trip to that point, was long forgotten and my new environment brought an easy smile to my face. Although I was forced to pay to do it, I swam in the heavy, salty waters of the Dead Sea. At the time I did not know it, but it would barely drop below 30°C during the daytime again for the remainder of my journey.

On the western shore of the Dead Sea were Israel and the West Bank, bare, sand-coloured mountains rising steeply out of the calm waters. Although the Jordanians are not as hostile towards Israel as many surrounding countries, there were still several military checkpoints dotted along the Dead Sea Highway and my passport was always checked before I was allowed to continue unhindered. At one particular checkpoint the officers seemed friendly and I asked if they would pose for a photo with the Ashes urn. They happily obliged so I pushed my luck and asked if I could pitch my tent for the night. There were very few places that seemed safe for camping and, bearing in mind the military presence and the paranoia about Israel, I did not want to be found alone in the middle of the night. The answer came back 'Yes', and I began to set up camp. A little while later, cooking in the porch of my tent as I enjoyed one of the finest sunsets of the entire ride, the officer came over to say goodbye, and to wish me luck. I assumed he meant good luck for the journey ahead, and perhaps he did. But what he should have said was 'Good luck persuading my colleague on night shift that you can sleep here'.

The sky was a deep red when his armed replacement trotted over less than five minutes into his shift. Although he spoke no English, I understood immediately that he wanted me gone. I have a rule: never argue with a man carrying an automatic weapon. Reluctantly I stopped cooking, stuffed my half-cooked pasta into a Tupperware, packed up the tent and all my strewn belongings, loaded my bicycle and pedalled off into the growing darkness.

An hour later I came across a factory and pulled up next to the large glass security hut at its entrance. I explained my dilemma to the guard, who spoke excellent English and turned out to be sympathetic. I think he felt like some company because he let me bed down at the foot of his desk. But my struggle continued. I was woken around 2 a.m. by an aggressive boot to my feet. The guard's supervisor was apparently adamant that I should leave. And so I did, packing up my belongings again and pedalling off once more to find somewhere to spend the second half of the night.

I was lucky. I did not have to pedal for long. In the dark I made out the outline of what turned out to be a half-built, bare concrete house, some fifty metres back from the highway. A staircase led up to an open roof. In the absence of anything solid that would stop me falling two storeys if I rolled over in my sleep, I laid my bicycle near the edge and my mat alongside it. It was warm and there seemed little chance of rain, so I did not pitch my tent but simply fell asleep to the distant howls of wolves. The following night I crept into a plantation and slept in a greenhouse between two rows of tomatoes. I was beginning to enjoy warm nights and the freestyle camping opportunities they allowed.

For the next couple of weeks I raced south, chasing the sun, on a mission to get some decent mileage done. I pedalled furiously, keen to give myself every chance of getting all the way to Mombasa by the end of March, the rough deadline I had set myself.

But there was another reason I pedalled so hard. While I was in Damascus my sister had sent me a link to an article in London's *Metro* newspaper. A friend of hers had advertised for companions to cycle from Cairo to Cape Town with her to watch the football World Cup. She had chosen three men, and they were due to arrive in Aswan, in southern Egypt, on 19 February. Although I did not regret taking on my challenge alone, I did sometimes feel like some company and if I was going to have it anywhere then the edge of the world's largest desert seemed like a pretty good place. It would certainly make the challenge less daunting and it was with that thought in mind that I endeavoured to make it through Egypt to Aswan to meet Lindsey and her cycling partners for the Sudanese leg of my journey.

Crossing my first desert north of Aqaba.

In southern Jordan I crossed my first desert, a two-day ride into the northern Red Sea port of Aqaba. I ate at Pizza Hut before deciding that I had to get out of the town as soon as possible; it was expensive and brash and I did not want such an incongruous city to leave me with a lasting and unrepresentative impression of that corner of the Middle East.

On 10 February I caught a boat from Aqaba across the Red Sea. About twenty minutes into the hour-long journey I stood on the deck, took out my map and looked around me. I was amazed that I could see the hazy coastlines of four countries: Saudi Arabia, Jordan, Israel and Egypt. I wanted to visit all of them, but it was for Egypt and Africa that I was bound.

SUDAN

PASSAGE TO SUDAN

Twitter, 18 February 2010
Proud owner of Sudanese visa. Immigration guy more interested in my football team than if I am going to disappear while in Sudan.

My companions and I watch in horror as hundreds of Sudanese lug their worldly belongings on to the unsteady, lurching vessel. The ferry is smaller than I had expected – perhaps fifty metres in length – and it is the only boat moored up to the long concrete jetty suffering like the rest of us under a fierce midday sun. The red, green, white and black of the Egyptian and Sudanese flags flutter on top of the ferry's bridge. High on deck, men lean over the warped railings, flailing at missiles thrown at them from below: cardboard boxes tied with twine, taped-up battered old suitcases, mattresses, chairs and unidentified objects wrapped in tarpaulins. On the jetty, women balance sofas on their slender, bewilderingly sturdy frames; children follow suit, lifting sacks of fruit and sugar from wooden pallets and straining under the weight. Men in long white tunics, or jalabiyas, carry less but yell more. One man is notable by his silence and stillness. He is to the left of the ship's only embarkation point, leaning on a dilapidated piano. His languid posture suggests he believes himself above the hullabaloo and presumably he is, because he is about to take a fucking huge piano on to a ferry. We cyclists may be on holiday but most of our ferry-mates seem to be moving their lives southwards, to Sudan.

I had spent the previous week racing through Egypt, detouring Cairo completely and forfeiting the chance to gaze at Luxor's ancient wonders. I had met my four new pedalling companions in Aswan. Lindsey, long blonde hair, endurance athlete, journalist and friend of my sister's, had gathered a team to cycle to the football World Cup in South Africa. They had started their journey in Cairo less than two weeks earlier. She was joined by John, Dicky and Duncan. John, tall and serious, cricket lover and frontman in a London band; Dicky, shorter, fit as a butcher's dog, ready for some hard pedalling; Duncan, full of life, a joker with a shock of bleached blond hair that was his most sober characteristic. He rode the same bike he had ridden from London to Taiwan two years earlier when he had bet a friend £1 that he could not cycle from Reading to the tallest building in the world. Naturally, he cycled with his friend to adjudicate. But a week before the two set off, someone told them that a new tallest building had been opened, in Dubai. Without telling anyone they detoured via Dubai, photographed themselves in front of the new title-holder and continued to Taiwan. When they arrived, Duncan presented his friend with a shiny one pound coin at a press conference at the top of the world's second tallest building. I was excited to be journeying south in the company of others. The road ahead somehow seemed less daunting, the adventure more exciting.

With Sudanese visas stamped into passports, and passports safely tucked into handlebar bags, my new friends and I navigated our way out of Aswan towards the ferry that would take us to Sudan, pedalling along a bustling main road that hugged the east bank of the Nile. It was a peaceful morning; men rested on moored feluccas, shielded from the already intense sun by giant white sails. Some smoked dope, others slept. More feluccas sailed gently upstream, leaning on what little breeze there was. Egypt hadn't seduced me like other countries but in racing through it so quickly I felt I had given it little chance to do so. There were always going to be some countries that I got to know less well and certainly I hoped to return to the Egyptian Nile one day.

My head wanted to pedal but my legs did not. Even after a couple of days off they were weary and leaden: too many Egyptian McDonald's perhaps? Still, after twenty minutes we were out of the city and well on our way to our next stop, bouncing along a sandy track bordered by low, dust-clad buildings that would lead us to the ferry terminal. I began to feel energy return to my legs. Young boys indulged in their favourite pastime of pushing old tyres along the side of the road with sticks and we did our best to dodge them. Booming voices shouted accusingly at us from deep within buildings: 'Want US dollars, yes?' or 'Exchange good price!'. Aswan may be two hundred miles north of Egypt's southern boundary but it is the only overland border linking it with Sudan, a fact explained by the presence of Lake Nasser, a vast body of water stretching from Aswan in southern Egypt, more than three hundred miles south to Wadi Halfa in northern Sudan.

Lake Nasser, or Lake Nubia as it is called in Sudan, is the physical result of the construction of the Soviet-designed Aswan High Dam. We reached its little brother, the Aswan Low Dam, a couple of hours before dark. A lasting monument to Victorian ambition, it was completed by the British in 1902, built to reduce flooding and support population growth in the lower Nile. But it did not prove high enough, and was regularly breached. As a result, thirty-six years after its completion, the Soviet Union offered the new President, Gamal Abdel Nasser, the funds to build a second dam, later named the Aswan High Dam. This vast structure was built over ten years from 1960, measures about two and a half miles across, and at its base is 980 metres thick. It is four miles upstream from the Low Dam, providing hydroelectric power and increased protection from flooding. It changed the geography of this corner of Africa and as a result, as well as being the largest, is arguably the most famously controversial reservoir in the world.

The lake has undoubtedly improved the lives of millions of people: it provides 40 per cent of Egypt's electricity supply; guarantees a year-round water supply to a region that has suffered annual droughts for millennia; and it has created an abundant and profitable fishing industry. But waiting at a dusty ferry terminal a few miles south of Aswan, looking out over the lake's tranquil northern reaches, I found it humbling and desperately sad to think of the human and cultural price that was paid during its construction. Hundreds of thousands of Nubian people, whose communities had for centuries been clustered along the banks of the Nile in southern Egypt and northern Sudan, were forced to abandon their villages. They were resettled further from the river on high, infertile ground that made their simple, subsistence way of life far less manageable. It wasn't just people who suffered. Tens of archaeological sites were dismantled block by block and moved to higher ground. Abu Simbel, built in the thirteenth century BC, had to be saved by the United Nations in 1968 and is now a UNESCO World Heritage Site. Plenty more sites were left where they stood, and now sit forgotten, deep under the colossal weight of water.

My vague knowledge of the lake's controversial history planted in me a seed of guilt at using it at all. But in the absence of roads linking Egypt and Sudan, Lake Nasser provides the only overland alternative to air travel between the two countries. A boat leaves once a week from a little port south of Aswan, where we found ourselves face to face with a throbbing assembly of humanity all attempting to clamber aboard to begin the long journey to the exotic-sounding desert town of Wadi Halfa.

We were whisked from one bored, uncommunicative Egyptian customs officer to the next in a masterful display of apathy; then to the Sudanese officers. I rolled my bicycle on to a set of blue metal scales and the dial jerked to the right. The customs official and I raised a collective eyebrow when the needle settled on sixty-four kilograms. My bicycle had never been heavier, loaded with water and food to keep me going throughout the long journey down Lake Nasser. I told the officer not to worry because, unlike me, he did not have to cycle it anywhere at all. Customs negotiated, I was ushered down a barbed-wire corridor slightly narrower than my bicycle, at the end of which I discovered the absurdity of being asked to weigh it in the first place. Several hundred furiously hurried and impatient people were barging, shoving, screaming and wailing their way on to the ferry with their life's belongings. In the absence of a better idea we crouched, gritted our teeth and piled head first into the mêlée, elbows at the ready and patience bending long before the ferry journey even began.

The entire process of boarding was both memorable and in defiance of physics. Everyone contorted their bodies into and around tight corners, sharing their sweat and growing filth with those they squeezed past. How the lady with four sacks of sugar on her back negotiated the narrowest staircase on the planet I will never know. There were tiny, private cabins off the corridors, where women sat in brightly coloured tob and hijab, huddled around makeshift kitchens complete with gas stoves, pots, pans and animated company. Although Muslim, the women did not cover their faces, and it was easy to see their eyes following me as I shuffled down the corridor. They were as intrigued by me as I was by them, a theme I

Life on board the ferry to Wadi Halfa

had already noted through Turkey, Syria and Jordan and one that would continue as I headed into Sudan.

When eventually I reached the deck I saw that life was equally fraught, but at least there was air. What there was not much of was deck space. It seemed we had been beaten to it by almost all the other passengers who had long before finished creating mini, shaded living spaces to make the journey as painless as possible. The passage was due to take seventeen hours and for us, it seemed, it would be an uncomfortable time. But after some sensitive negotiating through the medium of face contortion, finger pointing and thumb waggling, the five of us secured a small area the size of a coffee table and began to make it our own. We leaned our bicycles against safety railings protecting us from the waters below and puffed air into our inflatable mattresses. Creating shade was a little tricky but apart from working out that the bridge would provide some respite from the sun in the morning, there was little we could do. With our new home perfected, I set about my favourite pursuit of people-watching.

As we pulled away from the Egyptian shore a mere four hours behind schedule, I stood at a vantage point on the bridge near the officers' cabins, from where I could see the entire deck. I didn't mind our delayed departure. Time had grown gradually less relevant since I had left home. No trains to catch, no immediate deadlines to meet, no responsibilities, complete freedom. I enjoyed the movement southwards as we inched into the lake's slender body, slowly closing in on my next challenge.

I lied when I said I could see the whole deck. It was so crammed that every square inch of it was camouflaged by passengers and their many belongings. At the stern were two large, orange fibreglass lifeboats hanging precariously over both starboard and port. I could not help but notice there were about five hundred passengers and only two small lifeboats capable of carrying no more than fifteen each. I also noted that an alarming number of the Sudanese had positioned themselves in the deck space between the lifeboats. I did not know if, in doing so, they had betrayed knowledge of the vessel's desperate safety record or simply thought that was where they would find the most shade. I hoped it was the latter.

Most Sudanese men were dressed in crisp white, traditional floor-length jalabiyas (loose-fitting, long-sleeved and collarless). On their heads they wore taqiyahs (short, rounded caps that, as far as I could tell, were also nearly always white). Some had turbans wrapped around their taqiyahs (again, generally white). There were a handful of men in the less traditional, more practical combination of trousers and shirt, and a few in Premiership football club shirts. Happily, Liverpool seemed to be the most popular team by far with Manchester United, for once, a distant second.* There was not a single Sudanese woman in eyeshot. They were all below deck.

Towards the middle of the ferry I could see the ten white faces of our fellow travellers. I guessed they were 'overlanders' travelling the continent in extravagant 4x4 vehicles. Most had erected expensive looking tents and were chatting away: 'How many times have you broken down? Did you see the man with the piano? Do you reckon we'll sink and drown? Look how much furniture everyone has! Where have you come from? Where are you going to next?'

Below me, on the starboard side, was our camp. Next to us were a group of three traditionally dressed Sudanese men piling cardboard boxes on top of each other to form a circular wall. The boxes were full of CDs and they were unpacking, labelling and repacking each one. It was a task that would take the entire seventeen-hour journey. I had already discovered that every week they travelled back and forth between

---

* An uncanny number of the football fans I came across in developing countries were Liverpool fans. I never found out why, but suspected its popularity ran along similar lines as the explanation of the Argentinian national team's overriding popularity in Bangladesh. The story goes that television arrived in Bangladesh in the early 1980s when Diego Maradona and his team-mates were the best in the world. When they won the World Cup in 1986, Bangladeshi football fans took Argentina to their hearts. Around the same time Liverpool were the dominant team in England and Europe, so perhaps the developing world had taken to them for the same reason.

the two countries, buying in Egypt and selling in Sudan. For them the voyage was not an adventure into the unknown, but a regular commute; one that was a means of survival, rather than a means of discovery.

As the Egyptian border receded and we advanced under another red African sunset, life on board took on a placid, rhythmic quality. Even the deep groan of the boat's engine seemed to fade as night approached. Some passengers found contentment in quiet conversation or slept under giant tarpaulins, others sat blank-faced listening to meditative music I wanted to call desert-rock, but which I was sure had a proper name. It reminded me of the Malian band Tinawiren and I imagined the musicians in floor-length kaftans playing soothing electric guitar atop a Saharan dune; I suspect they were probably in a studio in New York.

Two Sudanese Liverpool football fans befriended us, keen to practise their English. 'Beckham very handsome!' the one in a Crown Paints-era shirt blurted, pointing at Duncan, before turning to me and saying, 'You Peter Crouch; he also very handsome!' Duncan found it easier to become mates with Crown Paints man than I did.

So instead of befriending local people, as dusk turned to darkness I switched on my head-torch and began reading a book I had picked up in Aswan. Dave Eggers' *What is the What* is a fact-based novel about the horrific experiences of Valentino Achak Deng growing up during the second Sudanese Civil War. I knew a little about the country's history but was keen to learn about individual stories which I always found useful in bringing a place alive.

The next morning I was woken by Kurt, a Swiss television journalist, and his crew who were up early to film while we glided past Abu Simbel. I could not imagine the effort it must have taken to move such a huge temple complex. Tourists, already arriving by the busload, looked like ants gathered below the sheer sandstone walls of its two vast structures. We were too far away, perhaps a mile, to be able to decipher any engravings, but the sun, which rose behind us, lent the complex a magnificent orange glow. After Abu Simbel the rest of the day was uneventful. I read, chatted and finally, as we neared the end of the journey, completed customs formalities with a handful of Sudanese officers dressed in military garb, in a stuffy room on the ferry's lower deck.

Abu Simbel, thankfully on the banks of Lake Nasser,
rather than underneath it.

I had now been on the road for over four months. The relatively slow speed at which I had crossed from village to village, from one country to the next, lent a sense of continuity and slow adjustment to my travel. Arriving in a new country by aeroplane is always overwhelming, with the differences between home and destination accentuated by the speed and ease of the journey itself. But on my ride I had rarely felt out of place; I always had a sense of belonging, perhaps aided by a sense of purpose. I may have looked like, and occasionally acted like, an intruder in foreign lands, but I did not feel like one. So as we approached the end of the ferry journey and caught sight of another dusty terminal, I felt little but anticipation. Sudan was the next, very natural step on my way to the

Ashes. I knew the road ahead was likely to throw up moments of surprise, shock, agony and heartache but, knowing that I had already surpassed my expectations by reaching Sudan in the first place, I felt ready to tackle it head-on.

A DESERT OASIS

I have known of Wadi Halfa since I was young. My dad was stuck there for ten days in 1972, having arrived off the ferry to be told that because it was Ramadan the customs officers would not be issuing visas. He would have to wait until after Eid. Stories of his travels through Africa have always inspired me to travel and his faded photographs of the port town suggested a wild, inhospitable desert outpost, an edge-of-the-world sort of place that I was desperate to see for myself.

About a mile from the Sudanese shore, other than the southern reaches of Lake Nasser and a red cargo ship moored to a small concrete pontoon, I could see nothing but sand. There were no buildings, no people. The sky was a piercing, deep blue, the sort we don't get in England. After sixteen hours chugging southwards, we were finally about to arrive in Wadi Halfa, but it appeared to have been wiped from the planet.

Our Sudanese travelling companions had long finished packing up their temporary shelters and kitchens and their anticipation was tangible. I knew how they felt. Most, like us, had lengthy onward journeys to complete, so the southern tip of Lake Nasser, while a step in the right direction, was merely the start of the next challenge. I imagined some of the places they might be heading for: Darfur, Port Sudan or, like us, Khartoum. Whatever their destinations, most looked happier to be at the Sudanese end of an impossibly cramped ferry journey because it meant they had made it home. For our part, we were just happy to be in yet another country none of us had ever been to before.

Upon docking, there ensued a perfect reversal of the scene played out in Aswan seventeen hours earlier, the only difference being that while in Aswan everyone was eager to secure space on deck, now all anyone wanted was to escape the confines of the ferry's bowels as quickly as possible. The captain was omnipresent, his role apparently to shout as loudly as possible, to as many women as possible. Corridors reverted to wrestling arenas furnished with piles of wicker chairs, cupboards and sacks of grain and sugar. While I tackled the corridors of hell with my bicycle and belongings, Dicky came up with a much more astute solution up on deck, attaching his loaded bicycle to a rope and, inch by inch, lowering it to John who had managed to escape to the pontoon below.

I eventually made it out again to see my four companions waiting for me. After dunking my bicycle into Lake Nasser to give her a pre-Sudan clean, we followed a line of trucks piled high with our Sudanese ferry-mates, hoping they would lead us to the still invisible town of Wadi Halfa.

Of course, Wadi Halfa did still exist. We found it nestled among banks of high sand dunes two miles south of the lake. I had passed through lots of border towns since leaving home – two in most countries I had visited – and found them to be strange places so reliant on passing traffic that nothing else seemed to matter. Transient hawkers peddled and vagrants lay about in the vain hope of being offered a better life, or at least some small change, by a passer-by. Wadi Halfa felt different, and I liked it straight away.

In every direction, above the rows of single-storey sand-coloured buildings were sandstone, conical hills. At the bottom of each one were burnt-out cars and other relics from decades past. There was one road that led south towards Khartoum – the road we would take the next day – and it was the only road that went anywhere. Others simply ran their short course to the edge of town before merging with the sand that did not come to an end for thousands of miles in all directions. The occasional splash of green palm trees provided colour and shade, but otherwise we were under siege from the world's greatest desert, the Sahara.

Men sat on carts pulled by donkeys, gently rapping them

The road south out of Wadi Halfa.

on their behinds when they paused for rest; there were almost as many donkeys as people. Taxi rickshaw drivers sat waiting for customers. The town seemed too small to need taxis, and trade can't have been roaring. If they were in England they would have been twiddling their thumbs but I expect they were not even doing that. Other men wandered lethargically through Wadi Halfa's sandy streets, smiling nonchalantly as we passed on our bicycles. I was interested to see what sort of reaction I would get on my arrival in Africa's largest country.* I got my answer when a group of villagers huddled under the shade of a café awning all offered a hand in welcome as we stopped to ask where we could find a hotel. One man rose drowsily out of his chair, steadying himself as he did so and walked us four blocks down to the only hotel in town.

It was difficult to reconcile this sleepy little desert oasis with a town that had played such an important role in the country's

* South Sudan achieved independence after a referendum in 2011. This split left Algeria, at 2,382,000 square kilometres – more than three and a half times the size of France – as Africa's largest country.

history. It was from Wadi Halfa that the British launched a series of attacks to defeat the Mahdist nationalist forces at the end of the nineteenth century, to begin a prolonged period of British and Egyptian rule. The Egyptians, under the control of the Turkish Empire, were the first foreign rulers of Sudan in the 1820s, when slavery became the country's *raison d'être*. By the 1870s the British were in control of Egypt, and with it came Sudan. The Sudanese nationalist movement, which had gained momentum during Ottoman rule, was thriving by the 1880s. The Mahdist forces, led by the self-titled Mahdi, an Islamic nationalist and spiritual leader named Muhammad Ahmad, won several important battles against Egyptian forces in the early 1880s. Eventually the British, who considered Sudan strategically unimportant and lacking in natural resources, decided to cut their losses and ordered Egyptian forces to withdraw. Major General Charles 'Chinese' Gordon, an aggressive, high-ranking British officer fresh from victories commanding Chinese soldiers of the 'Ever Victorious Army' in the Second Opium War and the Taiping Rebellion, was appointed Governor-General of Sudan and sent to oversee the withdrawal.

But Gordon soon discovered the scale of his challenge. With Egyptian garrisons scattered across the country and many already under siege, he was advised by London to concentrate on withdrawing the Egyptian and European population of Khartoum. He disobeyed orders, though, obsessed with the noble aim of securing the safety of every Egyptian across the country. As a result, the Mahdist forces were able to lay siege to Khartoum and Gordon paid the ultimate price when his forces fell in early 1885 and his head was chopped off and paraded around Khartoum on a stick. The Mahdi became ruler of the first recognisable Sudanese state.

But the British, who by the late nineteenth century had ambitions for Sudan, returned and from Wadi Halfa coordinated a successful campaign, culminating in one of the most one-sided victories in imperial military history at the Battle of Omdurman in 1898. Then, through the employment of the highly efficient Sudan Political Service, they set about making use of the vast and largely arid region. The Gezira Scheme, built between 1906 and 1925, eventually provided irrigation for 6 per cent of the world's cotton; the railway system became the pride of Africa. But economic success was short-lived.

As an Englishman new to Sudan, I found it difficult to feel completely guilt-free about the country's modern plight. Since shortly after its independence from Britain and Egypt in 1956, Sudan has been embroiled in one of the world's longest running civil wars of the twenty-first century, the seeds of which had been sown, at least in part, by my countrymen. Having sensibly administered the largely Muslim north as separate from the Christian-dominated south until 1946, the British eventually caved in to pressure from Khartoum and integrated the regions, making Arabic the language of administration in the south and appointing northern administrators to positions of power there. Christians were sidelined in the government of their own land, causing great resentment. When, in the 1950s, the British were preparing to grant Sudan independence, southern Sudanese leaders were not even invited to negotiations. From its birth in 1956 the new Republic of Sudan was in trouble.

The new government, from its base in Khartoum, enforced an increasingly repressive administration on Christians, especially in the south: in 1962 Christian missionaries were expelled; Christian schools were closed; government militia attacks on southern protesters resulted in small-scale fighting that eventually became civil war. The Addis Ababa Agreement of 1972, which gave a degree of religious and cultural autonomy to the south, never promised to achieve a lasting peace. When war came again in 1983, the government in the north fought not only for religious and cultural dominance over the south, but also for its resources. The south had water and oil. The north had neither, yet oil revenues made up more than half of Sudan's export receipts. Ferocious fighting played out for two more decades all over Sudan.

Once the giant of Africa, and the continent's greatest hope for peaceful coexistence between Arab and African, Muslim and Christian, Sudan has been embroiled in civil war for most of the last sixty years. Two million civilian lives have been lost in conflict; four million people have been displaced in southern Sudan alone. It is only since the Comprehensive Peace Agreement of 2005, signed by the government and the southern rebels, that relative peace and stability has emerged.

Wheeling my bicycle up to the doorway of the single-storey Hotel Defintood I felt safe and, strangely, like I belonged. I did not feel like I was in a country with such a tragic recent history. The manager of Hotel Defintood was polite and friendly, our rooms clean and simple. Despite having slept and rested for most of the past couple of days, we slept and rested some more and by early evening, having unpacked, repacked, fixed and sorted so that we and our bicycles were ready for the desert, John, Dicky and I felt like a game of cricket.

DESERT WHITES

The fact that John, Dicky and I fancied a game of cricket was unfortunate because, of course, we were in Sudan. If we had been a century earlier we would have had little trouble sourcing plenty of beflannelled Englishmen, marking out a twenty-two-yard strip and having a good old thrash about (as it no doubt would have been termed). As Richard Cockett explains in *Sudan: Darfur and the Failure of an African State*, the Sudan Political Service had a simple and, in hindsight, disgraceful recruitment policy. Ninety-two per cent of those hired had undergone the 'cold baths and cricket curriculum' of the British public school system which was seen as being the perfect preparation for the governance of Empire; not only that, but every one of them had gone on to study at Oxford or Cambridge; most studied law or history; one in three graduates appointed to the Sudan Political Service in its fifty-six-year history had gained a Blue at university. It was for this reason that Sudan became known by the rather uncomfortable name of the 'Land of Blacks ruled by Blues'.

Fresh from sporting excellence back home, these young

men of privilege recreated their achievements on the fields of the Empire. Tennis was popular because often there were not enough officers to play a team game like rugby or cricket (the British committed far fewer resources in Sudan than they did elsewhere; never more than 125 administrators to govern an area three times the size of Texas). But in towns and cities with larger British populations, cricket was played. In 1883 the *Sporting Times* recorded that 'On January 3 a cricket match was played at Suakim between the English Navy and the Soudan Field Force. Major-General Sartorius, Colonel Harrington, and Leiutenant-General the Honourable Fitzroy Hay, played for the latter. The game was drawn in favour of the former by twenty runs on first innings.' A couple of years later the Suakim Expedition of 1885 also seemed to have provided a good opportunity for these men to play cricket with regular matches played on coir matting.

Later on, bespectacled Jake Seamer, captain of Somerset in 1948, left county cricket for Sudan where he once scored a century before breakfast as matches started early to avoid the worst of the heat. Dick Stanbury was another former Somerset cricketer who became a District Commissioner in the Sudan Political Service, finding himself judge, administrator and police chief at the tender age of twenty-one (in later years he worked for the Foreign Office in Cairo and kept wicket for the Gezira Club against the first Pakistani team to tour England).

But since independence there has been little sign of cricket in Sudan. My research had turned up only one mention of cricket, in a report published in the 2006 copy of *Wisden*, about an enterprising game played by expats in Khartoum in 2005:

The Anzacs v Rest of the World fixture involving UN peacekeeping soldiers took place in forty degree heat two days after Christmas 2005 in a suburb of Khartoum on a field normally used for soccer. The ground had a six-foot high brick wall around it, which made a useful boundary. But the wall is used as the local toilet, adding to the lovely smell of Khartoum. On one side was a massive cemetery. Fortunately, no sixes went in there, as the Muslims might have been upset had we chased the ball, and we only had the one. We did have two bats and two sets of pads and gloves, which made changes of batsmen rather slow. And by the end, all the kit was a dusty grey. Both teams wore uniform boots and trousers, with T-shirts and hats. The pitch was swept down to the hard dirt, and the bumps taken out with a shovel as best we could. The Anzacs won by two runs, with two balls left. The umpiring was terrible.

Not exactly Lord's on a pleasant June afternoon but it had all the ingredients I had come to expect of my odd cricketing encounters: unusual surroundings; lack of meaningful protection; confused local population; dodgy wicket. Still, extensive research led me no closer to finding any other sign of cricket in modern-day Sudan. In fact, apart from the game played between the Anzacs and the Rest of the World XI, it seemed that the country's nearest recent connection with cricket came in the form of 1980s England left-arm spinner Phil Edmonds who, as well as provoking controversy on the pitch when he proceeded to read a copy of the *Daily Telegraph* while fielding at square leg in a Test match in Calcutta, also attracted unwanted attention off it by attempting to strike a controversial oil-exploration deal in southern Sudan. French oil giant Total claimed to have exclusive rights and Edmonds' efforts in Sudan apparently failed, just like the spread of cricket.

It was of course a shame that Major-General Sartorius, Colonel Harrington, Jake Seamer, Dick Stanbury or, indeed, Leiutenant-General the Honourable Fitzroy Hay were not available for a game with us in Wadi Halfa. But as we left the hotel in search of a suitable oval and some local people to introduce to cricket, John, Dicky and I agreed that it was great amateur cricket territory: firm and fine sand; excellent wickets; lots of space – an endless succession of open areas more than big enough for even the longest of hitters; sight-screens – plenty of white painted single-storey buildings; and local men, in their long white jalabiyas, were halfway to being dressed for the occasion. The only trouble we faced was that no one could fathom what the hell we were up to.

We created a sort of temporary wicket complete with dusty crease markings and a large, rectangular lump of stone to act as stumps. A group of men – most of whom were bus and taxi drivers sleeping the night in town before venturing into the desert the following day – sat and watched from a distance, but before long curiosity got the better of them and they wandered over for a closer inspection of the strange scene. Patrick Leigh Fermor's experience in Sofia came to mind: John, Dicky and I must have looked ridiculously out of place. But as it turned out, like the Serbs I had encountered in Belgrade, the Sudanese had the natural advantage of exceptional height and it was no surprise that those who showed an interest in our alien pursuit headed for the bowler's end – the fluidity of the bowling motion clearly appealed to their languid sensibilities rather more than the frenetic movement of batting.

When it came John's turn to bat, a man named Tahir insisted on turning his arm over. Having studied me waddling in from the Sahara End moments earlier, Tahir seemed to have learned his new skill quickly and his action was fluid despite the unhelpful loose cut of his tunic. The first ball that Tahir ever bowled was surely one of the slowest balls in history, a full toss that John stroked calmly to the sandstone wall acting as extra cover. A quick single was run. Tahir continued, and by about his seventeenth ball (little attention was paid to 'overs' on the playing sands of Sudan), he seemed to have developed a healthy and competitive dislike for both John and I. Perhaps he had seen clips of Jeff Thomson in his devastating pomp because he quickly became a fan of short-pitched bowling and seemed intent on hitting both of us on the head. It was the Sudanese equivalent of Bodyline, just seventy years too late and with less media attention.

Before either – or both – of us were damaged permanently I wrenched the ball from Tahir's tight grip and chucked it to one of the growing throng of local kids kicking their heels behind the bowler's arm. While a young boy in a Barcelona football shirt guided his donkey and cart across the wicket until they both stood at square leg (umpire or fielder, I was unsure), John handed the Mongoose bat to the smallest man at the ground who was brave enough to become the first Nubian batsman, ever.

It has been said that the instinct to throw and to hit is the basis of man's primitive armoury* and it is true; it is amazing what happens when you hand a man a lump of wood and tell him to whack an onrushing ball as far as he can. For the next five minutes the little man tried and succeeded in doing exactly that. The joy on his face had to be seen to be believed as his friends and colleagues hollered at the victory of novice batsman over novice bowler. I think the British imperialists of the last two centuries missed a trick in discouraging the Sudanese to take up cricket.

That said, we were unable to persuade the Sudanese that fielding was an enjoyable activity and the donkey cart quickly became the preferred fielding position – less sandy, more comfortable. When the number of fielders sitting on the donkey cart reached about fifteen, Dicky, who had returned to the hotel for a pee, happened to emerge back into the clearing with a football. He kicked it high into the twilight sky. Sudanese necks craned and as soon as their eyes caught sight of the round chequered ball my attempts at a cricketing revolution came to an abrupt end. Shirts-for-goalposts were in place in seconds; teams formed naturally into Jalabiyas vs Football Shirts; shoes were outlawed, although one poor man became the first to limp off after his right foot collided forcefully with a boulder acting as the penalty spot. Lethargic cricketing merchants became combative soccer warriors: aggressive in the tackle, highly competitive, incredibly competent. John and I were left alone, clutching a bat and a ball respectively, with no one to play with.

We were in Africa after all, the continent that lives and breathes football perhaps more than any other. Accepting

---

* H.S. Altham, *A History of Cricket, From the Beginnings to the First World War*.

Sudanese man with the Ashes urn.

defeat, we joined in and by the time bad light stopped play one strange English game was long forgotten and we had been beaten by several goals at another great British sport. Yet although I had failed in my attempts to persuade a handful of Sudanese of the joys of cricket, it struck me that if I had not had a cricket bat with me and if John, Dicky and I had not walked out on to a patch of sand and begun playing, we would never have enjoyed an afternoon of sport with fifty men of the desert. Still, if Dicky had not gone to find the football we might have played cricket for a lot longer.

SAND AND STARS

Intent on refuelling after our attempt at cricket, the five of us sat in the heart of a small, dusty square among Wadi Halfa's swollen ferry-day population, eating bread and delicious plates of fūl (fava beans with olive oil, parsley, onion and garlic). We weren't to know at the time that the frequency with which we ate that same dish over the coming weeks would render it borderline inedible.

Hawkers, salesmen and other local characters came and went, each telling tall stories we felt certain were told to every traveller who passed through. Still, no one believed our story either.

'We are pedalling to Khartoum, starting tomorrow.'

'No, no, no, no,' protested a man called Ahmed, wagging his finger from side to side. 'This is not possible. It is very far to Khartoum. Perhaps will take you one week on bicycle.'

I'd heard these sorts of protestations many times before. 'More likely three weeks,' I explained.

'Oh but desert is very dangerous. Bad people there, and dangerous animals,' Ahmed implored.

'I hope we'll be okay. I think we'll make it to Khartoum. Have you been there?'

'No have not been there,' he explained, before continuing with a story we hoped was untrue. 'In 1983 was speaking with traveller in my restaurant. Told me he was riding motorcycle to Khartoum, and told him he was crazy fool. But next day he left Wadi Halfa and rode into desert. Some days later we heard about white man get eaten in desert by animal the size of horse but very dangerous. The police brought his motorbike back to Wadi Halfa.' Ahmed turned and pointed to a sinewy man smoking a shisha on the floor outside a food stall. 'My friend now rides the Italian's motorcycle.'

I dreamed of horse-sized man-eaters that night. Next morning the sun woke me as it sneaked through a narrow crack in the ceiling of the simple hotel room I shared with Dicky and

Duncan. The door was made of steel and padlocked, with a barred window above; the walls were a cold, painted white concrete. The floor was cold and concrete, too, but not painted. I lay still, sleepy but happy amid the murmur of a nearby market and the constant braying of donkeys. Hotel Defintood was not a hotel by Western standards, but at least it was clean. I had slept well there, and was ready to ride into the desert.

In the shaded open-air corridor I found a young boy turning the wheel of my upside-down bicycle with his finger, smiling as he did so. I threw him a high-five as I passed on my way to the shower, a cold tap and bucket number that did a first-rate job of waking me up as I watched the skittish behaviour of two geckos running about on the wall beside my head. As I dried off, perched on my bed's string frame, eating a breakfast of leftover bread and jam, I considered that for the next few weeks food standards would probably take a sharp nose dive from those I had managed to maintain throughout the Middle East and Egypt.

I completed various tasks that needed doing before we left Wadi Halfa. None of us knew what to expect of the Nubian Desert. Where would we find food and water? Would we find towns, and, if we did, what would be in them? There were tyres and inner tubes to be repaired, food supplies to be bought (rice and pasta mainly), water bottles to be gathered (for now, at least six litres each for drinking and cooking), music to be uploaded, tools to be cleaned, bags to be made sand-proof and packed. Everything had its place. My bicycle was in good shape – just a few minor adjustments to the derailleur and brakes that had been rubbing since Damascus.

Dicky and Duncan were impatient to leave, but Sudanese customs came first and the office was not open until eleven o'clock. I suggested we finish customs formalities, wait for the heat of the day to pass and then head into the desert. John and Lindsey agreed. Dicky and Duncan were happy to pedal out in the heat. I had expected cycling in a group to be fun and a welcome change to the monotony of lone travel: stories and jokes to share, decision-making to offload. We had not even left Wadi Halfa yet and there were signs that it might not be as easy as I had expected.

As it was, this time the dilemma was taken out of our hands because negotiating Sudanese customs was a blur of white, pink, blue and yellow forms and folders that took more than four hours to get through. It involved four visits to a concrete prison-like pit and several visits to a man called 'the Captain', whose office off a shady courtyard reeked of a superiority complex. When the process was complete I was verging on suicidal, but at least we each had a piece of paper with lots of indecipherable words on it; and another that would have to be presented to a police station in each town we visited through Sudan. Finally, we were ready for the desert.

We said goodbye to Wadi Halfa that afternoon, riding south past single-storey, marine-blue concrete and sandstone compounds. Everybody waved at us and we waved back at everybody. At a police checkpoint just out of town, two friendly officers checked our newly acquired documents with the haste of a pair of dying tortoises. Still, seeing them let us pass made us content that our morning had resulted in something meaningful. Life had been slow in Wadi Halfa, it was slower at the checkpoint and it was about to get a whole lot slower in the desert.

Before long we saw sand and a road and nothing else. The wind was with us, which was a blessing. The low mountains that Dicky and I had marvelled at from a hill in town seemed less dramatic when we were among them, carving our path towards Khartoum. The riding was easy with the wind on our backs. The sun sank quickly and I sensed a palpable excitement in the group. We had all read about 'the Sudan', and also its recent troubles, but none of us had ever been there before; we had never been anywhere even similar. We knew we were not explorers, barely adventurers really, but riding along under a sky full of stars, we felt like both.

For days through the desert the rolling sand dunes kept my camera and imagination busy and I relished the company of four like-minded Brits. They had been on the road for less than two weeks whereas I had been cycling for five months, so I was keen to catch up on all sorts of news from home: football transfer rumours, the England cricket team, the continuing woes of the economy and, naturally, the weather. It made me feel closer to home, although in reality I was constantly moving further away. John and Dicky, especially, asked about my time cycling through Europe and the Middle East and I was a little surprised to find that the bad times seemed to have evaporated in my mind and I reported nothing but positive news from my travels. On 25 February I noted this in my diary, and wondered: 'Does this mean I am in a positive frame of mind to attack the coming months? I hope so, and hope it serves me well.'

Although the group tended to split during the day – Dicky and Duncan out front, Lindsey, John and me at the rear – by the time the sun began to set we generally pedalled along in a group. On our third night out of Wadi Halfa we all rolled along until well after sunset, with no need for lights thanks

Lindsey, Duncan, Dicky and me at some pyramids.

175

to a full moon that seemed to light up the whole desert. The road was wide, smooth and empty and there was no sound but the gentle hum of our tyres on fresh tarmac and a light, cooling breeze. We had covered well over seventy miles in the day, a rate that I needed to keep up if I was to dispel doubts about making it all the way to Mombasa.

We found a place to sleep between two dunes sculpted by the wind into a perfect campsite for five English cyclists. Tents up, Dicky cooked pasta and the rest of us lay on our backs, exhausted after a long day, staring up at the bright haze of the Milky Way arching from one horizon to the other. It was seven o'clock on a Tuesday in February; five o'clock at home. It would be dark there as well, but the moon would either be lurking behind a bank of clouds or diluted by the bright lights of London. I struggled to imagine friends under the same sky. They would be gearing up to leave offices and battle buses, trains, busy pavements. I tried to hear a sound but there was nothing. Even the wind had died. A continuous stream of shooting stars raced across the expansive sky while satellites glided slowly through our little corner of the universe. I had left home for such moments; to sense the enormity of our planet from the saddle of a bicycle and to go in search of its diminishing corners of serenity and silence. I found one such place in the Nubian Desert and considered it likely that I would never again feel so far from home.

Duncan was first to break the enormous, splendid silence, launching into an uninhibited version of Monty Python's 'Galaxy Song'. We all joined in for the second verse. John's less resonant, but equally adept, rendition of Jay-Z's 'Girls, Girls, Girls' followed. Then, just as Lindsey readied herself for a solo, clouds of sandflies burst in on our star-gazing and we sprinted for our respective tents as nature put an end to one of the most magical nights of my entire journey. I was just happy to have shared such a night with friends.

A LESSON IN DESERT CAMPING

Every day on the road brought new sights, smells and sounds so that there was little time to dwell, always something new to enjoy and appreciate. But there was routine, too, and for me it is the seemingly conflicting relationship between these two things, the new and the quotidian, that makes travel by bicycle so alluring.

Each day I pedalled huge distances, I listened to the same songs over and over again, I thought of home, I wondered what I would do when I finally *got* home, I attempted to speak to local people using sign language, I watched the sun rise, I was asked my name, and whether I was married, I watched the sun set, I dreamed of doing it all over again, I dreamed of the end. And each night I slept.

Camping became one of the many routines of my journey. While it was necessary for me to keep pedalling in order to reach Australia by bicycle, it was just as important that I slept and, although my budget allowed for occasional nights in hostels and cheap hotels, it was a tent that was my default home come dark. The search for a place to sleep was a boring task that became a gratifying ritual and an unexpected daily highlight of my ride.

In the Sudanese desert my companions and I were occasionally lucky enough to find ourselves in a town and there was no need to camp. These were enjoyable evenings that gave us an opportunity to belong for a time, to explore markets and to watch local people. 'England I love you' was a common greeting from people in small towns like Dongola and Delgo, at least once they discovered where we were from. Hotels were crudely built: mud walls, no electricity, bucket showers. Prices reflected simplicity. In Dongola we paid fifteen Sudanese pounds, the equivalent of two British pounds, for a windowless twin room with string beds and no mattresses in the Lords Hotel (more likely named after the Lord's Resistance Army, the military movement led by Joseph Kony and accused of murderous campaigns in the region, than the home of cricket).

Out of the towns, we camped. Security was always the most important consideration but despite the eternal sand and space that Sudan offered, we sometimes found it difficult to decide upon a safe place to spend the night. The roads we used may have been far from civilisation, but remoteness meant danger. We were often warned by strangers in villages: 'Must be careful, there are many bandits on roads at night', or 'Do not enter next village, many bad people there'. Although we were never sure whether to trust such warnings, we felt it was better to do so than ignore what may have been genuine advice gleaned from personal experience. In the absence of any decent getaway vehicles five foreign cyclists would have been easy prey for even a trainee bandit.

On my journey until Sudan I had often enjoyed camping close to civilisation – sleeping in a ditch five metres from speeding traffic was fun if the alternative was not sleeping at all. In Sudan, if we found a police checkpoint near dusk, we liked camping there. We were usually greeted warmly by bored, uniformed policemen who were either desperate for company or desperate to show us their automatic weapons. Their road-side homes tended to consist of one or two Portakabins, outside of which were a handful of white plastic chairs underneath large, branded Pepsi umbrellas. We liked staying in such places because we were often served tea and chatted with educated Sudanese about their country. We rarely learned what they did not like – they were not willing to discuss political matters.

If we did not find bored policemen to hang out with, or a town to stop in, the expanse of the desert had to do. It was hardly a chore. Camping in remote parts of the Nubian Desert is one of my abiding memories of the whole journey. But deserts are endlessly shifting piles of sand, so there are not many places in which it is easy to find a good hiding place. Lugging heavy equipment miles off the road is not an option, so a safe place close to the road was what we looked for. Timing was important, too. It did not occur to me until my night's sleep depended on it that the closer you get to the equator the faster the sun sets. If we put our tents up half an hour too early they would overheat; too late and we would be unpacking, pitching, changing and cooking in darkness, all as sandflies nibbled away at our pink English skin.

Most of the time finding a safe place to sleep in the desert meant sheltering in obscurity behind a dune or under a bridge. With about an hour until sunset, at around six o'clock, as we pedalled we began to scan our surroundings for a safe pitch. If someone spotted what looked like a suitable camp, we all pulled over, considered its suitability and sent one of the group to scrutinise the site. Access was important so we checked the distance from the road and the depth of the sand. If it was less than an inch or two, we would go for it. Any deeper and we knew we would struggle to lug our heavy kit to the site and tended to carry on until we found a more suitable location.

Once the pitch was agreed, it took several runs back and forth to get all the gear to the camp. Wind direction and sunrise dictated the layout of our tents. If possible we would camp to the west of a dune so that the sun did not make the morning too uncomfortable (it was often 30°C shortly after sunrise). There were five of us and only four tents so the men took turns to share.

A peaceful early morning in the Nubian Desert.

Dicky and Duncan were the most efficient and one or the other was always the first to have their tent up. Lindsey and I took our time, while obsessive compulsive John laid out all his belongings neatly on to a tarpaulin before deciding what to do next. Dicky would normally cook for all of us on his fuel stove. Rice or pasta were staples and cheese and a green vegetable occasional luxuries. I had a tub of pre-mixed salt and pepper that provided a bit of seasoning. When I lived in London I occasionally stumped up enough cash to eat at a decent restaurant but I never anticipated any meal as much as I looked forward to those in the Nubian Desert. Food was fuel and nothing more. Having refuelled for the following day, we needed to rest so, despite attempts at bonding around campfires, food was always followed swiftly by a well-earned sleep.

TEAM VERSUS INDIVIDUAL

As long as we woke early enough, mornings spent under a fly net in the desert were enjoyable. They were cool rather than cold, sedate (no rush-hour traffic) and, although they brought with them the promise of searing heat and sweaty labour later in the day, they also carried expectation: of whom we might meet, of what we might see and always of an unfamiliar world so astonishingly different from our own.

A couple of mornings after our Monty Python/Jay-Z singalong, it was cool and still. We packed up our tents, boiled water for tea and, after consulting maps and feeling confident that the next settlement was thirty miles – or two and a half hours – south along the Nile, got back on the road.

We rode together. By ten o'clock Duncan's thermometer read 45°C, and after forty miles there was no sign of a village. We consulted the map and pedalled on, expecting another village soon. We were each sweating litres, unable to replace fluids quickly enough. After fifty-five miles we had no water left between us and still there was no sign of life along the road. Nothing but sand stretched to the horizon in all directions. I regretted wasting water by boiling it for an early morning cup of tea. I was the weakest in the group, which, considering I had been on the road for four and a half months longer, was a little embarrassing. I was shivering all over, despite the intense heat, goose pimples covering my arms and legs, my neck aching and mouth bone dry.

Then John spotted a vehicle that seemed to be stranded on a dune high to our left. It began moving, sand spraying sideways from beneath its wheels; not stranded after all. When it reached the main road we flagged it down and tipped our heads backwards, glugging imaginary water in the hope that we could make ourselves understood. The driver pointed behind him, from where he had appeared. That was when we noticed that the lorry had in fact been on a little-used, but nevertheless existing, sandy track. It climbed up a dune some twenty metres high and seemed to continue over it. Thanking the man in the lorry, we followed the sandy track for no more than a mile until we had a view of a sweeping bend in the Nile. There we found several thatched mud huts bordering a dirt road that ran parallel with the river, and with it a posse of villagers sitting around under a bamboo shade. The five of us staggered towards a six-foot-high terracotta urn and, checking inside for flies, gratefully drank our body weight in water. I will never again use the word 'thirsty' without remembering how I felt just before we arrived at that oasis.

Studying our various maps as we rested, we could not figure out why the villages were shown to be roadside settlements on our map, whereas in reality they were a mile off the road, closer to the Nile and hidden behind sand dunes. Then John looked at *his* map for the first time – a more recent, 2009 version – and noticed that there were two roads marked: a recently laid tarmac road and a dirt road that ran closer to the Nile and had several villages marked along it. We worked out that we had been riding the new tarmac road and that it must have been built only a few months earlier, which explained its absence from our old maps.

We found out that evening that the road we had been

pedalling since Wadi Halfa had, in fact, been completed by Chinese engineers just six months before our arrival. I had mixed feelings about this discovery. I know others who have cycled from Wadi Halfa to Khartoum and described days of pushing their bikes through thick sand and riding on tracks 'rutted like a washboard'. So I felt grateful that we had been provided with an alternative, a perfectly smooth tarmac road that I rated as the best surface I had ever ridden on.

But whereas the old road meandered from village to village, presumably as it had for hundreds of years, the new road bypassed villages entirely, having the effect of denying much-needed passing trade to desperately poor villagers. Thanks to the push for improved transport infrastructure, largely funded by the Chinese, the villagers will have to adapt or get left behind.

Having rehydrated and filled up more than ten litres of water bottles each, we made sure we bought biscuits and fruit from the villagers before heading back to the tarmac road to continue on our journey.

The following day Dicky and Duncan pedalled ahead again: they were out of sight within the first few miles. With forty miles under our belts, John, Lindsey and I arrived to find two lone bicycles leaning against a concrete pillar by the side of the road. We looked around. There was no sign of our friends; there was no sign of anything but the two bicycles, a lone concrete pillar and several thousand square miles of sand.

Then we heard a strange, hollow whispering. Lindsey peered over the edge of the road where the sand had formed a small hollow and there was Dicky's head, peeking out from inside a narrow, shallow tunnel.

'An hour we've been here,' Dicky piped up.

'Didn't take long for your forehead to burn then, did it?' Dicky touched his forehead and winced. He and Duncan had done well to find the only shade for miles around but the tunnel was not deep enough for his whole body. The day had turned out to be the hottest any of us had ever experienced.

Duncan's thermometer read 53°C and cycling in such heat made your head feel as if it would explode. But, as ever in Sudan, we enjoyed a tailwind, which made everything else seem all right.

That afternoon, Dicky and Duncan again pedalled off quickly and disappeared once more. Their desire always to be on the move, and moving fast, had, since Wadi Halfa ten days earlier, been the cause of growing tension between the five of us. Whereas I tried to approach each day as a way of life and was quick to take a break or stop for a photo, Dicky, especially, attacked cycling as a challenge that had to be overcome. He was eager to reach his evening's destination and enjoy some well-earned rest. That was simply how he dealt with the challenge in front of him. I did not blame him; in fact I admired his bloody-minded pursuit of record days in the saddle. Part of me wished I could have done it that way, but I knew my limitations and had to settle for a more sedate pace.

It was not just speed that was divisive. Five individuals meant five different personalities, moods, habits and egos. Just as it was natural that one person cycled faster than another, so it was obvious that some would need more breaks, eat more slowly, drink more often.

Traversing Europe and the Middle East, although I had often wished I had a companion to share my experiences with, I was aware that life was made easier by my position as a lone cyclist. When I did have company, my lead role was never challenged. In Europe, James had not only respected my physical limitations but also, perhaps because he felt I needed to learn my new trade, had not questioned my role as decision-maker; when Serpil was with me in Turkey and Syria, she had followed my every move with a video camera rather than worrying about the pace I was pedalling or the time at which I ate. On my own I enjoyed making every decision there was to make. Generally my wheels turned at exactly the pace I wanted them to, the exception being when exhaustion caught up with me. If I wanted to spend an hour repacking my panniers before setting off, I did. If it was snowing and I did not fancy cycling, I did not. If I was hungry, I ate. If I felt tired, I crashed out in a bakery or on the floor of a petrol station. I slept where I wanted. I chatted with who I wanted, and when I wanted. I stayed for a week in Budapest because I met cool people I got on with. I altered my route, adding several days to my ride through Turkey, because I felt like visiting Cappadocia. Decisions were made painless by solitude and it was on the long, hot road towards Khartoum that I resolved to return to my solitary existence when we got there.

ATBARA

A stout man in long white jalabiyah, taqiyah and thin-rimmed glasses shuffles through the sprawling, labyrinthine streets of Atbara, the town in which he has lived for seventy years. He is leading us down a dusty alley of compacted sand and jagged rocks. We walk our bicycles past a group of men kneeling and stooping around a low table, placed carefully under the shade of a palm tree. They chuckle as we pass, and who can blame them? It has been a long few days cycling and camping and we are dusty and filthy. Modest single-storey dwellings form the neighbourhood, crudely constructed in simple stone. Roofs are corrugated tin. Outside a bright blue painted wooden door the man pauses, turns to face us and urges us to follow him into a large courtyard. 'This is my home. Now it is your home. You must rest.'

Five minutes earlier, on the main road into Atbara where trucks, cars, motorbikes, bicycles and donkeys combined to ensure we were forced to negotiate traffic for the first time since leaving Aswan, the man had asked us where we were staying the night. We had all shrugged before he told us to follow him.

It was only now, in the confines of his shaded courtyard, that he introduced himself as Muhammad, a local Arabic teacher. 'I have been to my sister's funeral today. These are all of her belongings.' He gestured to the sack he had carried slung over his shoulder all the way from town. Lindsey consoled Muhammad but he would have none of it and instead showed us around his sprawling, yet modest home. Set around several courtyards, it was a compound of mud shelters, each crumbling and painted a blue that would once have been bright, but was now faded. Herbs, vegetables and plants stood in pots under a bamboo shade and a long hosepipe snaked from kitchen to courtyard and courtyard to living quarters.

Palm trees and jasmine provided more shade, coaxed to provide maximum protection from the relentless sun. There were beds dotted around, too, perhaps twenty in all, some inside but most outside under shade. Next to one bed was a curtain and when I peeked behind it I jumped in surprise: twelve goats stood staring at me, teeth bared. There were about fifty domestic pigeons dotted around the compound, too, as well as a number of chickens and a giant tortoise that had been born three days after Muhammad.

'Before, I lived here with my two wives. I divorced them both on the same day two years ago because neither gave me a son.' I looked for a sign of jest, but there was none. 'Now my sisters live here with me. I used to have thirteen siblings; now we are just three.'

Muhammad's brother-in-law, newly widowed, lay on one of the outdoor beds waving and grunting as if to suggest nothing could have been more normal than having a group of English cyclists invade your house. Noises came from most corners of the compound: pots clinking, bare feet shuffling, water running, music playing, girls giggling. Quietly and casually, various of Muhammad's relatives appeared and disappeared. None was surprised to see us. There were no questions, only food, shelter and the offer of some beds for weary travellers. It was hospitality, Sudanese-style.

'Come, I will show you to your bed.' Muhammad led me just a few yards across the courtyard and shooed a couple of pigeons off a steel-frame bed. 'I hope this will be suitable.'

I nodded, and was reminded of a quote by the American author James Michener: 'If you reject the food, ignore the customs, fear the religion and avoid the people, you might better stay at home', before dumping my belongings on the bed next to a goat pen. 'Of course, this is perfect, thank you, Muhammad.'

I managed half an hour's kip before I was woken for food. Fatimah, one of Muhammad's two remaining sisters, had prepared a feast of roast chicken, eggs, tomatoes, onions, goats' cheese (all from Muhammad's compound) as well as flatbread, falafel and a mysterious looking dip, all cooked on the floor of a room that acted as the kitchen during the day and her bedroom at night.

'Keep the noise down, would you?' My bedside companion at Muhammad's house in Atbara.

We sat in a circle around the tray of food and picked at it with our fingers. Immediately to my right sat a girl for whom John and I developed an instant fascination. Ente'saa was Muhammad's staggeringly beautiful niece, with huge brown eyes and a perfect smile framed by a pink taqib that she draped over her head. I could not stop looking at her, although it seemed that my interest was not returned. She spent the whole meal whispering to Lindsey, too shy to speak English aloud, asking her what it was like being a girl in England and concerned, above all, that Lindsey, as a twenty-seven-year-old woman, was not yet married.

The feast at Muhammad's.

Appetites replete, Muhammad offered to show us around town. On the way, we passed a vacant stall where he used to sell sweets each evening. He could no longer afford the rent, so had given it up. Most of the other stalls were empty, too.

In the evening, on a dusty road lit solely by hanging household lightbulbs, we ate goat stew sitting at plastic tables and chairs outside a busy local restaurant. An endless succession of characters came and went, friends and colleagues of Muhammad's who were keen to meet the only white people in town. It turned out that each one was even keener to let us have their forthright views on the country's political and economic woes. A man called Osama, a mechanical engineer who had lived in Atbara since moving to work on the railways fifty years earlier, was particularly damning of his country's plight. 'Sudan is a corrupt dictatorship. The President is a bad man and his ministers are even worse. His government is interested only in helping friends from the same tribe. I am always told "Don't do this, don't do that" by uneducated policemen. There is nothing I can do. Many friends have moved abroad; many more have just disappeared.'

At the time I remember being surprised at finding such passion and frankness in a sleepy desert town. But then, I was not aware of the important role Atbara played in the modern history of Sudan: it was once the centre of the country's labour movement and the home of Sudanese communism; even in the twenty-first century it is still renowned as a hotbed of political activism.

The story goes that after the British and Egyptians had defeated Sudanese rebels at the Battle of Atbara in 1898, they set about linking the then small desert oasis with the Mediterranean in the north, Khartoum in the south and Port Sudan on the Red Sea coast. It was from these terminals that cotton, then Sudan's main export, was shipped to Britain and other corners of the Empire.

Atbara quickly became known as 'the City of Steel and Fire', and owes its status as one of the country's most notable towns to its central role in the expansion of the railways during this period. With such a booming population of railway workers, Atbara naturally became the centre of the country's trade union movement, starting with the Railway Workers' Association, which was formed there in 1947. In the early 1950s there were up to 25,000 railway workers in Atbara alone, making up a huge proportion of the country's working class.

From these workers grew a labour movement that in turn formed the core support for the Sudanese Communist Party.

Communism won a huge following all over Africa because it offered a compelling alternative to the injustices of imperialism. But in Sudan it prospered more than elsewhere because of the strength of the agricultural and railway trade unions. Atbara became home to the Sudanese communist movement and the Sudanese Communist Party became one of the largest, and one of the best organised, political bodies in Africa. It was not until 1971, when President Nimeiri destroyed an attempted coup by the Communist Party and executed its leaders, that communism was defeated once and for all in Sudan.

Another man, a Christian wearing a suit and tie, introduced himself to us as John. 'I worked for many years on Sudan's railways. I was sacked for political reasons in 1990. Now I am an active member of the Sudan People's Liberation Movement. We are working towards independence for the south.'

John encouraged Muhammad to take us home via the railway yard, and ended up joining us himself. It was a short distance from the town centre, crammed with ancient, rusty locomotives, parked on tracks, that did not seem to have moved in years. 'When your people were here our railways were the best in Africa; now they are ruined, just like everything else in this country.'

The decline and fall of the British Empire had, in fact, been responsible for the demise of Sudan's railways. With the defeat of Sudanese communism in the seventies and improved links with the West, the railways, which once formed the power base of the trade unions and Communist Party, were deliberately left to run down and today are a shadow of their former glory.

John accompanied us towards Muhammad's home before stopping at a dusty crossroads and pointing towards his neighbourhood. 'You must come to eat dinner at my house tomorrow. I would like you to meet my beautiful daughters. They need husbands!' It was a tempting offer, but one which, sadly, we could not take up.

*

Thirty-six hours after we first arrived in Atbara we found ourselves back in Muhammad's compound, eating another meal prepared for us by Fatimah, a breakfast of cheese and tomatoes this time. Ente'saa was there again and although she still directed her speech solely at Lindsey, she had become more confident in her English. 'Why must you leave? Why cannot you stay in Atbara?' she asked.

Lindsey told Ente'saa simply that she would miss her, but she had to get to South Africa. Like me, Lindsey and her team had a promise to deliver on, a goal to achieve. I often felt that there was a conflict between bicycle travel as a journey of discovery and the attempt to achieve a stated goal; in my case, reaching the Ashes in time for the first Test match in November 2010.

As a traveller I occasionally asked myself what would happen if I jacked it all in, hung out for a while; stayed still. No one would mind if I spent a few months fishing on the banks of the Atbara River with Muhammad and teaching at a local school, would they? Sponsors would forget about me and family and friends would forgive me in the end, surely? I have failed plenty in my life, so why was I so adamant about achieving my goal this time?

Meeting people like Muhammad and his family made moving on difficult. Atbara was a town where thirty-six hours earlier I had known no one. Now I had friends there and a new perspective on the place. Rather than being the latest dusty highway town on my route, it had become a reference point for my journey through Sudan. In years to come I might meet a Sudanese man in England and while I will have forgotten all about other towns that had slipped by, Atbara will be fresh in my mind. I will ask him whether he has been there and I will recount the story of my time there with Muhammad and his beautiful niece. It is people, after all, who make a place memorable. Oh, and goats, too.

However, I also wanted to move on. I believed that the reason I had enjoyed my time there, just as I had in many towns around the world, was because I was a visitor. It was our status as travellers, and particularly our means of travel, that drew us to Muhammad and opened a window into the lives of an ordinary Sudanese family. Having offered us accommodation and food, the last thing Muhammad expected us to do was outstay our welcome. We were expected to continue our onward journey.

As we began to pack our belongings, John asked where Muhammad was. It was a good point: none of us had seen him all morning. His family either did not know where he was or did not want to tell us. It was lunchtime, and tempers were beginning to fray and patience bend by the time he finally returned, shuffling through the low blue door into the compound. He was straining under the weight of five translucent yellow plastic bags.

'I know you will be safe on the long journey ahead, because Allah is watching you,' he said, pointing upwards. 'But I look after you, too. These are for you.' Muhammad gave one bag to each of us and inside was tea, milk, sugar, biscuits and soft drinks.

With that final gesture of goodwill from Muhammad, we said our goodbyes, promised to keep in touch and pedalled back along the dusty alley of compacted sand and rocks towards the main road, bound for Khartoum.

FAT CAMP

The cycle from Atbara to Khartoum was 210 miles, a distance we would normally have attempted in three full days. But as we waited for Muhammad to appear we decided that, although in Atbara we had been fed handsomely, we were unlikely to find such satisfying nourishment on the road south; Sudan had, after all, been both a culinary as well as a literal desert and we were all, rather shamefully, desperate for some red meat. We opted for a two and a half day ride to Khartoum, and knew it would test our physical resolve.

Slow progress on our way out of Atbara meant that we only

managed twenty-five miles before dark, leaving 185 miles in two days. The following day we hammered down on our pedals, enjoying a tailwind again, confidence growing that we could make it to Khartoum for a burger the following day.

On one particularly deserted stretch we were surprised to come upon a lone Frenchman walking in the same direction as us.

'Where are you going?' Lindsey asked the man.

'The Meroë Pyramids!' he replied, pointing at a high dune off to the left.

As we pedalled on, the dune eventually gave way to a magnificent view of hundreds of two-thousand-year-old Nubian pyramids. A Korean camera crew were filming Sudanese men on camels, racing across the desert towards the ancient site. We chatted with some Spaniards who worked for the United Nations in Khartoum. They advised us where to find beer in the otherwise dry city: the British High Commission. They also told us we looked knackered and we told them we felt it.

Later that afternoon, in Shendi, we stopped for water and shade and I saw my face for the first time in days, catching a glimpse in a shop mirror. I looked a mess. I was gaunt, my shoulders shrunken, cheeks hollow and a bristly red. My forehead and ears were burnt and peeling, lips cracked and eyes bloodshot. My hair, although filthy with sand, dirt and sweat, was virtually white-blond. The dust and the intense sun had taken their toll. I recognised the need for several days of food, and planned on eating plenty in Khartoum; red meat of course.

That night we slept without tents in a dry riverbed surrounded by nothing but sand. In the morning a few cattle-herding nomads woke us and asked for food. No wonder they needed it; there was no sign of vegetation anywhere. We gave them some leftover jam and bread; it was redundant, so long as we reached Khartoum that night. It was one hundred miles away.

We set off and within five miles John had a puncture. He fixed it, but another came almost immediately. There was no shade and Duncan's thermometer read 51°C. We stood over

John to give him some shade as he fixed the tyre. We had been blessed by an absence of punctures in Sudan, but our luck seemed to have run out. Lindsey got one, then I did. The metal rims of my bicycle were too hot to touch so in the ridiculous heat I wore gloves to change the tyre.

Towns came thick and fast near the end of the day and we knew we would make it. Simple concrete buildings, shops and local eateries lined the highway on the most enjoyable ride into any city I can remember. Everyone we cycled past cheered us as if they knew the hardship we had had to endure to reach them. Any pain there had been in our legs disappeared, to be replaced by adrenalin.

We cycled through the colourful souks and mosques of Omdurman, where the Mahdi was buried after his death in 1885 and where, as recently as 2008, a Darfur rebel group had engaged Sudanese government forces in heavy fighting with the aim of overthrowing President Omar al-Bashir. Still the locals waved and cheered as we sped past, a temporary, foreign blur in streets that generally dealt only in the familiar: market traders, street hawkers and an endless stream of dilapidated vehicles near the end of their own long desert journeys.

A mile-wide bridge marked our arrival in Khartoum and we leaned our trusty bicycles against the railings, exhausted. I have always loved the name: KHARTOUM. In the atlases I studied during geography lessons it had stuck out on the page; a city that screamed remoteness, history and old-school adventure. Now I loved it even more. I could not believe that I had made it there, and on a bicycle with four others who had become good friends. We marked the group's achievement with a team photo on the bridge. The recently opened five-star Corinthia Hotel, or the so-called 'Gaddafi's Egg' on account of Libyan funding for the development, stood resplendent in the background. A few half-finished tower blocks dotted the silhouetted skyline, too, as if to say 'Not so old-school now, am I?'

Sudan certainly seemed to be a one-city nation. Whereas in the desert we had been lucky if we'd found tarmac roads and water, let alone stocked shop shelves or a cash machine, in Khartoum there were international banks, a stock exchange, four-lane highways and Italian restaurants. We welcomed the change. Often when I reached a major landmark on my journey my mind turned to the next challenge; but arriving in Khartoum I did not have the energy or desire to think beyond a few days' rest and some juicy burgers.

Lindsey had arranged for us to stay with a friend of her mother's in Khartoum. We were directed by a young man (he was apparently our hostess's bodyguard) to a large building in the affluent al-Riyadh neighbourhood, where Osama bin Laden had owned a pink and white stucco house in the 1990s. The building we found ourselves in turned out to be a fitness centre. Exhausted after a long day on the bikes, we were given a minute to freshen up before being led through corridors to the double doors of an auditorium.

Peering through the glass, I saw several hundred seriously overweight Sudanese in fancy dress, listening intently to a lady standing at a lectern on the stage. The bodyguard opened the doors and ushered us inside, at which point there was silence as the room stared at us. The lady at the lectern looked excited.

'We have been expecting you!' she exclaimed into her microphone, pointing to five chairs beside her on the stage. Us boys gave Lindsey questioning stares. Lindsey shrugged and went with it.

The lady began speaking in Arabic to the assembled throng and when she had finished the room erupted into applause. I did wonder if she had told them: 'Just four months ago, these skinny Brits were huge, just like you!'

We were asked to introduce ourselves to the audience. Lindsey dived straight in.

'My name is Lindsey and I am cycling a bicycle from Cairo to Cape Town. We are very pleased to have made it across the desert to Khartoum.'

Gasps of disbelief were followed by enthusiastic applause, led by a man in a Japanese sumo wrestler's outfit complete with fake 'toothbrush' moustache who clapped particularly vociferously. It was all very strange.

'My name is Dicky and I have done the same as Lindsey. It's great to be here.'

More over-the-top inhalations and a few cheers.

'My name is Oli, and I have cycled here from London. I am cycling to Australia to watch a cricket match.'

There was some hollering; quite a few confused faces.

John and Duncan introduced themselves before a long line of questioning began, led by the sumo wrestler.

It turned out the lady onstage was our hostess, Dr Hiba, a famous Sudanese television personality through her weekly aerobics show aimed at targeting the growing problem of obesity in Sudan. Outside her television work she ran evening classes for obese people where she trained them in healthy living. I never found out where fancy dress came into the equation, but Fat Camp was a weird and welcome introduction to Khartoum. Often the first impression I got of a city came not through interaction with its inhabitants, but simply via people-watching. It made a pleasant change diving straight into an everyday situation, even if it was a bit of a surprise.

After a couple of nights sleeping on the floor of the fitness centre we were introduced to a few Eritrean refugees who had some spare floor space in their flat. They were humble young girls who had arrived in Khartoum after walking more than three hundred miles to escape their homeland. They were busy most of the time so we barely saw them. Instead Dr Hiba's bodyguard, Fawaz, looked after us during our time in Khartoum, driving us to all corners of the city in a blacked-out Range Rover. Dr Hiba joined us when she could. When John and I mentioned that we had developed a penchant for Sudanese music they took us to a record shop, paid the girl behind the counter to kick out the other customers and asked her to burn some local tunes on to CDs for us. While we waited we had the run of the place, and the sound system, and danced to a soundtrack of reggae, rap, hip-hop and traditional Sudanese music with a famous Sudanese television star and her bodyguard while a healthy crowd formed on the other side of the shop window. Footage quickly made its way to Budapest for László to edit.

A DIFFICULT DECISION

I loved Khartoum and I loved Sudan.

Of course, we could have pedalled off to Darfur looking for trouble and we would have found it pretty easily, but Sudan is a big place and the danger spots are easy to avoid. Apart from one incident when we were chased down an almost empty desert road for the apparently criminal act of taking a photo of an oil pipe, we had been made to feel welcome everywhere we went. We never felt in danger despite the instability that war has inevitably brought to the country.

Yet sit in a pub with some mates and tell them you plan to cycle through Sudan and you can expect some pretty strange looks. I know; that is exactly what I did six months before I left home. 'You're pulling my leg, right? I've read about Darfur, mate. Sounds dodgy!'

In the West we are fed bad-news stories from Sudan on a daily basis. The atrocities in Darfur have grabbed headlines for decades; the civil war between the north and the south is the world's longest running and often features in Western media. In fact, I cannot remember ever having seen a good-news story about Sudan in the press back home.

Admittedly it is not just Sudan; while I was writing this book I was interviewed by a *Guardian* journalist about a new project I am working on. When I asked his angle, he said that he was fed up with reporting on bad news from Africa and fancied writing a story about something a bit more positive.

Quite naturally, the preconceptions we develop about distant countries from the comfort of our armchairs often become misconceptions. And whereas preconceptions can be right, misconceptions cannot. Although I tried desperately hard not to, I arrived in Sudan with a head full of preconceived notions of what it would be like. Some were right: food was cheap; the pace of life was slow, almost stagnant; there was a lot of sand. But I had been wrong about so much more.

The news I had been fed over the years had forced me to think of Sudan as a one-dimensional picture of tyranny and repression rather than a multi-dimensional jigsaw of a million pieces. When I read that President Omar al-Bashir had been indicted for war crimes by the International Criminal Court I wrote the entire country off as a failed state and forgot that the ordinary Sudanese had probably never visited Khartoum, and cared little about the country's politics. He just wanted to feed his family.

Cycling through Sudan reminded me that under despotic regimes there still exist good, honest people.

Now I had tackled Sudan and spent a few days recuperating in its capital, I was forced to think about the road ahead. The rough schedule I had set myself (remember the map back home, the index finger and thumb used to mark my route?) told me I should already have been in Mombasa, which from Khartoum still lay more than two thousand miles – or six weeks' cycling – to the south.

For a while I had been worried about not reaching Mombasa, mainly because I had said I would go there and didn't want to fail to reach a goal. But I had also been concerned about cycling across India during the monsoon season (which started in May), not because I did not fancy getting wet, but because I thought I might miss out on so much cricket.

But I did not regret the weeks I had spent in places like Budapest, Belgrade and Istanbul. I have never been good at rushing anything and the modern trend of racing around the planet on a bicycle did not appeal. I preferred to take my time, live a place and get to know its people. Besides, those cities had been highlights of my ride precisely because I *had* stopped and taken time to explore them; I had found reasons to hang around, including cricket.

The choice was to continue on the road to Mombasa and

risk the journey turning into a race – something I never intended it to be – or cut my losses, forget about the boat from Mombasa to Mumbai, swallow my pride and fly to Mumbai to continue my journey. It was a big decision, and one that I spent days mulling over.

Then something happened that pre-empted my dilemma. I went in for a slide tackle while playing five-a-side football at the British High Commission in Khartoum, and tore a hamstring. I groaned in pain as Lindsey tried to massage it out after the game. The next day I could barely walk, nor the next. There was no way I could pedal on. I chuckled at the notion of picking up the phone and calling the England and Wales Cricket Board to ask them to delay the Ashes for a couple of months because, if I hung around in Khartoum before pedalling south, I would have had no chance of reaching Brisbane in time for the start of the series.

Friends and family got in touch, telling me how disappointed I must be; and I was. Although I had never considered that my ride would be an unbroken path from London to Brisbane (how could it be, when I was cycling from one island to another?), I did want to pedal as much of it as I could.

I was still undecided and feeling sorry for myself when, in the Eritreans' flat one evening, I was confronted with the oldest, Samha, who was in floods of tears. She and her new husband had been interviewed by the Australian government a few weeks earlier and had just received the news that they had been accepted for a sponsored move to the Gold Coast.

'Isn't this good news?' I asked.

'Of course, of course it is good news, Oli. But now we must make the decision. Do I leave my friends and family in Eritrea forever, or do I start a new life where I know nobody, on the other side of the world?'

Samha's extraordinary dilemma was enough to convince me that my problem was a high-class one.

I boarded the next plane to Nairobi, spent a few days sorting out Indian and Bangladeshi visas, and flew to Mumbai to do battle with the subcontinent from the saddle of my bicycle.

THIRD INNINGS

INDIA

Batsmen walk out into the middle alone. Not Tendulkar. Every time Tendulkar walks to the crease, a whole nation, tatters and all, marches with him to the battle arena – C. P. Surendran, 'Would You Like to be Reborn an Indian?'

Sunday Times of India, 26 April 1998

Only the most foollhardy or ill-imformed tourist would dare venture to India from April to September.

Sarah MacDonald, *Holy Cow*

FOOLHARDY OR ILL-INFORMED?

A chorus of male voices talks excitedly outside my room. My Marathi being what it is, I can understand little of what is being said, but three words keep cropping up. One is 'cycle' (a bicycle is never a bicycle in India. It is always a 'cycle'). The others are 'mongoose' and 'bat'. I get up from my bed and open my padlocked door to find five men on their haunches around my bicycle. Their interest is so intense that they do not notice me at first. One is busily trying to rip apart my brake levers while another inspects the bottle cages, fine as they are. A third man is immersed in the metallic pleasures of my rear wheel and a fourth and fifth are stroking the handle of my cricket bat as if it is a cherished family pet. If my bicycle had feelings, right now it would feel claustrophobic and fucking terrified.

Iᴛ ᴡᴀs 4 April, and my first morning in India. Beads of sweat tumbled down my cheeks, landing softly on the pillow one after another, joining the mess made by my matted, sweat-soaked hair that lay drenched between my scalp and the dirty white linen of the pillow. I lay still, staring vacantly at the ornate ceiling mural – two cows pulling a wooden harvesting contraption across a field while a mustachioed man looked on, smiling. The smell of scrambled eggs wafted in from the kitchen, which was also the hotel reception, and directly outside my room.

My only previous visit to the subcontinent seven years earlier had been with an old friend, Simon, when we'd backpacked around the Golden Triangle of Delhi, Agra and Jaipur. I remember us wandering casually and unconcerned through customs at Delhi's Indira Gandhi Airport, blissfully unaware that nothing, not even a mother's warning that India would be 'something of a culture shock', can prepare a man for his first experience of an Indian airport Arrivals Hall.

After successfully negotiating the 'Nothing to Declare' section, rounding the corner we were confronted with a wall of humanity, writhing in unison, arms waving, teeth bared and creating a desperate, orchestral scream of 'Taxi, sah, taxi?' We ran the gauntlet of kicks, shoves, screams and halitosis, fighting to remain in the company of our backpacks until one particularly persistent and odorous taxi driver outnegotiated several other particularly persistent and odorous taxi drivers, to bundle us into a dilapidated Ambassador and charge roughly ten times the going rate for the fifteen-minute journey to our pre-booked hotel in Majnu-ka-Tilla, Delhi's Tibetan quarter.

The taxi ride was terrifying and on more than one occasion almost fatal. My diary entry at the end of my first day in India read: 'For the Indian driver, a car horn seems to be far preferable to indicator lights, mirrors or a seatbelt. Most seem to drive as if life, and indeed death, means little.' Back then I would never have entertained the notion of returning seven years later to do battle with horn-happy Indian drivers from the saddle of a bicycle.

This time it was Mumbai's Chatrapati Shivaji International Airport. In light of our experiences in Delhi, I had mentally prepared myself for a scramble. I also had the advantage of having in my possession an exceptionally heavy cardboard box the size of a bicycle to use as a battering ram if push came to literal shove. I readied myself in Baggage Reclaim, puffed out my vastly diminished chest as far as it would go and headed for 'Nothing to Declare'. Braced for carnage, I wheeled the loaded trolley nervously into the Arrivals Hall, only to be greeted by no more than a few dozen tired looking faces, most waiting to give returning relatives a big hug.

I must admit that, having prepared myself for an onslaught, I was somewhat disappointed at the mild scene before me. No hugs for me. I was on my own and delighted. I walked purposefully and with ease to the airport's exit where I unpacked my bicycle and began reassembling her. It was, however, during the reassembly of my trusty two-wheeled chariot that I first suspected being in India might test my patience. A crowd of onlookers began to congregate, and by the time I was ready to jump on and pedal to the nearest bed, I was surrounded by enough coiffed young men to fill a boutique cinema. They were not so interested in me, but were purring alarmingly at the sight of my sleek gear shifters and electric-blue bicycle frame, and swooning over the newly oiled, smooth surface of my cricket bat.

Now here I was, the morning after, in a grotty hotel confronted with a similar group. My first two social encounters in India, first at the airport and now in my hotel, helped me compute five things:

- That I was about to cycle two thousand miles with a cricket bat strapped to my 'cycle', through a country full of Indians.
- That Indians were interested in 'cycles'.
- That Indians were more interested in cricket than 'cycles'.
- That I was about to embark on my biggest challenge yet.
- That, perhaps, I was more foolhardy than ill-informed.

KONKAN COAST

I spent a few days in Mumbai, initially to adjust to life inside a humidifier and then to explore the place. My time there reminded me why I had wanted to visit India again, and I marvelled at the differences with Africa: the people, the buildings, the parties and, of course, the cricket.

Mumbai gave me my first opportunity to experience the unbridled devotion to cricket in Indian society. Since pedalling out of Dunkerque six months earlier I had often found that the barrier to my understanding of a situation or place had been linguistic. I guessed that India would throw up the same issue, especially in rural areas, and hoped that a common love of cricket would make life a little easier. Besides, surely understanding India's attitude towards cricket would be a great way to start understanding one of the most religiously, ethnically and culturally diverse countries on the planet. I suspected that a love of cricket might be one of the few passions shared universally.

For my first week in Mumbai I stayed with Rob, a friend who was in town helping to organise the Indian Premier League (IPL), which was back on Indian soil after a year in South Africa. He lived in Bandra, an upmarket neighbourhood favoured by Bollywood stars, cricketers, bejewelled South Asian goddesses, knackered transcontinental cyclists and a seemingly inexhaustible number of air-conditioned Italian restaurants, out of reach to all but the wealthiest of Mumbaikers. One night I had a drink with Marcus, the chief executive of Mongoose Cricket, who had arrived in town bearing two new bats: one for me and one for the Australian flat-track bully Matthew Hayden, who was in town on IPL duties. I could barely lift Hayden's and was grateful that mine was lighter; I assumed Hayden would not be cycling thousands of miles with his.

For my last few nights I managed to wangle a free room at the Cricket Club of India on the back of my cricketing odyssey. The manager seemed to take a liking to me and let me hang out with greying old men in sports jackets and cravats in the stately club room that overlooked the hallowed turf. There I wrote my diary, read voraciously and drank my body weight in freshly squeezed orange juice and Earl Grey tea.

The Delhi Daredevils were in town to play the Mumbai Indians, which meant the media were around, too. I did a couple of local television and newspaper interviews and word got out that there was a foolish cricket fan pedalling his way to the Ashes. In their quest for any cricket-related story, national media outlets began hauling me in front of television cameras to ask me who my favourite Indian cricketer was. I knew to answer that it was, of course, Sachin Tendulkar.

During one television interview with bearded Bollywood stud Gaurav Kapur, held on the outfield of the Cricket Club of India, Tendulkar passed a couple of yards to my right and I was quickly left alone as the whole crew swarmed around the great man. We did finish the interview once he had gone, and that evening fifty million Indians tuned in to *Extraaa Innings* expecting to see clips from IPL matches but instead got my thoughts on cricket in the Balkans.

Away from cricket, Mumbai was as frantic as I had expected. A morning spent at Chatrapati Shivaji Terminus was an education. It was built in 1887 to commemorate Queen Victoria's Golden Jubilee, and for more than a hundred years it has been the stage for one of Mumbai's greatest performances. At 11.30 each morning, a train pulls into the station and thousands of men known as dabbawallas – identically dressed in traditional white dhoti (sarong), shirts, sandals and wearing distinctive Gandhi-style caps – emerge as one pulsating unit. It is a lunchtime rush hour like no other. It is not the office workers who are commuting, but their food. In a city where every second counts, Mumbai's dabbawallas are food deliverymen, balancing cylindrical metal tiffin boxes on their heads to distribute lunch to office workers across the city.

Mumbai is set to become the most populous city in the world by 2020 and I was staggered at the fast-paced development in every district. There seemed to me little doubt that life for millions of Mumbaikers was improving, but I could not help notice the proximity of brand new shopping centres, hotels and residential developments to the slums and filth and child beggars. I wondered whether millions more of the city's inhabitants were being left behind.

Certainly it is not unusual in the developing world for five-star hotels to sit adjacent to slums. More confusing were the billboards that advertised skin- and tooth-whitening treatments in a city where 99 per cent of the population could not afford such luxuries, even if they knew what they were. I had heard Mumbai was a city of contrasts, but perhaps it will become even more so as the rich get richer.

Whatever Mumbai's fate, I felt ready to leave when I did. The Gateway of India is another monument to Empire built to commemorate the visit of King George.V and Queen Mary to Bombay in 1911. Standing beneath its vast arch it seemed these days to commemorate nothing more than the failing engines of small, wooden, semi-submerged passenger ferries. Still, I found one that promised to take me the short distance to Mandve, from where my Indian adventure would begin in earnest.

My first impression of Mandve was that it did not really need a name because it was not really a place. It seemed to consist solely of a short wooden pier and a couple of tatty wooden shacks with men in string vests hanging around outside them. But I was delighted to be there, not least because, when I breathed in, I inhaled a considerable dose of tranquillity and relatively fresh air. Mumbai sits just a few miles to the north but it may as well be a million. As is often the case after time confined to a city, I was excited by the onward journey once again.

Pedalling away from the small ferry terminal, I was glad to be progressing cheerfully inland on a road that was shaded by overhanging palm branches; and it soon became clear that there was more to Mandve than I had initially thought. I peered into the thick jungle, making out small wooden dwellings where large families were playing out their daily routines. Women hung clothes among vivid bursts of frangipani, kids played cricket in the occasional clearing and old men cycled ponderously, waving at everyone they knew. And they knew *everyone*. Scooters and cars drove considerately, patiently. It was a veritable Eden, just a few miles outside one of the world's great metropolises. It was not like the India I knew.

I came across a group of teenagers playing cricket on a patch of sand beside an abandoned building. Three stumps were painted in black against a bare concrete wall and although they had a tennis ball, they used a sanded-down plank for a bat. A chorus of 'mongoose bat, mongoose bat!' rang out when they noticed me. The Mongoose bat had only been invented a few months before I'd left home and was a different shape from ordinary cricket bats. It was designed with the hitting demands of Twenty20 in mind, with a shorter surface and longer handle adapted to increase bat speed. Of course, I knew Indians had fallen in love with Twenty20 cricket owing to the commercial onslaught of the Indian Premier League, but I was still surprised that knowledge of the Mongoose had made it to rural Maharashtra, and even more perplexed as to how the teenagers had identified it from such a distance. I had two on me and pulled out the older one from beneath my rolled-up tent. Seeing their faces when they caught a glimpse, I decided to give it to them as a gift. Both parties benefited: they were over the moon with their new willow weapon and I was happy to be pedalling onwards about three pounds lighter.

I warmed to the riding. As I pedalled into increasingly remote countryside life became more peaceful than anywhere else on my journey. I had not expected to find tranquillity in India. If Mumbai was another country, then home, and England, were another world. I rode south whistling, mimicking the tropical birdsong that accompanied me. I ventured deeper into thick emerald forest. I passed fishing villages where men rowed colourfully painted fishing boats just as their ancestors must have done. Toothless women called out at me from the doorways of their proudly maintained, modest wooden houses. I weaved my way through jungle settlements where I found women washing clothes in ancient stone bathing pools covered in bright red water lilies. Children dived and swam, but when I passed they stopped and stared. I stared back, intrigued. Sometimes I pulled up to offer villagers a go on my bicycle while I tore around on their Hero Honda motorbikes. When it was time to sleep I pitched my tent on perfect, deserted sandy beaches where sari-clad young girls swam in the Indian Ocean, and where there was more cricket. Always cricket.

I encountered river crossings, struggled with indecipherable – to me if not to everyone around me – Hindi road signs and marvelled at an endless succession of forts in varying states of decay. Janjira Fort was an almost perfectly maintained fifteenth-century island fort out to sea off the tiny village of Murud. Built by fishermen originally from wood, as protection from pirates and thieves, it was demolished by an Abyssinian explorer who rebuilt it in stone with walls that still towered above crashing waves 350 years later. It was the only fort on the Maharashtran coast that survived every attack from the Portuguese and British. Alone, I ate paneer and roti on the beach that it overlooked.

One evening I pedalled through the fishing village of Kelshi. Its beach was fringed with palm trees that did a good job of camouflaging hundreds of stilted wooden shacks, the homes of some of the villagers. While hundreds of pairs of eyes watched me from behind the foliage, I found a patch of soft sand suitable for my tent. As I prepared to put it up a smart looking man approached, wearing the standard Indian male uniform of collared shirt, khaki trousers and sandals, complemented by a thick moustache. His name was Sanjay, and he was the village doctor, on a two-year placement from his practice in Mumbai. The government had sent him to Kelshi to provide expertise in dealing with snake bites and scorpion stings. He was on call twenty-four hours a day, seven days a week because, he told me, a villager was bitten or stung every single day. Kelshi was so cut off that a few years ago a hundred villagers a year were dying as a result, but since he had arrived not a single villager had been killed. There were tens of villages like Kelshi along this coastline and according to Sanjay the government had saved thousands of lives since implementing the initiative.

Sanjay also told me to move my tent away from the undergrowth at the back of the beach – *snake territory*. When he was gone I did so, but asleep some time later I woke with a fright. Quick as a flash I flicked on my torch to see that I was not being attacked by a snake, but that something much larger was standing in the doorway of my tent. It was a man, who had apparently unzipped my tent and was staring at me sternly. My first reaction was to reach for my cricket bat which I often kept at close quarters during the night but, as my sight adjusted to the light, I saw that he was old and, I guessed, unlikely to rob me. Still, he was in no mood for niceties.

'Cannot sleep here. Move now please Mister.' The intruder reached into the front pocket of his collared shirt where he found a comb (as far as I could gather, almost all Indian men kept a comb in the chest pocket of their short-sleeved shirt. They pulled them out and began attending to their locks at the most extraordinary moments. Still, as far as I was concerned the man in my tent won the award for 'Most Inappropriate Moment to Comb Hair') and a business card. He greased his hair with saliva, then combed it, then passed me the business card. I could not understand a word because it was written in Marathi.

'Cannot sleep here. Move now Mister please. I am officers of customs.' The man did not know much English, but I did not expect him to. I showed him my bicycle, maps and cricket bat, but seemingly they got an endless stream of English cricket-playing cyclists washing up on Konkan beaches and there just was not room for all of us. It was a moment I had long been expecting: my first run in with a pompous Indian bureaucrat. Still, I was not jubilant that it was happening inside my tent on a beach at eleven o'clock at night after having cycled seventy miles in 45°C heat and 90 per cent humidity. The combination was not a good one and led to a severe sense-of-humour failure on my part. But my options were limited; he seemed increasingly militant.

'Cannot sleep here Mister.' The beach at Kelshi, where
I slept for half the night.

'Cannot sleep here Mister. Please move now because customs officials I am.' His voice was raised. I was not getting out of this one. Encounters with jobsworths were a constant feature of my ride, especially in developing countries. I had passed through parts of the world where so many rules and laws seemed to be universally flouted that it always seemed to me a little unfair to pick on a harmless foreigner on a bike. Of course, a sneaky backhander would normally have done the trick but I was unwilling to oblige such demands so, in a state of mild rage, I got out of my sleeping bag, out of the tent and spent half an hour loading my bicycle while Customs Nazi hovered over me, arms folded. Then I pedalled by moonlight into the thick jungle. After an hour I found a temple, and slept fitfully on the stone floor, dreaming of killer snakes until I was woken seven hours later by a man who took me for breakfast at his family home.

Back on the road after breakfast, I waved at children dressed in crisp, clean, blue and white uniforms on their way to scruffy, single-storey village schools. I was scruffy, too, in torn shorts, a filthy, sweat-stained long-sleeved cotton shirt and open sandals that had seen better days.

A succession of six-seater rickshaws carrying more than twice as many passengers passed. In cities I got barked at by passing traffic but on the Konkan Coast I was blessed with languid howls of encouragement that could only have come from those accustomed to a peaceful way of life. My nocturnal intrusion at the hands of Customs Nazi was merely a diversion from the Konkan Coast's otherwise straightforward, serene charms. Sometimes I would have a mango or banana thrown my way and I would thank my benefactor with a wave and a Marathi 'Aabhari Aahe!' or 'thank you!' The narrow stretch of coastline south of Mumbai is a little-explored oasis of serenity with not a tourist in sight; the perfect contrast to the big city. I could not keep the smile off my face.

TRUST

I had expected to pedal the Konkan Coast for three days before heading inland on the 1,600-mile journey across India. But hills and heat ensured it took six days to pedal roughly 250 miles, leaving me in the Arabian Sea port of Ratnagiri, from where I planned to head eastwards. When I got there I sought the most trustworthy man I could find and left my bike with him; unlocked because I had left my lock in Mumbai. 'No problem sir, your bike will be safe with me!' promised the jovial owner of a roadside dhaba.* Meanwhile, I was bound for the beaches of Goa for some much-needed R&R.

The bus journey to India's most famous seaside state reminded me why I was not using public transport to get to the Ashes. I read the Lonely Planet guidebook all the way to Goa in order to avert my eyes from the horrors of the road, and was delighted and surprised to escape with my life six hours later. Whoever wrote the guidebook did not seem to like Goa that much, and certainly was not sold on Calangute: 'For many people it's just a busy, noisy and tacky Indian Costa del Sol, and the thought of spending a single night here is enough to make them shudder.' For reasons I found hard to fathom, I decided that Calangute sounded exactly what I was after. I think, perhaps, I fancied some reverse escapism to make me feel like I was not as far from home as I seemed.

As I wandered Calangute's palm-fringed, sandy streets I refused several hawkers' attempts to lure me for a midday beer in bars with names like the Sportsman and the Honey Pot, and instead concentrated my efforts on finding a quiet spot where I could sleep for forty-eight hours. Rani and Nani Guesthouse was a lovely little family-run Portuguese colonial mansion, built in 1928 by the ancestors of the current owners. Its mature garden had a view over the mouth of a small river that separated sleazy Calangute from thick jungle that gave a hint of how Goa must once have looked.

I was delighted to find that I was one of only two people staying at the guesthouse, but after an evening spent with the other guest I wished I was alone. Brad was Australian and Brad, apparently, loved the 'energy of India'.

'What do you mean by that?' I asked.

'What does anything really mean?' came Brad's obnoxious response.

---

* 'Dhaba' is the name given to roadside restaurants across India. They serve as truck stops and since most truck drivers in India are of Punjabi origin, food and music from that region are common. I tended to be unadventurous in my choice of food, largely to minimise the risk of sickness, and almost always opted for 'boneless' butter chicken, two roti and a Pepsi.

Looking back, I pin-pointed that conversation as the moment my intense dislike of Brad began to develop. It only matured as the evening wore on, and I was forced to listen to a series of deluded theories on the meaning of spiritual travel and laughable explanations of Tibetan proverbs. After dinner I was able to escape, claiming exhaustion, which, thanks to Brad, was now mental as well as physical.

The rest of my time in Goa was spent reading on the veranda overlooking the Indian Ocean, watching the cavorting of moneyed Russian tourists, racing on a moped around densely forested hills that shrouded impressive colonial villas, playing cricket with Rani and Nani's two sons in the garden and avoiding Brad. After two days spent recuperating, I was ready to head back to Ratnagiri to find my bicycle and begin the five-hundred-mile stretch to Hyderabad.

One of the eternal problems with travel to poorer parts of the world is that, as a Westerner, one is always seen as wealthy. It did not matter that I did not *feel* rich; compared to many people I came across, the support I received from Betfair and Mongoose Cricket made me a wealthy man. As a result, I would always struggle to appear equal, especially somewhere like India.

That did not stop me trying. In order to fit in as best I could, I always sought ways to make myself blend in with my surroundings and to gain the respect of those I came across; ways of minimising my difference. Of course, my modest mode of transport helped, but my bicycle, even if no longer shiny, still looked impressive and was burdened with a lot of expensive kit, unlike any Indian bicycle I ever saw. I had expected my appearance to help, too, but looking about me whenever I was surrounded by a group of Indians, I noticed that everyone seemed to be dressed in clothes that were as smart and clean as they could afford. The Indians are a proud race and I suspected that when they saw me in my rags, with unkempt, filthy hair, their respect for me was limited.

So I landed on a new approach. I decided that an effective

way of showing someone that I respected them was to demonstrate that I trusted them. That is why I left my bicycle and a pannier-full of belongings with the dhaba owner in Ratnagiri, sitting unlocked in the corner of his bustling roadside café. My decision had been based on the fact that I was not willing to haul my bicycle to Goa for a couple of days; I therefore decided to test my trust theory.

On my return from Goa I walked nervously through the open dhaba doorway, casting my eyes about for any sign of my bicycle. The owner appeared, greeting me like a brother back from years at war. 'Mr Oli you are mostly welcome. Goa very nice yes? I wash your cycle! Was very filthy. Come, you like idli?'

As I tucked into a specially prepared idli and mild masala, a sinewy man with a crooked nose wheeled my bicycle over and leaned it against the table. Whoever had cleaned it had made a better fist of it than I had ever managed. The rims sparkled, the gears were mud and dirt-free and the tyres were black rather than a pale grey.

I felt good for having trusted the dhaba owner and his clientele and, from the welcome I received on my return, I guessed he was proud that he had looked after it so well. It was the first time I had entrusted my bicycle to an Indian, and it was far from the last. In most towns from then on I would pull up and leave my bicycle with someone as I set off in search of nourishment.

The reality was that, if my trust turned out to be misplaced, an Indian family could have eaten for months off the proceeds of the sale of my bicycle. But not once was I let down; in fact, I was always rewarded, often just with the satisfaction at having made a new friend, but sometimes with an interesting experience that added colour to my subcontinental bicycle ride.

Weeks later, in Rajahmundry, the cultural capital of Andhra Pradesh, I left my bicycle with an ageing man called Vivek, the security guard at the town's dilapidated cricket stadium. If he could guard a cricket ground, I reasoned that he could sure as hell guard a bicycle.

When I returned a couple of hours later Vivek handed me an envelope stuffed with papers that were warped and yellowed by time. 'I read sign on your bicycle. It is honour to meet you. When I was young, I dreamed of going on similar journey,' Vivek explained as I began leafing through the contents of the envelope.

I was staggered at what I found: tens of photocopied letters to governments around the world, including the United Kingdom, France, the United States and Canada, in which Vivek begged for permission to cycle across their countries; letters to Indian companies, too, dated between 1982 and 1990, asking for money to help fund an 'Around Globe Bicycle Challenge'.

'When I was young man my dream was to cycle in Olympic Games. When I realised I missed opportunity I started to dream about cycling entire world.' The Indian head waggle can mean a thousand different things, and as Vivek's head began to veer from left to right, he looked sad. 'But I am poor man, and nobody would help me. As you see, I write many letters, but I get no money.'

Vivek ducked into his security shed and hauled out a rusty old bicycle complete with three sets of handlebars for different riding positions. 'This bicycle has been all over India. Every state I have cycled, but never out of India.'

I looked down at my state-of-the-art bicycle and felt slightly ridiculous for thinking I needed such an advanced machine. I raced Vivek through the crowded streets of Rajahmundry on my way out of town and by the time I had reached its limits he was out of sight ahead of me.

The following week, in Orissa, one of India's poorest states where almost 50 per cent of people live on less than a dollar a day, I left my bicycle in a town with a shopkeeper who spoke English fluently. When I came back armed with biscuits and water ten minutes later a crowd of around two hundred people, almost all men, was surrounding my bicycle. I stood on a step above them all, held my cricket bat aloft and shouted 'SACHIN TENDULKAR!' The men cheered in unison and

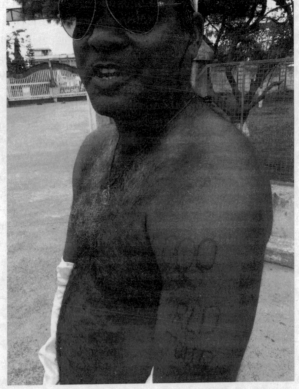

Vivek, Olympic rings tattooed proudly on his arm.

what had been a relatively calm gathering became a border-line riot. I pedalled out of the village to chants of 'SACHIN, SACHIN!'

Trusting Indians with my bicycle went so well that I did not buy a new lock until I reached the last country on my journey. On countless occasions I left my bicycle with strangers and each time my faith in humanity soared.

Now, in Ratnagiri, I tried to pay the dhaba owner for the idli but he refused. 'You are friend now; friends do not pay. I wish you happy journey to Ashes matches.' He would not let me argue, so I just pedalled off, enthusiasm renewed for the road ahead.

CHEATING AND CRICKET

I am riding the hard shoulder of a busy highway seven miles west of Sangli when a motorbike pulls up beside me. It happens several times an hour and at the end of a long day in the saddle I do not acknowledge its presence, keep my head down and my legs turning.

'Excuse me mister foreigner, but what is your good name?'

I peer across at two men riding a Hero Honda. The driver is a round man with glasses and wiry, unkempt hair. Around his abdomen are resting the arms of a smaller man in jeans and T-shirt, grinning from ear to ear. I pedal on; I just want to be left alone; I want space.

'What is your good country? What is your good purpose?'

These guys are persistent. I haven't got the energy to continue ignoring them so I pull up and cave in to their questioning.

'My good name Kapil. My friend good name Amit. We film-makers from Sangli; we make recent film about problem of infanticide in India. We like to show you our town because it is most beautiful town in all Maharashtra.'

Five days earlier I had left the coast at Ratnagiri and begun the long journey across India. My route was relatively flat at first, wide, shallow valleys guiding me through towns and villages of mud and crude bricks with little going for them. Every day roadworks dominated my immediate environment as thousands of women shovelled gravel on to newly flattened tracks. Watching them made me pleased to be on my bicycle; it looked like back-breaking work that, I noticed in India, was nearly always done by women. Beyond the roadworks subsistence farms stretched into the distance on either side of the road. Women, again, were bent double as they harvested by hand whatever crop their arid field would take. Most seemed to live entirely off the land and, judging by their sinewy figures, most only just managed.

I saw no outsiders and, in truth, could see little reason for tourists to visit this part of India, except to witness the desperate conditions that a large proportion of more than

1.3 billion people in the country are forced to put up with.

Each day I was on the road by sunrise and an hour later the heat was too much to bear. Since leaving the coast any breeze had disappeared. I tweeted: 'Impossible to replace fluids quick enough. Put simply, this is the hottest, most unpleasant weather I've ever encountered.'

Taking photos was impossible because the camera lens was permanently steamed up. I tried everything to keep the sweat out of my eyes. I used a redundant T-shirt to wipe the beads away, but within seconds they were back, salt stinging my eyes. I found a barber in one village and, for a good price, persuaded him to part with his spray bottle. In a move that I decided was tactically astute, I strapped the bottle to my handlebars so that I could spray water on to my face when the heat got too much. But after ten minutes in the sun the water was too hot to spray on to skin and I had no way of keeping it cool.

Sweat worked its way from my forehead, down my brow and into my eyes in such volume that I could barely see where I was heading. On a bicycle, the plankton of the Indian road network, I was often reminded of my mortality by speeding, out-of-control trucks and buses doing impressions of dodgems. Sight was therefore preferable to blindness but I found no way to conquer the constant dripping and, in the absence of functioning eyebrows, which only now did I realise must be faulty, there being no other purpose for them I could think of, had to resign myself to a sweaty fate. I was such a sweaty mess that, when two young men pulled up on a motorbike and asked if I was the Englishman who had appeared on *Extraaa Innings* before the Delhi versus Mumbai game, I gave them short shrift. Even when they asked me to write my signature on their bare shoulders I could not muster the energy to laugh, although I signed them anyway.

By the time I reached the foothills of the Western Ghats there was enough breeze to make life a little less unpleasant. Buses passed and I gathered the energy to wave on the off chance that there were passengers inside who might wave back. When I felt like it, interaction on the road kept me sane. As one bus passed a few inches from my handlebars, ten hands appeared through its open windows, followed by ten confused faces which quickly turned to smiles when they saw me waving furiously. The smiles disappeared only when the bus merged with the horizon a few hundred metres ahead of me. India blessed me with mental images that I will cherish forever.

The Western Ghats are a range of mountains spanning a thousand miles along the length of India's west coast in the states of Maharashtra, Goa, Karnataka, Tamil Nadu and Kerala. I had not looked at my map hard enough to know I was approaching them and so was grateful that I did not have to climb them on my own; instead, I cheated.

A continuous line of trucks passed me and, as the road was beginning to steepen, the white-vested passenger of one truck gave a toothy, brown grin that betrayed a lifetime spent chewing paan, before gesturing for me to hang on to a chain that was dragging along the road behind the truck. I managed to grab it and spent the next hour and a half – and twenty miles – clinging on for dear life. Although my legs enjoyed the effortlessness of the climb, my hands did not, and were aching like hell for days.

A couple of hours before Kapil and Amit accosted me on the road into Sangli I had been pedalling an unusually peaceful stretch of road bordered by thick deciduous forest when I heard the distant rumble of a public address system. It was a sultry April afternoon and most villagers had sought shade from the heat of the day. The distant rumble got closer and by the time I saw where it was coming from, it was deafening.

A red and white striped marquee stood in the corner of a field, facing a dusty cricket ground. Groups of men sat on their haunches around the boundary, holding hands and taking pictures with their mobile phones. More sat on their haunches – always on their haunches – under the shade of the marquee, being slowly deafened by the commentator, who was clearly enjoying having the stage to himself.

Rested legs, sore hands; clinging to the truck as we
climbed the Western Ghats.

I made my way to the marquee just as a wicket fell and
everyone rose to their feet in unison, hollering encouragement for the bowler. I was told it was a village match between
bitter local rivals. The commentator's voice echoed off the
escarpment beyond square leg and boomed for miles around.

Two balls later, a concerned, deathly silence. The new
batsman had launched a leg-spinner straight into the air and
two fielders closed on the ball to attempt the catch. One stopped
as he neared it; the other did not. When he made contact with
the electricity pylon ten metres from the wicket at short extra
cover the crowd gasped. He fell to the floor in a heap. Silence
was followed by chaos as men rushed on to the field from all
corners. The man was out cold when he was carried from the
field, shirt and trousers bloodied from the collision.

As the attention of the crowd turned towards the bloodied

invalid, I decided to take my cue and leave. But the men in the marquee would have none of it. Before I left, the commentator insisted I take with me a gift as a good luck offering for the remainder of my journey across India. And so it was with a winners' medal draped around my neck that I cycled the road to Sangli, wondering to myself which of the poor players would have to go without at the end of the match. I hoped it was not the man who had got to know the electricity pylon. I also hoped he was still alive.

'Have a medal son!'

Now, some hours later, I was chatting to Amit and Kapil on a busy highway hard shoulder, seven miles from Sangli. I introduced myself. When I told them the purpose of my travel, and that as film-makers they might be interested that I had filmed my journey since Belgrade on a small handheld camera, they got very excited indeed.

'This is most exciting indeed,' asserted Kapil. 'You must come with us for purpose of make film about game of cricket in Sangli. We are perhaps only Indians who do not like cricket but we would like very much like to help you find some cricket in most beautiful town of all Maharashtra.'

Amit nodded enthusiastically, like a puppy on a parcel shelf.

I was sold.

As the two made their way tentatively down the hard shoulder on their Hero Honda I followed, pedalling furiously just to keep up and wondering how, in such monstrous heat, people could get excited about anything that was not a fridge or an air-conditioned room. But then I was in India, a country in which even two self-confessed cricketing non-believers were enthusiastic enough to suggest finding me a game in their hometown and filming it.

Since 1721, when British sailors are said to have enjoyed a game among themselves in the port of Cambray, cricket has become so embedded in Indian culture that now, in the twenty-first century, it is less a sport, more a religion and national obsession. I have heard it said that the only Indians who dislike cricket are economists, who worry about its effect on absenteeism from factories and offices around the country, especially when the national team is playing a big match against bitter rivals Pakistan. Kapil and Amit had proved that theory wrong, but I did not doubt there was some truth in it. Indeed, during a recent one-day international between the two teams, it was estimated that the television audience in India alone exceeded the entire population of Europe.

Indian professional cricketers are fêted like few other sportsmen on the planet. The praise heaped on such Western sporting stars as David Beckham, LeBron James and Roger Federer is nothing compared to the adulation poured on even the most average of Indian international cricketers. Play cricket for India, and the unconditional, crazed love of your countrymen is almost guaranteed.

That said, there is one cricketer who stands head and shoulders above all others, who is perhaps the most famous living Indian and certainly the country's most marketable commodity, having signed sponsorship deals with tens of companies since arriving on the international scene in the late 1980s. He is the greatest Indian cricketer of all time, 'the Little Master', the batsman Sachin Tendulkar.

When it comes to cricket, Tendulkar is arguably more idolised by his own people than any sportsman, ever. Indian cricket commentator and leading journalist Harsha Bhogle once wrote that 'if Sachin plays well, India sleeps well'. Indeed, one man recently got himself in such a state over his idol's failure to reach a hundred international hundreds that he hanged himself.

There is another story that goes some way to explaining the esteem in which Tendulkar is held by his countrymen. Chasing 279 for victory against Pakistan in Calcutta in 1999, Tendulkar clipped a ball from Shoaib Akhtar to deep square leg. Turning for the third run, he watched the ball being hurled in from the boundary. Shoaib did the same and the two collided, with Tendulkar just shy of his ground when the ball hit the stumps. He was given out, sending one hundred thousand Indian fans into a frenzy that soon became a riot. Play was suspended for an hour before Tendulkar spoke over the loudspeaker, appealing for calm. Eventually the riots calmed and the game resumed without further incident. Pakistan won the match.

The great man cannot leave his home in Mumbai without disguising himself with a fake beard and he lives a life shielded from his countrymen by the length of his bodyguard's arm. He spends a lot of time in London these days to escape the public and media attention. In some ways it is sad, I suppose, to be so loved by your people, yet unable to walk among them for fear of being mobbed.

When Kapil, Amit and I had finished a late-night vegetable curry we wandered the streets of Sangli with a cricket bat and video camera in search of a game of cricket. Before long we had quite a following, with an army of coiffed, greasy teenage boys in tow, all trying to cop a stroke of the cricket bat as we dodged a stream of motorbikes on which young girls in saris rode side-saddle behind their boyfriends. A cinema emptied, its audience spat out on to the street to mingle with the brown and white cows, the street vendors and the bicycles. Shopkeepers did a roaring trade, showing no sign of shutting up for the night, their bright interiors lighting up the dark streets. The tables of open-fronted restaurants spilled out on to the streets, merging with the chaotic traffic.

This being India, we found a game easily enough. The dustbowl took up an entire block and was surrounded by a low barbed-wire fence. Dim floodlights lent the red earth an ethereal glow. A marquee ran the length of one boundary, housing a commentator and a number of dignitaries burdened by self-importance. Marathi music blasted from a sound system controlled by the commentator's young sidekick, who stroked his fluffy moustache as his head bobbed forward and back, out of time with the beat. At fine leg stood a series of five-metre-high banners on which were printed the slightly spooky faces of various managing directors and chairmen of companies that had clearly put their names to the event. It was eleven o'clock on a sultry May night and hundreds of people had gathered to watch the under-eleven teams of two local neighbourhoods battle for bragging rights.

I often wonder how cricket has come to mean so much to so many Indians. Why cricket rather than any other sport, for example? Lots of people I have spoken to believe it to be a symptom of that fact that Indians are a small race; diminutive and slight, hardly suited to the physical demands of games like rugby or football. Others say the British nurtured cricketing enthusiasm for more than two hundred years on the subcontinent, so it must be down to them. But although the British introduced cricket to the Indian population, they can hardly be congratulated for the spread of the game. When the Calcutta Cricket Club was formed in about 1792* it may have been the first cricket club outside

* Although it is not known exactly when the club came into existence, a copy of the *Madras Courier* dated 23 February 1792 reported cricket fixtures between the Calcutta Cricket Club and Barrackpore and the Calcutta Cricket Club and Dum Dum. The club, therefore, was certainly in existence by then.

Dustbowl cricket: who knew the toss of a coin could usher pandemonium?

Britain, but that is not to say Indians were permitted membership. In fact, until as late as the mid-nineteenth century the British simply fenced off vast areas of India's major cities for use as cricket grounds by their aristocracy and civil servants whenever it took their fancy. The first cricket club for Indians was not founded until 1848, when the Parsi population of Bombay formed the Orient Cricket Club. Hindus were a little slower to beat down British obduracy, only forming their first club, the Union Cricket Club in Bombay, in 1866.

I prefer to go along with an explanation put forward by Ramachandra Guha in *A Corner of a Foreign Field: The Indian History of a British Sport*, in which he suggests it was an event in 1946 that sowed the seeds of cricket's longevity in India. At the beginning of that year Mahatma Gandhi's Indian independence movement was based in football-mad Calcutta. But later in 1946 Gandhi made the decision to relocate his organisation to Delhi, where cricket happened to be the number one sport. Guha argues that, had Gandhi and his organisation remained in Calcutta, football may well have become the country's national sport, and not cricket.

Guha also goes on to suggest that around the time India achieved independence from Britain, cricket, although popular, was not considered by everyone to be a pastime suited to Indian culture. In 1946 the General Secretary of the All India Congress Committee, B. V. Keskar, stressed his view that cricket would not survive the disappearance of British rule, saying that it could only do so in an 'atmosphere of British culture and language'.

If B. V. Keskar were still alive he would, presumably, be somewhat surprised at cricket's explosion since the British gave India back to Indians, and particularly at its boom since their World Cup win in 1983. That event, more than any other, gave the Indian people and cricketers the confidence to believe they could be successful at the very highest level. It acted as a catalyst for participation across Indian society and, aided by huge economic growth, India has now become the undisputed financial powerhouse of international cricket and home to some of the highest paid sports stars on the planet.

Keskar would also undoubtedly be surprised that a game between a handful of nine- and ten-year-olds in Sangli, one of hundreds of similar-sized towns in Maharashtra alone, was able to draw such a raucous crowd. Although I was not allowed to join in the game, Kapil hardly had to use his powers of persuasion to get me a hit between innings, followed by a stint commentating on a couple of overs when the second team batted; nor to get local people to speak to the camera.

'Who is your favourite English cricketer?' I asked tens of excitable kids who stood staring at me, crowding the lens.

'Andrew Symonds!' came one reply, 'Brett Lee!' another.

'They're both Australian,' I told the boys, despairingly.

'Herschelle Gibbs!'

'No, he's South African.'

'Matthew Hayden! Shane Warne!'

'More bloody Australians!' I muttered under my breath.

Their stares were confused now. Each was desperate to be the first to receive a congratulatory high-five.

Finally, 'Andrew Strauss!' came a barely intelligible wail from a gangly kid at the back.

I was pleased that English cricket was alive and well in India.

The following morning my two companions and I visited the Sangli Cricket Stadium, where a state match was taking place. I was invited to toss the coin to decide which team batted first, and even enjoyed sticking a key into the wicket* with the camera trained on me.

'You wouldn't let a bunch of grannies play on that back home,' I said to the camera. Although the standard of play was high, facilities were desperately poor, with a roughly mown, uneven wicket and an outfield of bare brown dirt, rather than the lush green grass one would find for such a game back home. Cricket might be India's passion, but that clearly does not mean funds make their way into deserving hands.

The remainder of the day was spent at Kapil's parents' house, editing a short film about my time in Sangli that made its way back to László in Budapest; he was gathering quite a collection in case he did decide to make a film of my journey.

'You must promise to send us footage from other parts of world, Mr Oli,' Amit said as I hauled my right leg up and over my bicycle the next morning. 'Outside world is very interesting to us indeed.'

I promised to do so, before pedalling away from Kapil and Amit on the road towards the capital of Andhra Pradesh, the thriving, writhing metropolis of Hyderabad.

---

* The legendary former England opening batsman turned commentator, Geoffrey Boycott, developed the habit of sticking a car key into the wicket during his pre-match pitch reports for television. Boycott did this in order to assess the hardness and moisture of the pitch, both factors that affect the decision of the captains when they're weighing up whether to bat or bowl first. It is no longer permitted, partly because it was considered bad for the pitch and partly because there are rules for everything these days.

With Kapil and Amit at the Sangli Cricket Stadium.

TOP OF RANKINGS, CURRENTLY

It was 340 miles from Sangli to Hyderabad, a five-day journey that took me across the state line from Maharashtra into Andhra Pradesh. One state down, three to go.

I stayed with a local friend in Hyderabad. Uday knew the city's temples, bars, tourist attractions and restaurants inside out. Hyderabad is the home of biryani, a dish traditionally made of basmati rice and lamb and invented in the kitchens of the Nizam dynasty that once ruled the city. For five years back home I ordered a biryani takeaway most Sunday evenings, but it was not until I tasted the real thing that I realised I had been paying good money for a poor imitation.

When Uday had work to do, I hung out with Anantha, a keen cricketer and film student whom László had found on the internet. Armed with a video camera, Anantha accompanied me to various engagements around the city as I attempted to delve a little into the city's cricketing culture. We had a hit

Men in the streets of Hyderabad: surely there is a comb
in one of those top pockets.

with some kids on a patch of dirt next to some disused train
tracks; visited the national stadium, where the IPL team Deccan
Chargers play their home games; I gave a talk about my trip
and a coaching clinic at the Hyderabad Sports Academy, where
immaculately turned out former street kids got to spend their
days playing as much sport as they had the energy for. Before
I left we lined up for a photo beneath life-sized cut-outs of
Pelé, Sir Donald Bradman, Nadia Comăneci, Michael Jordan,
Muhammad Ali and Pete Sampras. The director of the academy
seemed to place great importance on the kids not only playing
as well as they could, but on behaving in a manner reminiscent
of some of the greatest icons in sport.

On my last day Anantha and I travelled to Hyderabad's
HITEC City, a manicured suburb of gardens and glass office
blocks at the centre of Andhra Pradesh's technology boom.
Microsoft, General Electric, GE Capital, IBM and Accenture
all have offices there and it's also the home of Facebook's
fourth largest office. If you find yourself on the receiving end
of a call-centre call from India, there is a fair chance the caller
is sitting in a sparkling new office in HITEC City, Hyderabad.

But Anantha and I were not there to visit call centres. We were there at the invitation of a man called James Bond, a Google technician who had been following my journey online, and who wanted to show us something in the basement of his office.

In most office blocks around the world the basement acts as either storage or car park. Google headquarters in HITEC City is no different; there is the space to accommodate hundreds of cars. What *is* different about that particular basement is that, in a corner well lit by an open stairwell, there is a netted area about the size of an Olympic swimming pool, reserved solely for cricket.

It was lunchtime when James, Anantha and I visited. A basketball net hung loose and redundant from the wall. Creases and popping creases were marked in white twenty-two yards

En route to Google HQ.

apart on the bare concrete floor. Yellow-painted lines were drawn under mid-off's feet; they were motorcycle parking spaces, but they were never used.

Fifteen or twenty Google technicians stood in a queue, barefoot with suit trousers rolled up to the knees, waiting to bat. Each had brought their own bat to work with them and they leaned on them uniformly, seemingly unaware of the enervating heat.

'We play every day, before work, at lunch and after work,' one player told me. 'There is batting league. I am top of rankings, currently.'

'Do your bosses not mind you playing so much?' I asked, naively as it turned out.

'Of course not, they encourage us. My boss is most avid cricketer in whole Google.'

If I needed any persuading that cricket was India's first love, my visit to Google was confirmation. Not until I arrived in Kolkata* would I see such love for the game again.

James Bond with the Ashes urn.

* The city was named Calcutta by the British and remained so until 2001, when it was changed to Kolkata to match Bengali pronunciation. However, many Bengalis still refer to the city as Calcutta.

HYDERABADIS ON WHEELS

7 May 2010
Dear Oli

I got into the love of bicycling recently, it is five months now, ever since the thought came that I have become part of the population that create pollution and affect ozone layer and what not. So I took up to cycling again after my college days, and now bike to work every day. I have done a few solo century rides since, as I seemed to develop a greater interest in cycling.

I have two kids aged 16 & 12. The elder also developed an interest in cycling . . . my wife is a home-maker.

Me and my family will be pleased to have you at my home. Let me know your plans.

On a different note, I am a member of Hyderabad Bicycling Club and manage the Go Green Initiative's Hyderabad wing. I would love to organize a bicycle ride with our members during the weekend if it is okay. You will find a nice set up bikers who will be very pleased to meet you and share thoughts. Let me know, if that is possible?

Krishna

Since Mumbai, news of my exploits had spread on the blogosphere and social media platforms across India. Whereas in Mumbai it was generally local television and newspapers that were interested in my ride, by the time I reached Hyderabad national broadcasters and newspapers were getting in touch. In many towns and cities I passed through I was asked for an interview and every day I had tens of new India-based Twitter followers and emails from people across the country offering everything from accommodation to games of cricket. It was incredibly humbling. I had set out on a bicycle ride in the pursuit of a rather selfish, single-minded adventure. I never dreamed that people beyond my family and friends would be interested in following my progress.

And so it was that after a week in Hyderabad I found myself in the gaze of various television camera crews as I prepared to leave the city. I quite liked being on camera by that stage and felt comfortable talking to journalists because I had at least a few stories to tell.

As the cameras continued to roll and the questions kept coming, Krishna turned up on his bicycle. I had received his email during my stay in Hyderabad and, although I did not stay at his house, had arranged to leave the city with him and other members of the Go Green Initiative. In a country that pumps out around 1.2 million tonnes of carbon a year, it was nice to see a group of enthusiasts willing to take action by getting on their bicycles.*

I have already said that Indians like 'cycles' a lot. Before 1898, tens of millions of Indians simply had no means to travel.

With members of the Go Green Initiative,
before pedalling out of Hyderabad.

* In May 2013 I received excellent news from Krishna who told me that, thanks to incessant lobbying by members of the Hyderabad Cycling Club, the goverment of Andhra Pradesh has agreed to begin construction of fifteen miles of cycle paths in Cyberabad, a suburb of Hyderabad.

Road networks were poor, horses were expensive and railways connected very few towns and villages outside the major cities. When the bicycle first arrived in India at the end of the nineteenth century, it perhaps did more to alleviate poverty than any other vehicle before or since, giving farmers and villagers a chance to travel beyond their daily environment.

Yet, more than a hundred years later, despite the fact that around 30 per cent of all city journeys are still made by bicycle, the average Indian no longer dreams of cashing in his savings to buy a shiny, steel bicycle. He dreams of owning a motorised engine instead: a car, a truck or even a rickshaw. Whereas once the bicycle was king, now it is the preserve of the poor and the athletic.

Recreational cycling is a growing pastime in India, as it is across the world. The machine that changed the fortunes of billions of Indians now helps millions of them to get fit. Krishna was in the 'get fit' category, and I admired him for his newfound passion. By the time we were ready to leave the group was around thirty strong, a motley crew of varying shapes, sizes and ages and we pedalled one of metropolitan India's most chaotic road networks behind a cavalcade of police motorbikes.

The police had agreed to allow Anantha to ride backwards on the back of a motorbike so that he could film us cycling behind him. He said goodbye at the top of the first long climb out of the city. At noon the mercury hit 50°C in the sun and we were out of the city, riding up a steep incline with fifteen-ton trucks whizzing by. My companions seemed unfazed by their proximity; they were used to it, they said. I wondered if I would ever get used to it.

Although most riders kept up a faster pace than me and my mobile-home-on-wheels, one by one they dropped off to return home. When the group numbered just four, we stopped for a curry at a roadside dhaba and spent half an hour moaning about the staggering heat. I was glad it was not just me, but Indians, too, who complained when it got too hot. Apart from the weather I had little to moan about.

I loved involving Krishna and his Go Green team in my ride out of Hyderabad and was pleased to play even the smallest of roles in promoting my favourite mode of transport as a healthy, environmentally friendly way to get around.

But after lunch the group was one again, and I pedalled down a gentle hill wondering what other surprises India held in store for me.

A DAY IN THE LIFE OF A CYCLIST IN INDIA

I fall back on to the bed, staring at the large red swastika painted on the wall and then at the ceiling, fan whirring noisily and perilously in its centre. I wonder how so many dark stains have found their way up there. Is that really a knob of butter next to the smoke alarm?*

Ten minutes earlier I had been asleep in a box room in yet another rancid hotel, this time in Eluru, a hub for tobacco, palm oil and Persian carpets in eastern Andhra Pradesh. I had been on the bike for three days since Hyderabad and had almost made it to India's east coast.

A knock at the door woke me. The darkness suggested it was early, and I checked my watch. It was early indeed: 4.30 a.m., an hour before sunrise. I groaned and the intruder heard me.

'You like cold water, sah?' The voice carried from the corridor because a pane of glass was missing from the window frame above my door. I realised that my restless night spent vigorously scratching had been down to the mosquitoes that had found their way into my bed and under the sheet. Most of them seemed to have enjoyed the taste of my left ear lobe which, during another sweaty night on the subcontinent, seemed to have tripled in size.

I hobbled out of bed, opened the door and was met by a head that nodded gently from left to right and back again

---

* It was a knob of butter, although I never discovered how it got there.

several times. In the middle of the man's face, below his nose and just above his chin, sat a smile the size of Mumbai's new landmark, the Rajiv Gandhi Sea Link Bridge. I had slept for only a few hours and, I am afraid to admit, could not muster the energy to smile back.

'Yes, I like cold water. I like cold water a lot. But I don't like being woken up at half past four in the morning to be asked if I like cold water. I don't want cold water right now,' I thought, but did not say.

'Not now, but thank you for the offer,' I replied, at the same time frowning to convey my displeasure at his interest in my nocturnal drinking habits. The waterboy turned on his heels and shuffled down the dimly lit corridor, no doubt disappointed that the only foreigner in Eluru had not fallen for his liquid charms.

Now, staring at the knob of butter, contemplating more sleep, I realised that my early morning intruder had done me a favour. The sun was still below the horizon. In a couple of hours the air would be so heavy that breathing, let alone cycling, would be an immense task. I decided to get on the road early.

Standard traffic on the road across Andhra Pradesh.

The build-up to the monsoon had been gaining in intensity since I'd set out from Mumbai, making life in the saddle increasingly unbearable. The past few days since Hyderabad had been some of the most unpleasant, stuck in the thick of Andhra Pradesh's hottest May since records began – or maybe since time began, I could not remember. Each day I was pounded by the sun for up to ten hours and my head throbbed with every pedal stroke. I was caked in sweat twenty-four hours a day and the volume of unruly traffic since Hyderabad had also started to take its toll on my sense of humour.

I staggered out of bed and lugged my bags down the open-air staircase, taking care to dodge a piece of half-chewed naan bread lying on the landing floor.

By the time I had attached panniers, tent, cricket bat and sleeping bag to my bike a crowd of twenty confused insomniacs was surrounding me. One of them spoke good English. His name was Johnson; he was a Christian from Kerala, in the south of India. He told me that he had a family – a wife and two children – whom he saw once a year, for two weeks each

The confused insomniacs.

June. I asked if he missed them. 'Of course,' he admitted, 'but I would miss them even more if they starved because I could not feed them. I cannot find work in Kerala, so I am here.'

As his interest in me and my bicycle waned he pointed across the road to a tyre repair shop where, he said, he lived and worked. Johnson's family and friends in Kerala were more than a thousand miles away. Meeting him was a welcome jolt to my increasingly self-pitying demeanour. I vowed that the next time I got homesick or moaned about the humidity or suffered mosquito hell I would think of Johnson and remember that life could have been a lot worse.

Before I set off for the day I asked one of the confused insomniacs to look after my bicycle while I went to the loo. Inside, I opened the only cubicle and found a rabid-looking dog hiding behind the door, dribbling. It watched me pee. Solitude really is too much to ask for in India.

At six o'clock I was finally on the road; but, as ever in India, I was not alone. My early start was supposed to help me avoid heat and traffic, but the sun was already beginning to sneak above the horizon and, far more worryingly, a steady stream of trucks hogged the width of the road. There was little I could do but keep an eye on my wing mirror (a recent addition to my bicycle's growing armoury; I had been warned I would need it for cycling on the subcontinent. I was grateful for the tip) and veer carefully off the road whenever I felt like I might become road kill.

Come seven o'clock I needed shade, but there was little. The landscape was largely featureless, tobacco plantations and paddy fields stretching for miles in all directions. What trees there were did not offer the kind of all-consuming shade I was after.

I spotted a roadside tree in the distance. The prospect of ten minutes of shade got me excited and I let out a whoop! of delight. Shade would bring relief the like of which I never thought I would know on a simple bicycle ride. Approaching the tree, however, my elation turned to dust. A handful of men, dressed sparingly in lungi and leather sandals, had beaten me to the only shelter for miles around.

As I got closer I saw that the men were all asleep, while tens of women, presumably their wives and daughters, performed back-breaking work in the fields at the bottom of a small escarpment. Seeing an opportunity for a hassle-free break while the men slept and, spotting a patch of shade next to the hard shoulder, I quietly dismounted, using the cricket bat to prop up my bicycle. I had taken to using my bat for all sorts of things lately: it came in handy for flattening earth to create a comfortable camping spot, acted as a door-stop in the absence of a lock in most cheap motels and even made a great vegetable chopping board. Panniers came in handy, too. I removed one to use as a pillow and lay down on the hard ground, careful not to make a sound.

But seconds after I closed my eyes, before I had time to think to myself, 'Wow, I'm so lucky to have found shade under this beautiful tree without waking up the other shade-dwellers', I heard a rustling near me. I squinted to see an emaciated figure leaning on a tree branch that he was using as a walking stick, staring at me from his prime position in the heart of the shade. He woke up one of his friends with the stick, rapping him firmly on the legs. An extended groan of pain and, quick as a flash, most of the men were awake and making their way towards me. They did not speak and, although they seemed friendly enough, they fixed me with the kind of stare only a young child could get away with back home: open-mouthed and brainless.

At such times it was easy to forget that most villagers around the world were just as curious about my presence as I was about their lifestyle. The difference was always that I was the trespasser, the outnumbered visitor thousands of miles from home.

In fact, the men were probably wondering who the open-mouthed white man with a blank, brainless stare was. I tried to speak to them but we could not understand each other and although I did not want to appear rude, I did not have the energy to mime.

Eventually, twenty men were surrounding me so closely

that I felt like I was in a huddle after taking a wicket, but without the feeling of happiness I would have had on the cricket field.

The temperature was nudging 45°C before eight o'clock and getting warmer. I remembered the previous night's news feature about hundreds of elderly people who had died of heat exhaustion in the past few days in Andhra Pradesh alone. Being on a bike in such debilitating heat made me feel pretty elderly, so perhaps I should watch out, I thought.

As the crowd around me grew bigger I flapped my arms about like a kid learning to swim, desperate to demonstrate that I wanted some space. But the men did not understand and simply came closer in the hope that proximity would lead to greater comprehension. The only thing to do was to move a few metres along, which I did. But I was followed. Frustration was well set in now.

Eventually, despite heavy legs, a heavier sweat and being slightly less relaxed and more tired than I had been five minutes earlier, I decided to pedal on in search of another, less populated shady spot. I passed a few trees offering shade but under each one there were men sleeping and I was not eager to repeat the earlier scene. I gave up my search, donned my wide-brimmed hat instead and got on with the business of churning out miles.

Some hours later, towards mid-morning, I neared the outskirts of a town. The town had been the centre of my attention for a couple of days for the simple reason that I enjoyed repeating its name: Tadepallegudem, Tadepallegudem, Tadepallegudem. Tadepallegudem had occupied my thoughts for hours in the saddle. I imagined that while I pedalled its wide, clean streets the faint aroma of jasmine would tickle my nostrils. The drivers would, at the very least, possess a brain each, but might even be thoughtful and calm. There would be a clean restaurant that served Caesar salad, shepherd's pie and strawberry Cornettos, and an internet café where the internet would actually work. No one would fiddle with my bike's gears while I was looking away, or kick the wheels, just because . . .

I arrived in Tadepallegudem, where the vision disintegrated. It was a squalid, dusty, typically frenetic town where I jostled for space among hundreds of string-vested men pedalling rusty steel cycles. All I could find was a filthy roadside dhaba where I drank a 'Thums Up', the Indian equivalent of Pepsi, served to me by a prepubescent waiter whose left hand remained stuffed inside his boxer shorts for the duration of my stay. Then I gave the internet café a go. The man there told me 'inturnet no wuking', and I was back on the road a few minutes later. Tadepallegudem was just the latest of thousands of nowhere towns around the world whose anticipation kept me motivated and occupied my mind for days, before disappearing under my wheels in a flash.

On the outskirts of town a man on foot began chasing me shouting 'Are you missionary, are you missionary?' over and over. 'Yes, a cricketing one!' I replied, standing on my pedals to get away from my pursuer. Five minutes later I came across a particularly dilapidated dhaba, outside of which a man squatted as he took a shit against the wall. I did not enjoy the sight, or the sound effects.

I saw another man being carried out of the same dhaba by five or six others. His body looked leaden and I thought he might be dead, but I was told he had just passed out drunk. I checked my watch. It was 11.30 a.m. It was not the first time I had witnessed morning intoxication in rural India, so I was not surprised. I had seen fights fuelled by alcohol, drunken rants directed at dhaba employees. A few days earlier I was forced out of a shop by a man wielding a huge whip. He could hardly walk, and cracked his leather weapon as he stumbled from one shelf to the next, ransacking the place and destroying the poor shopkeeper's livelihood in the process. The owner was calm and resigned, as if he had seen it all before.

I once watched a documentary in which Harsha Bhogle travelled to some of the poorest corners of his country and discovered village after village mired by inebriated men. He was not surprised by such rampant alcoholism because, he concluded, life for most Indians was so very tough. Another

Indian cricket writer, C.P. Surendran, wrote that watching Sachin Tendulkar go out to bat gave a 'pauper people . . . relief, remission from the lifelong anxiety of being Indian'. India is estimated to house one-third of the world's poor. Life for hundreds of millions is a daily battle for survival and, just as cricket is the ultimate escapism for so many in this country, so the availability of cheap alcohol provides an alternative form of escape for millions more, particularly in rural parts. I often wondered about the hypocrisy of pumping billions of dollars into new hi-tech cities like Mumbai and Bangalore when the bulk of Indians struggle by on less than two dollars a day.

Despite the drunkard and the fellow having a shit, I did eat in the dhaba. It was as squalid as expected, with more cockroaches than paying customers and a kitchen that would have made Gordon Ramsay say 'Fuck' quite a lot. The waiter cleared his throat as he approached and when he reached me, leaned across, put one hand on a railing and expectorated effusively on to the street, narrowly missing a near-naked child playing with a ball in the dirt. In fact, there seemed to be a lot of near-nakedness going on. At the table next to me was a man wearing only underpants, covered head to toe in chalk. The barrier to me finding out more about this old man was, as so often in rural India, language. I moved on, none the wiser, and slightly more confused about what to make of this extraordinary country.

Back on the road I got a puncture in my rear tyre, my fifteenth since leaving Mumbai. Indian roads were less forgiving than those in other countries, the result of errant wire, metal and nails that lined highway hard shoulders. I pulled up next to an affable looking, toothless old guy, wearing what his dishevelled appearance suggested was his only set of clothes.

'You know where I can fix this puncture, sir?' I asked, doing my best impression of an Indian accent. (This was a tactic that I had developed on the subcontinent. I found if I spoke in my normal accent I could barely make myself understood, so across India tended to mimic the local accent. It worked, without exception.) My pump had broken during repairs in Sudan and I had yet to find a replacement. Besides, hydraulic pumps always did a better job of providing me with higher pressure, which made cycling easier.

'Yes, young man, just three furlongs down the road, past the dhaba, you will find a car mechanic. He will help you,' replied the old man in perfect English.

I was startled, firstly at his equestrian approach to measuring road distance, and secondly at his surprising grasp of English. Whereas almost every young Indian boy or girl I met spoke excellent English, even in the most remote of villages, I had come to expect puzzled looks from old men when they were confronted with my language. The friendly old equine dude was clearly an exception to the rule.

I could only guess that, after independence, the English language understandably played less of a role in Indian life, but that the recent economic explosion meant it was undergoing a revival. Some weeks later in Kolkata, a friend told me that India is reputed to have the most English speakers of any country on earth. I was pleased to learn that, along with cricket, the British had left another lasting legacy.

I fought to keep my laden bicycle upright as I wheeled it away from the old man and, sure enough, found a mechanic three furlongs down the road. 'Hello, foreigner,' the man said as I leaned my machine against a wall that seemed to bend as I did so. It was a strikingly accurate greeting that seemed to be favoured by the rural underclass across India, the word 'foreigner' always pronounced in a curious Welsh lilt. Of course, I was never able to forget that I was a long way from Wales because across the Severn it is rarely 50°C.

The mechanic had me back on the road in no time and I was soon a foreigner with a newly patched-up tyre. The afternoon wore on and was, as ever, punctuated by a raft of events that I would have considered wholly unusual in most countries, but which were routine, even mundane, in India. A motorbike sped past me and the driver waved; nothing unusual there, except that he had five double mattresses balanced on his head.

Another motorbike appeared in my wing mirror, two young boys riding it, both of whom had to be under twelve years old. As they passed me, they turned and waved. I gestured at an oncoming truck but their eyes remained fixed on me and my bicycle. They stared at me while the truck passed no more than a few inches from them, and then they careered off the road at speed. Just before they reached an escarpment, which led ten metres down into a jungly ditch, the driver used all his experience to rescue them. When the bike was under control again, they turned to bid me farewell, smiling and waving furiously as if the truck episode had not happened.

Then came a third motorbike. The driver cut me up so I had to pull over. He asked for my autograph, email address and phone number before he even said hello or asked me my name; oh, and he tried to stroke my hair with his four-inch long fingernails, at which point I stopped the nonsense and pedalled on, the end of my day within reach.

I felt weak and dehydrated throughout the last hour because, for once, just when I needed one, there were no roadside shops. But after eighty-five miles I did eventually make it to my evening stopover just after sunset. Gandepalli was less 'town', more 'random collection of buildings in the middle of nowhere', and I did wonder why it was even marked on my map.

The search for a cheap place to sleep was refreshingly hassle-free: there was only one option, the confusingly named Gandepalli Manor Place View Resort; confusing for obvious linguistic reasons, but also because the hotel had no view, was not a manor house and did not form part of a resort. I considered suggesting to the management that, for the sake of accuracy, they rename it the Gandepalli Humid Pit and perhaps adorn the entrance with a banner that read 'Welcome to Squalid, Rat-infested Hell', but instead I just checked in. Within five minutes I was sitting on the floor of the bathroom, washing myself under a trickle of cold water. My diary entry for the day read simply: 'I ache all over. I have never been more tired. I haven't the energy to write. I will try again in the morning.'

Before I left home I could never have imagined being as staggeringly tired as I was each evening in India. My head ached constantly, my legs were barely able to climb stairs, my mind was numb; every atom in my body screamed for respite from the noise, the heat, the long, long days in the saddle. I rarely had an ounce of energy left when I collapsed into bed each evening and I loved the feeling: pure exhaustion born of strenuous exercise that I knew had been worthwhile. I could think of nothing more satisfying.

Bed also allowed for reflection. I rarely had time to reflect upon my journey until each day had come to an end; there was simply too much going on around me as I pedalled. But when the heat had subsided a little and I sat back to enjoy rare privacy at the end of a day, I reminded myself how lucky I was to be seeing India from the saddle of a bicycle.

I mustered the energy to spend a few silent moments peering out of the window of my room in Gandepalli, watching the low-key street scene being acted out below. Although it was barely a town, there was still plenty to look at and I considered that if you stood or sat still in India, wherever you were, day or night, you would see an abundance of things that, in equal measure, confused, astounded, worried and delighted: a man carrying fifty live but sedated chickens draped over his bicycle's handlebars; a kaleidoscopic swarm of pilgrims sleeping on the streets at night, safe in their numbers; a few cows nonchalantly tucking into a fruit-seller's livelihood. A traveller who opens his eyes in India can never be bored.

1.3 BILLION : 1

I spot a cold drinks stall and there is no one there. I buy a Pepsi – fifty rupees more for a cold drink to pay for the cost of running the fridge – and now the stall is crammed full of curious locals. The owner is not happy because none of them will buy anything from him. He takes out his anger on me by shouting and motioning that I should move on, which is fine because all I wanted in the first place was some shade and a drink. Most of the villagers are fiddling with my bike or trying to open my panniers. I leave the stall quickly because I JUST WANT TO BE ALONE!

I cycle on. I pass trucks parked in the slow lane of the highway because the driver is tired and is now sleeping under his vehicle. Buffalo lock horns, play-fighting in front of oncoming traffic. Phlegm and urine fly at speed from the windows of every type of vehicle, and often hit me. I stop for a lunchtime bite and my surprisingly tasty food is, as usual, delivered to me by a thirteen-year-old boy who scratches his balls, picks his nose and spits on the floor as he approaches my table. He carries my portion of naan bread in his right hand, which is caked in dirt and sweat. Next to me are two middle-aged men rolling around on the floor pissed as anything. They are spitting, too.

India was undoubtedly a highlight of my journey to Australia but it was not a road without obstacles. In the weeks and months after my trip I was often surprised to hear myself telling people how much I had loved it when for so much of the time I had absolutely hated riding across it.

The ride from Rajahmundry to Gandepalli was typical of the way my days panned out. After settling upon my route way back in Mumbai, a simple act that took less than a minute of map-gazing, I scoffed at those who warned me about the heat in April and May, particularly in central India. Perhaps I should have foreseen frustration around the corner.

I felt claustrophobic and suffocated. Generally I was forced to stay in cheap hotels, never paying more than £6 or £7 (I had tried camping on the relatively sparsely populated Konkan Coast, but it had proved close to impossible to find a well-hidden spot, even there), and although the crummy guesthouses offered relative privacy, it was scant relief for a man cycling along with a cricket bat strapped to his bicycle. Of course, it was partly my fault, but as soon as I clambered off the bike at the end of another torrid day I was public property, set upon by swarms of young men eager to play cricket or have their photo taken with me. I could not tell them, partly because I could not speak their language and partly because I just could not bring myself to, that I was too tired to speak let alone make friends.

In Tuni, on the night before I arrived on India's east coast, I was fast asleep at eleven o'clock when I woke to an incessant, urgent rapping at the door. I got up, opened it and found four shy smiles; a man and his three sons.

'Photo please,' the man said, pointing at my face from less than a metre away.

'What world are you in?' I said under my breath, getting ready for the man to take a photo.

'No camera please mister,' the man explained.

I understood him immediately. This had happened over and over in India. He wanted a photo of himself and his sons, but he did not have a camera. He wanted *me* to take the photo with *my* camera and send it to him by email. Grudgingly, I granted him his wish, went back to sleep and sent the photo the following morning.

Getting hassled when I wasn't riding was tough, but it was okay because I had my bicycle. Time in the saddle meant time to myself, for thinking of home and daydreaming about the future, for wondering what I would see next and where I would sleep that night.

Oh no, not in India.

In India I rarely had more than a few seconds to myself on the road before a motorbike pulled over or nearly ran me over and the driver or his passenger asked, 'Which good country your homeland is?' or 'You is come on good cycle from where sir please mister?' One morning I counted how many motorbikes attempted to halt my progress: twenty-three before midday. And it was not just motorbikes. On another afternoon, back on the road after lunch and a wash, a truck passed and the driver waved. I did not wave back and for my sins I got a bottle of urine thrown my way, splashing my bags and bare legs.

Friends often wrote to ask whether I got bored cycling so far all on my own. In India, I prayed for boredom and all I got was loneliness. I asked myself how I could have been lonely in a land of 1.3 billion people. I had not been lonely anywhere else, even pedalling the remotest stretches where there were very few inhabitants. Although I did not figure it out at the time, I was lonely *because* there were so many people, not in spite of it. In India, I did not really know anyone; it was a land of 1.3 billion strangers. That is a lot of people not to know.

The state of my health, I am certain, played a part in my fragile state of mind. Each day's cycling took all I had and I often collapsed on to a flee-ridden bed at the end of it, long after dark, and fell asleep in the filthy T-shirt, shorts and sandals I wore for pedalling. Although 'cycling fit', I sweated buckets, was gaunt and thin. For one particular ailment I blamed myself. One sweltering afternoon I had been crossing a dam when a man shouted up at me from a semi-submerged concrete bar spanning the vast width of the holy Godavari River. He had driven his motorised rickshaw along the bar and appeared to be cleaning it; slightly odd behaviour, but he continued to shout up at me so I found a way down and pedalled along the bar, enjoying the spray sent up by my wheels. The man just fancied saying hello, which was fine, but his two sons were swimming in the river beneath the dam and they beckoned me in. I stripped down to my cycling shorts and dived in, relishing the instant relief the cool water brought. The following day I got an itchy head and headache, neither of which disappeared until I left Dhaka, in Bangladesh, five weeks later.

The claustrophobia, the loneliness, the poor health, the heat, the endless poverty; they all made me retreat inwards. In every other country I had welcomed a roadside chat however difficult communication might have been. I had joked and raced with passing cyclists, stopped for a rest when café owners waved furiously for me to take tea with them. I had smiled my way through Europe, the Middle East and Africa, firm in my belief that it was the best way of making

The rickshaw owners cleaning their chariots in the Godavari River.

new friends. I had rarely been impatient, never shouted at people and certainly never questioned my sanity.

But halfway through my journey in India I began to fail at all those things. I hated myself for doing so, but I became less willing to engage with people, less animated with the ordinary Indian who just wanted to say hello. I still entrusted people with my bicycle, or chatted when I felt like it, but I was less happy and carefree doing so. My emotions, which I had always considered to have under at least a modicum of control, eventually got the better of me.

It was on the road into the east coast city of Vizakhapatnam that my state of mind came to a head, when I came across a road sign that bridged the four-lane highway.

KOLKATA 997KMS

At certain times during my ride through almost every country I had suffered moments of self-doubt or despair caused by something or someone: another rainy day in Europe, my first hill climb, being shoved into a roadside ditch by a passing motorist or struggling into yet another tormenting headwind.

But never had I felt such utter desperation and helplessness as the moment I saw that simple sign. Motivation, an essential tool for the long-distance cyclist, drained out of me. I struggled to imagine getting through another ten days; the notion of pedalling for even another day horrified me. I leaned my bicycle against the signpost, sat down and cried my eyes out, wondering why the hell I had put myself through all this.

I promised myself there and then that I would return to India one day, but that, when I did, it would not be on a bicycle.

YELLOW BRICK ROAD – THE FINAL STRETCH

A banana and peanut butter sandwich has done me well for breakfast most days in India, and it does me well today; the day I hope will take me within spitting distance of Kolkata. Finally, after days in the doldrums, the end is in sight and I am enthusiastic about riding again.

By lunchtime I have covered seventy miles and I consider making a push for India's eastern capital. It will be my longest day in the saddle by far, if I make it. But energy levels are high, fuelled by adrenalin and impatience at finally crossing the Indian subcontinent.

By nightfall I have covered 110 miles; thirty-five to go. I stop in a roadside dhaba and fill myself with my second butter chicken of the day, accompanied by four roti. I remember that I have always struggled on the last leg of various sections of my journey, and tell myself 'Not this time'.

The last two weeks and one thousand kilometres to Kolkata felt like two thousand. I struggled to get back on the bike each morning, India maintaining its ability to confound, frustrate and confuse. One moment I would be down on the country and its people, the next I would think it was the most magical place on earth; the most honest representation of the human spirit. I knew, deep down, that if I could make it to Kolkata with my sanity intact I would cherish the ride there as providing some of the most memorable times of my entire journey.

After my breakdown beneath the signpost to Kolkata, I had given myself a couple of recuperation days in the next town, Vizakhapatnam. On the second of these days, I joined hundreds of locals in a bar watching the final of the cricket World Twenty20, in which Australia were taking on the surprise package of the tournament, England. As the relative inexperience of Paul Collingwood's side began to get the better of the more fancied Australians, the bar grew more raucous and partisan with chants of 'Kevin Pietersen, Kevin Pietersen' echoing on to the streets. As the only Englishman in the place I was the focus of sustained high-fives and congratulatory remarks, which I accepted gratefully, while admitting I had very little to do with the victory.

I don't know how it happened – I must have been followed back to my hotel – but the next morning I was woken at six o'clock by seven members of a West Bengal youth cricket team at my door. They were in town to take on their Andhra

Pradesh counterparts and had heard I was in possession of a Mongoose bat; could they have a look? I felt pretty refreshed after a day off, so joined them for a game of corridor cricket there and then in the hotel. A few other guests must have heard the racket outside their rooms and appeared in the corridor but when I apologised and suggested we stop, they would hear none of it. Instead of complaining to the hotel management they simply either joined in or watched. India's love of cricket, in all its guises, really does know no bounds.

A couple of days later the border crossing into Orissa marked an immediate increase in squalor and poverty as well as a weather shift. Stall-vendors and shopkeepers were forced to work around the clock because if they did not eke out every last rupee they would starve. Litter was strewn everywhere, houses that looked unfinished, but were possibly just rundown, lined the highway in staggering density and unclothed children played in puddles of mud formed by the arrival of rain. I compared my despair with that of the people of Orissa, ordered myself to toughen up and pedalled on.

Rain lashed down on the road into Berhampur and I arrived a sodden wreck. While I was eating a man with a pencil moustache, in a suit, approached and told me that his fiancée had never spoken to a foreigner before and that he was sure she would 'be honoured' to meet me. 'Sure, where is she,' I asked. 'She is upstairs. We are getting married in one hour and her mother and sisters are making sure she is prepared,' the man replied.

The man's brother took me upstairs and I spent the next twenty minutes chatting with his wife-to-be, beautifully clothed in traditional Hindu dress, through the interpretive skills of one of her sisters. I expect the wedding went on for most of the night but I passed out shortly after demolishing a goat biryani, so heard nothing.

A week later, with Kolkata in my sights just 250 miles to the north, the end of one day brought me to a large, Gothic-style building on top of a rare hill. As I passed its long, tree-lined driveway a man ran towards me, pursued by ten or fifteen young kids. When they reached me they grabbed my bicycle, wheeled it to the front door of the building and bombarded me with questions about who I was and where I had come from, and whether they could have a go with my Mongoose bat. The Mongoose bat continued to enthrall.

It was an orphanage for 250 boys and girls, set up ten years earlier to help cope with the aftermath of a devastating earthquake that killed hundreds of people in the region. Most of the kids were away, visiting distant members of their families for the weekend. The twenty or so who remained had absolutely no one willing or able to take them for a few days. After a game of cricket on a stark, windswept hilltop, I put a slideshow with photos of my journey together and, on the only computer in the 'Technology Lab', spoke to them about the places I had cycled through. All they were interested in was where I had played cricket, and whether I would give them my Mongoose. I did, as a matter of fact.

Now, with twenty miles to go until I reached Kolkata, the traffic built up and the highway widened. The stifling humidity relented with the arrival of a welcome downpour. My legs that had served me so well – increasingly so – propelled me forwards; my shoulders were hunched, mind focused on nothing but Elton John's *Greatest Hits* playing on my iPod. It was the only album I had had for the entire Indian leg. 'Bloody "Nikita",' I mumbled, 'sod your fucking "Yellow Brick Road".'

Car, motorcycle, truck and rickshaw horns – the other enduring soundtrack to my ride across the subcontinent – blared, but now I smiled when I heard them because I knew it would not be for much longer. Swarms of yellow Kolkatan taxis and beaten-up, lurching buses surrounded me as I scoured the road for spaces to squeeze through, weaving my way past miles of near-stationary traffic; nearly there.

By the time I reached the Hooghly River in central Kolkata my odometer told me I had ridden 145 miles and the tears came, each one a reminder of all that India had given me and had made me endure. I was surprised that I had made it, both alive and with my mind relatively intact and I leaned back to enjoy the raindrops on my face as I pedalled down dimly lit Sudder Street. I could not have been happier to be back in a big city. I had made it.

LAUGHTER, ELECTIONS & CORRIDOR CRICKET

László, ever keen to build on his film project, had come up with more cricket-loving, film-making enthusiasts for me to hang out with in Kolkata. I arranged to meet them in a Parisian-style café on Park Street on my first morning and found a group of bright young students in their late teens and early twenties: Antoreep, Deeptesh, Deeptarko and the beautiful Ritu and Sanjana. Over the course of my stay they helped me fill up my newly concave stomach with pizza, pancakes and Marmite on toast. I drank beer and ate steak, for the first time in weeks, in a dingy bar called Oly Pub and cheered with other diners as the resident rat – 'Oly Rat' – ran around the room. We watched England's batsmen hit a weak Bangladesh team all over the park. We also explored their favourite corners of a city that, despite the multitude of differences, I found to be strangely similar to London. I think it was the green open spaces that made me feel quite at home, as well as slightly homesick.

It was great to spend time with locals, something I always enjoyed doing in a new city. They were passionate about film, cricket and about their city, and gave the impression of believing there were never enough hours in the day to study, earn money and develop their other sporting or artistic interests. Antoreep, especially, frequently worked through the night on one film project or another. Life and passion oozed out of them, just as it does from most Indians. Perhaps it is a symptom of the circumstances of everyday life there.

For so much of the past few weeks I had been unable to take a step back from all that India had thrown at me and laugh.

It was a feeling I was not used to, so when my new film-making friends offered me the opportunity to put things straight I jumped at the chance.

It was five o'clock on a Sunday morning when a knock at the door woke me. This time, unlike so often in India, it was a welcome alarm. As condensation ran down the walls of my windowless, airless room and on to my already sodden pillow, I quickly dressed and joined my new friends for the short journey to south Kolkata.

Unusually for India, there was little sign of life on the streets. Activity barely ever stops in any Indian city but that day was an exception because it was West Bengali election day and local people had been advised to leave home only to cast their votes.

The journey was therefore virtually traffic-free and half an hour later I was standing in a park overlooking a lake as the sun rose above it, holding hands with two Indian octogenarians in fluorescent leisurewear. The city's younger urban elite walked, ran, cycled and roller-bladed past, flexing their muscles in sleeveless tops and listening to iPods strapped to their arms. But this was not for us. After performing a series of yogic stretches, we had formed a circle with several other Indian men, all in their later years. Then, still holding hands, the elderly men and I bent double before rising up in unison, lifting our hands above our heads and letting out forced laughter that lasted several seconds. 'Ha, ha, ha, ho, ho, ho, ha, ha, ha, ho, ho, ho!'

Dr Madan Kataria, a Mumbai physician, invented Laughter Yoga in the mid-1990s. He believed that if you increase the amount of oxygen in your body through light enjoyment, changes in the physiology of your body occur so that you start to feel happier. There are now Laughter Clubs all over India, and about six thousand in more than sixty countries around the world. It is done in groups because eye contact with someone who is willing to laugh supposedly multiplies the effect.

At the end of two months' pedalling across India I needed

all the happiness and laughter I could get and I was amazed that it seemed to work. The laughter may have been forced at first, but after a while my octogenarian friends and I were rolling about in genuine hysterics. I promised myself I would seek out a Laughter Club if I returned to life in London and use it as a way of combating the stresses of the city.

In the Indian subcontinent's endless search for spiritual answers to everyday issues, I could not help thinking that Laughter Club was one of the more sensible approaches. The name of Dr Kataria's book, *Laugh for No Reason*, seemed to sum up my morning's activities quite nicely and on the drive back to Kolkata I felt the mood that had engulfed me for weeks begin to lift.

I needed to be in a more positive frame of mind for my afternoon's activity because a journalist from the *Calcutta Telegraph* had called to ask me for a foreigner's take on Kolkata on election day. We toured the city, from commercial Park Street to New Market, me on my bicycle and the journalist, Poulomi Banerjee, in her car. Apart from hordes of policemen, the streets were still deserted. Bunting put up by the various political parties hung from street lamps and trees on every street. Cycling was, for once in an Indian city, a pleasant pastime.

The Indian Communist Party had ruled West Bengal for decades but by the time Poulomi and I turned up at one of their polling booths, the faces of their party members suggested they knew they were on the way out.

So I thought I would try to cheer them up. I told them all about my morning spent laughing with a bunch of old people and suggested that, because it had done me some good, it might work for them, too. We began a series of yogic stretches and before long I was rolling about laughing for the second time in just a few hours, on this occasion accompanied by a handful of communists.

Their loss in the election was announced the next morning, but I was pleased to have been able to give them some joy during what I expect was an otherwise miserable few days.

I had to be out of India by 1 June, two days hence, as my visa was due to expire, but it seemed only right that I should squeeze in a game of cricket before heading for the Bangladeshi border, a day away.

Jadavpur University is one of India's finest academic establishments and, I was told, also home to one of Kolkata's most celebrated cricketing tournaments: the Jadavpur University Inter-Faculty Corridor Cricket Championships. The Championships, sadly, had just ended, with Antoreep having scooped the 'Best Batsman' award for the second year in a row. (No wonder he was eager to show me the famous corridors.) Still, he assured me there would be cricket.

When we arrived there was nothing happening. Students were lazing about on the grass in any patch of shade they could find (I felt like telling them how lucky they were) and cricket seemed to be the last thing on anyone's mind. But a word with Antoreep's English tutor set the wheels in motion and within ten minutes there were tens of students – male and female – gathered in the English Literature corridor – conveniently about the width of a cricket wicket – chatting excitedly about batting orders and bowling tactics.

I can safely say that I have never watched or taken part in a more fiercely contested, competitive game of cricket in my life. Batsmen raged when they were given out (for hitting the ball on to the wall full toss) and bowlers argued with calls of no-ball or wide. If I had expected some leniency as a result of my status as a visiting Englishman I was to be sorely disappointed. I was given out first ball, leg before wicket. I fared better when we bowled but was unable to help the English Literature faculty defeat their bitter rivals, the Engineering Faculty, and my team-mates and I loped off for a barely earned Tibetan curry.

It was a fitting climax to India, a country that had nearly broken me. Stinking rich and hopelessly poor; welcoming and daunting; noble and immoral; good fun, rewarding and endlessly frustrating; but there was always cricket.

I hoped that my onward journey, first into Bangladesh

and then through South-East Asia, would give me some respite from the daily grind I had faced crossing the subcontinent; as it turned out, I was to be sorely disappointed.

Antoreep batting in the corridors of Jadavpur University.

BANGLADESH

I T TOOK ME four days to reach the Bangladeshi capital, Dhaka, from Kolkata. My first impressions of this new country were twofold; there were more mosques – Bangladesh being a predominantly Muslim country – and everywhere seemed to be flooded. I put the latter down partly to Bangladesh's position as one of the world's lowest lying countries, and partly to the monsoon. It had well and truly arrived and I found myself wheeling my bicycle in and out of low wooden shelters at regular intervals, to be stared at by bearded strangers who probably wondered if I was mad. When the rain relented I stopped in sprawling villages to play cricket with local kids whose games were already under way.

In one village, at the edge of a bridge that crossed a small river that formed part of the Ganges delta, a woman in a burkha waved at me so I waved back. I was stationary, glug-

Crowds always formed to watch games of cricket with
even the fewest of competitors.

ging water and taking in the view. The woman crossed the road and, seeing my unbuttoned shirt, slipped a hand inside my cycling shorts and, to my surprise, cupped my crown jewels. I was shocked, but not as shocked as the woman when an old man ran out of the thick bushes behind her waving a stick above his head, shouting something in a local dialect. When she had scarpered the old man calmed down, gathered himself and told me, 'Bad woman, many bad woman here.' I could only guess she was an opportunist prostitute, but thankfully I never did find out.

A sea of Argentinian flags welcomed me into Dhaka itself. With the football World Cup now just around the corner it was clear where Bangladeshi hearts lay. I was met by Chris Austin in Gulshan One, a central commercial district where crumbling factories stood cheek by jowl with modern apartment blocks. I met Chris at a particularly nice house. He was, at the time, country head of the UK Government's Department for International Development (DFID). He also happened to love cricket and, during my two-week stay with him and his family, he introduced me to members of the Bangladesh Cricket Board at the Sher-e-Bangla Cricket Stadium. In an airless boardroom I sweated my way through an hour-long presentation about my ride. Once it was over it felt good to escape; I had not been in a boardroom for months and did not intend to be in one again for a while.

With members of the Bangladesh Cricket Board at the
Sher-e-Bangla Stadium, Dhaka.

Chris also took me to the British High Commission to play squash and tennis, and to the British Club to watch England's opening game of the 2010 World Cup from South Africa. It occurred to me, while watching, that Lindsey, John, Dicky and Duncan would have arrived at the end of their journey by now. Although I was increasingly excited about the road ahead, part of me was envious that they had completed what they set out to do, and would soon be on flights home to loved ones.

It was while Chris and I were watching the match, among a crowd of expats from all over the world, that he tapped me on the shoulder and whispered in my ear, 'I think you're in there, mate.'

I looked at him, confused.

'That blonde, I think she likes you.'

While we were watching the football I had been chatting idly to a Danish girl called Camilla, but until Chris pointed it out it had not even occurred to me that she was attractive; much less that she might fancy me. I had been on the road for so long that cycling and travel had become my life. I had not kissed a girl since leaving home. I had, I began to think, become asexual.

Camilla and I ended up spending a couple of weeks together. I had intended to spend as little time in Dhaka as possible, stopping only to persuade the Burmese authorities to issue me with a visa before pedalling off to the border. But the Burmese Embassy officials refused even to let me through the wrought-iron gates at the front of their compound. As my frustration grew and my indecision about the future of my ride mounted, so I began to like Camilla more and more. The thought of leaving her made me miserable, and I damned the decision I had made to cycle to an event with a scheduled start date. For a few days I buried my head in the sand and pretended that Dhaka was the end of my road. But I knew I could not continue like that, and began looking into viable alternatives.

I wrote a letter to a Burmese cycle tour agent:

10 June 2010
Dear Yan-Naing

I was passed your details by David from the British Foreign Office in Dhaka – I gather you have met him in Burma recently. I am currently in Dhaka, having travelled here by bicycle from London over the past 8 months.

I really want to visit Burma but am unsure about whether I can or not. David thought you might be able to advise me of the current situation. Ideally I would cross into Burma from Bangladesh and cycle all the way down to the border with Thailand at Kawthoung in the south of the country. But I think it will be tricky getting into Myanmar like that, so I thought maybe I can fly to Yangon (where I see you can get a visa on arrival as of last week, which is great!) and then get on my bike and cycle to Kawthoung and cross into Thailand instead. Like I said, I really want to visit your country.

What do you think my options are, if any, and do you know someone who might accompany me, or at least vouch for me, while I am in the country? I am really in a hurry now as I must be in Singapore by the end of July.

Any ideas most welcome.

Kind regards and all the best,
Oli

Four days later I received a reply:

14 June 2010
Dear Mr Broom,

Mingalarbar from Exotissimo Travel Yangon, Burma! ('Have an auspicious day!')

My name is Ye and I am a travel consultant from Direct Sales (TA) department. I have got your below email from our guide, Ko Yan Naing, and I have noted that you would like to make a cycling tour in Burma.

Please be informed that, according to the regulations, foreigners are not allowed to do the road travel from Bangladesh border into the country, as well as from Mawlamyine to Kawthoung Border. The possible way is that you can fly to Yangon, then you can do cycling in permitted area, then you can fly out again from Yangon. Please also note that there is no flight between Bangladesh and Burma. The most convenient flight is via Bangkok as there are several flights daily.

I am looking forward to hearing from you soon.

With best regards and

Kyan Mar Chan Thar Par Sae! (Burmese way of wishing at end of letter 'Be Healthy, Be Rich!')

Ye

My plans to cycle through Burma were dashed. While I could have pedalled around the countryside close to the capital, Yangon, that was not what my journey was about. Besides, the prices offered by Ye were astronomical, and far beyond my budget.

I was gutted, my route interrupted yet again. Chris put me in touch with a man who owned a shipping company and I briefly flirted with the idea of pedalling to the southern Bangladeshi city of Chittagong to catch a boat; but his contact knew of no ships leaving in the coming weeks that I could jump on, or even pay to board and, besides, it would have meant skipping the length of Thailand.

Frustrated, I booked a flight to Chiang Mai, via Bangkok, the next morning – if I was to pedal through Thailand then I would do so from the top – and I prepared myself to leave. I thought of asking Camilla to join me, but she had work to be getting on with and I needed to pedal faster than I had ever done before. I hated saying goodbye to her as she left me outside Chris's house.

THAILAND, MALAYSIA AND INDONESIA

'. . . and I rose up, and knew that I was tired, and continued my journey' – Edward Thomas, *Light and Twilight*

CHIANG MAI RAM

TWO WEEKS IN Bangladesh had given me time and space to prepare my head for the challenge of Thailand. And, in truth, I did not expect it to be one of the toughest legs of my journey. Friends who had been there told me about the easy pace of life and the incredible food, and although I had not arrived the way I intended, I got a sense that I was going to enjoy my time there.

It came as bad news, then, that, on my first morning in Chiang Mai, I felt the first signs of a sore throat and fever. I went to a clinic where a young doctor told me, 'No wuly mister, thloat infection no plobrem', and gave me some antibiotics to cure it. My throat got better but everything else deteriorated and that was how I ended up six days later in a bed in Chiang Mai Ram Hospital, on an intravenous drip with breakbone, or dengue, fever.

A mosquito-borne disease not unlike malaria, it takes two weeks for the symptoms of breakbone to appear and, far more worryingly, three months to disappear. With no specific cure available, I just had to sweat it out and hope that my white blood-cell count would begin to climb. But as I lay in that hospital bed all I could think was that waiting for a full

On a drip in my hospital bed in Chiang Mai.

recovery before pedalling onwards was not an option. The Ashes, the purpose of so many miles undertaken on my bicycle, the result of so much sweat and so many tears, would have been and gone. Could I really keep biking with dengue fever? Or was this the end of the road?

My phone rang. It was Becca, the friend who had first inspired me to cycle to Australia. She was in Bangkok on her way back to England after a year living and working in Sydney and wondered if I wanted some company on the bike over the next couple of weeks. I admitted to her that I was considering quitting; that the doctors had advised me against getting back on the bike even if I did not have to have a blood transfusion, and that there seemed little point in carrying on. But Becca did not let up and promised to get on the next flight to Chiang Mai – if I was well enough to cycle, she would join me; otherwise, she would do her best to make me feel better about the whole sorry episode.

That night I slept straight through and woke feeling physically much better, although my mood was still low. Then a doctor arrived bearing good news. My white blood-cell count was in the safe zone and I would not need a blood transfusion. Better still, I was given the go-ahead to get out of bed for some much-needed fresh air, and to go back to the hostel.

This good news and Becca's phone call flicked a switch in me. I realised that I had been defeatist for too long, telling myself that nobody back home would mind if I quit now because I had made it so far and that, anyway, I could not ride on with dengue fever. *Of course* people would be disappointed in me. More importantly, *I* would be disappointed in me. If my journey to Australia had ever been in doubt, it wasn't any more.

EMACIATED, HOPEFUL

The last time I had seen Becca I was a pasty, overweight chartered surveyor. After nine months on the road and the best part of two weeks in bed, I was now a pasty, emaciated cyclist. When she saw me for the first time in the street outside my hostel, she gasped and told me I could easily have hidden behind a lamppost to surprise her. She looked pleased to see me, though, and I felt glad she was there.

I had not seen much of Chiang Mai, so we wandered the clean, calm streets that were such a contrast to everywhere else I had been over the past months, and along the canal to find somewhere cheap to eat. It felt strange being in the company of a good friend for the first time in eight months. I had got used to being on my own, had learned to appreciate the silence that comes with lone travel; kept thoughts to myself instead of blurting them out to a companion.

Becca asked so many questions about what I had seen and done and how I had felt doing it all alone. But I did not want to answer every question because I felt I could not do justice to all that I had experienced and because, well, the journey was mine. I was not yet ready to share it.

So while I could have told her any number of things I had never told anyone, I kept most of it to myself, stored up for a later date. Instead we spent our first night in Thailand chatting about home and mutual friends over a bowl of pad thai. Lots of people we knew had got engaged or had babies since I'd left home. That felt strange, too; I still could not have felt further from marriage or fatherhood.

In bed that evening, on my last night of fourteen in Chiang

I was painfully thin thanks to the effects of dengue fever.

Mai, I read the final few chapters of a book called *First Overland – London to Singapore by Land Rover*. The author, Tim Slessor, and his five companions were student scientists who made that epic journey in the 1950s, travelling through many of the same countries as I had cycled across. They reached the end in Singapore to a huge media fanfare and the last line of the book reads: 'As an American journalist opined, "I guess you boys have run plumb outta road." We guessed we had. And it was most satisfactory.'

Singapore is the southernmost tip of mainland Asia. I was aiming to ride two thousand miles from Chiang Mai to Singapore and, if I managed it, I guessed I would find it most satisfactory, too; I would have run out of road and my mind would turn to finding an ocean passage to Australia for the final leg of my journey. But on the night before I left Chiang Mai, I was just grateful to be in the company of a friend, to be out of hospital and optimistic that the worst of my illness was behind me.

CLIMBING A MOUNTAIN ON A BICYCLE: PART II

Through forests of teak, we zigzag alongside a churning river, deep within the smooth grey walls of a narrow canyon. A crested serpent eagle soars above us and our progress slows to a snail's pace. Guinea fowl dive in and out of the thick green under-growth, gibbons and macaques swing from vines as they screech eager warnings: TWO CYCLISTS IN THE JUNGLE!

Becca and I had reservations about the road ahead, and they centred on both the route and our physical states. Firstly, I had chosen to ignore conventional wisdom which said 'cycle in a straight line to Bangkok; it will be flat and easy'. Despite my depleted condition I fancied cycling west towards the jungle and mountains bordering Burma in the hope that the ride would be more beautiful, less chaotic and better for the soul. Secondly, neither of us was sure how we would cope with cycling anywhere, let alone up mountains. Becca had not sat on a bicycle for almost a year.

Nevertheless, we aimed to be in Mae Sariang, overlooking Burma, on the morning of 5 July, my thirtieth birthday. That gave us three days to get there. I did not have a clue if I had made the right decision, but I did know I wanted to avoid highways as much as possible. I had ridden enough of those on the subcontinent.

We bought Becca a cheap mountain bike, plundered Chiang Mai's entire stock of mosquito repellent, sun cream and Haribo, and rode west out of town along a tree-lined country lane that would not have been out of place in Provence or the Loire. It was less than twenty-four hours since I had left hospital and, because of the delay in Bangladesh, almost a month since I had pedalled more than a few hundred metres; but as soon as Becca and I began moving, many of the frustrations and fears of the past few weeks disappeared. I had missed movement and the feeling that I was finally advancing towards my destination again sent my spirits soaring. Equally satisfying was the fact that, whereas in Africa and the subcontinent I had been the subject of every gaze, in Thailand nobody seemed to take any notice of us. There were no shouts of 'Muzungu!' or 'Foreigner!'. I briefly wondered if I would eventually miss being the centre of attention but quickly told myself that that was a foolish thought. Becca and I were as anonymous as I had been across Belgium and Germany, and I loved it.

We reached the sedate little town of Chom Thong, a place I would remember for two things: the best strawberry milkshake of the tour and the first hit-and-run accident I had ever seen. As we sat outside a small café sipping our milkshakes, a speeding car ploughed into an old lady on a scooter, sending her skidding across a T-junction. The driver glanced at her briefly before speeding off. No police came but a few locals helped the old lady to her feet, she got back on her scooter and tootled off, blood pouring down her leg, as if nothing had happened.

I may have been happy to be back on the bike, but I found the cycling far from easy. All the work I had done to get fit over the past nine months seemed to have been wasted by two weeks in bed. I was forced to adjust my expectations. Our first day out of Chiang Mai was a fifty-mile day that felt like one hundred and fifty, but just as I had done at the very start of my ride, Becca and I set ourselves ridiculously small four- and eight-mile goals to achieve. When we reached each one, we rewarded ourselves with a Haribo and a roadside break.

Despite being conscious of drinking plenty of water, I often felt faint, my mouth parched. I regularly took time out to sit by the side of the road, glugging water and eating peanut butter and jam sandwiches. I wondered if my body was telling me it was not ready to be back on the bike for hours each day. It would not have surprised me. I still weighed only sixty-eight kilograms and just a couple of days earlier had been on an intravenous drip.

When we reached Ob Luang ('Grand Canyon') National

Park the road steepened and we decided we did not have the energy to attack the climb that day. Near sunset we took the opportunity to camp on a rare patch of grass beside a narrow canyon, overlooking the river. Fireflies lit up our camping spot as we ate a bowl of burnt noodles and onions. I had lived with Becca for three years in London; I should have known better than to let her cook for me again.

All night the tent was pounded by heavy rain and we dripped with sweat inside. The following morning it was time to tackle the climb.

'My heart feels like it's about to explode out of my temples,' Becca remarked as she inched her way up the steepest section of road either of us had ever seen, let alone cycled. Her heart did not explode, though, and we ploughed on through Ob Luang National Park. It was the closest she came to complaining all day, and I took much-needed strength from her no-nonsense approach. She often pedalled several hundred metres ahead of me, spurring me on. I knew that, if it were *my* first big hill climb, I would not be in such high spirits. If, throughout the day, she had turned to me and asked why the hell she had chosen to cycle with me, I would have forgiven her. She had already let slip that, had she not come to see me she would have spent these two weeks partying on a sublime beach in Indonesia with a bunch of Swedish friends, before flying home. I knew which option I would have taken, given the choice.

But we reminded ourselves how lucky we were to be there, despite the sweat and the pain and the effort that it was demanding of us; certainly I preferred climbing in the heat to doing it in the snow. But further into the climb we began to care little for the macaques and the guinea fowl and the eagles, our enthusiasm dampened into submission by exhaustion and confusion. Sometimes the gradient was so steep that – despite the fact that they were loaded down with ten kilograms of kit in each pannier – I could not cycle without my front wheels rearing sharply off the ground and I had to be content with pushing the bike for the first time since Kent. That was a struggle, too, my open sandals slipping as I hauled my heavy bicycle higher and higher.

Climbing in the mountains of northern Thailand
meant every corner offered spectacular views.

'How can we still be climbing?' I wondered aloud, peering upwards and ahead and seeing nothing but deep blue sky. 'Fucking hills, end will you?' I remembered the same feeling climbing the Petrohan Pass into Sofia and was reminded that hills play nasty tricks on a man on a bike, each bend disguising itself as the last.

There were no cars to encourage us as there had been in Bulgaria; just the odd woman on the verge, carrying on her head a bucket full of water or a basket of fruit. They did not offer encouragement, but stared blankly at us as we passed. To urge my legs to keep pumping away I imagined myself as a character in *Butch Cassidy and the Sundance Kid*. There is a sequence in the film when the infamous outlaws are being tracked on horseback but they are unable to lose their pursuers. Paul Newman's Butch, eyes fixed on the menacing figures fast approaching, turns to Robert Redford's Sundance and says something like 'There's no way I could do that, could you? Who are those guys?' It is the moment in the film when we begin to doubt if the pair will ever make it to their Bolivian bank robbing nirvana.

Of course, I wasn't robbing banks and I was no outlaw, but perhaps because I had been alone in the wild too long I found it fun to imagine the women were thinking the same as Butch and Sundance as I passed, wondering who I was and where I had come from.

Two hours of climbing became three, then four, and we were caked in sweat that, although uncomfortable, at least kept us cool in the stifling humidity. We needed a storm, that's what we needed, but it didn't come.

Eventually, after seven hours in the saddle and half an hour for leftover burnt noodles, we reached the clouds and the summit was in sight. Still climbing, pain dissipated as our minds came to grips with the fact that we had as good as made it. It would have been the toughest climb of my life but for the camaraderie brought by the company of a good friend.

Finally, we stood at the summit, gazing through occasional clouds at the creased mountain range swathed in thick jungle. There, in front of us, lay Burma. I cursed the Burmese authorities again for not even agreeing to meet with me in Dhaka but was pleased that, although I had not been permitted access to ride across, I had at least seen it.

And we were further rewarded for our efforts. The rest of the ride was easy, a twenty-two-kilometre descent of mind-boggling beauty with views of Burma that came and went as the jungle thickened and then opened out, and eventually we arrived in the beautifully scenic frontier town of Mae Sariang. Three days in and I was coping all right.

BURMA AT THIRTY

Diary entry, 5 July 2010, Mae Sariang

I always imagined enjoying my thirtieth birthday with friends at home, reminiscing about the good old days. Oh well, what's a birthday if it's not a reminder to grab every opportunity thrown your way and be sure you make of it the best you can. I'm thirty.

I remember being eighteen like it was yesterday. I'll drink with friends next year, and the year after. For now, I'm happy celebrating with the freedom of the road.

We took a day off today. An old bloke sat cleaning his bicycle in the entrance to the café where we had lunch. Syd, an Australian from Adelaide doing a year-long tour of South-East Asia. I asked him where he was headed and he said, 'Nowhere really'. Not sure I could travel like that, so directionless. I suppose I admire him for being able to get on the bike every day though, without a specific goal.

I tried to talk cricket with him but he wasn't interested. He asked if he could join us tomorrow, didn't mind which way we are going. So from tomorrow we are three, at least for a bit.

The next morning was typically hot and humid, although I found neither nearly as problematic as I had in India. There was little traffic and few people, so we had space and time to ourselves at the beginning of the five-day ride to Mae Sot.

We pedalled a road that ran parallel to a murky brown river, both threading their way like filaments south through lush valleys of paddy fields and jungle, bringing water and life to all they touched. On the other side of the river lay Burma, vines clinging to the vertical granite cliffs as they soared eighty metres out of the water.

The landscape was different on our side; less wild, with a smooth tarmac road and any encroaching vegetation clipped back so as not to damage passing traffic. It seemed to be a decent metaphor for the immense differences between life for those on one side of the river and those on the other. In a small wooden café – where the toilet was in a bathroom and the bath had seven catfish swimming about in it – I asked the owner if he had ever been to Burma. He had not, yet his house was positioned at a particularly narrow section of river, no more than twenty metres from Burmese territory.

Our side of the river offered gentle, rolling hills which we climbed out of our saddles to tackle, and enjoyed freewheeling down the other side. Syd often rode ahead, more efficient in everything he did; a result of tens of years of taking himself off to the world's wild places and cycling on his own. I had rarely studied the movement of another long-distance cyclist, but it struck me how differently he did everything: from pedalling to map reading, storing his food and water to his riding position; the cadence he maintained in his technique up hills. I felt envious of the ease with which he seemed to do it all. Syd and his bicycle appeared to be one efficient, smooth-running machine.

Zig-zagging my way up another Thai hillside while Syd is already pushing.

'Is that how I look on a bicycle, Becca?' I asked, as Syd slid effortlessly up another hill.

'No way, you make it look much harder,' came her honest response, and it occurred to me that perhaps I was not a very good long-distance cyclist after all.

That same afternoon Becca noticed an old man in a conical hat tending to his rice field. We pointed ahead and asked him if we could expect easy riding on our onward journey.

More uphill? Becca can't hide her disappointment.

Taunting Australian Syd: 'You're not getting your hands on the Ashes, mate!'

'Oh yeeaaaaa, vely frat all way to Mae Sot now my fliends. Good ruck, enjoy!'

ENCOUNTER WITH A BEARDED LEFT-ARM SPINNER

'Oli Broom? Is that Oli Broom?'

I peer across at the man on the computer next to me, the skin on his face barely visible beneath a veneer of thick, matted hair. I do not have a clue who he is.

'Still tweaking it?' asks the beard, his left wrist rotating clockwise and back.

I stare into his eyes, but still nothing.

'Your left-arm spin. How is it these days?'

We both laugh.

'Terrible,' I reply.

'Mine too,' admits the beard.

I am in Mae Sot on the Thai–Burmese border. I know no one here and it is unsettling to look this camouflaged man directly in the eye, knowing he knows who I am, and being so utterly clueless about his identity.

Three days earlier Syd, Becca and I were enduring further punishment in the hills, despite the rice farmer's promise; up, up and up through dense jungle. By the time we summited six hours later I felt incredibly weak. I was sweating and shivering, despite the heat. I had been struggling to keep up with my two companions for days, was still unable to put on weight and often felt faint and dizzy.

I worried about the road ahead. To pedal long distances and climb hills you have to be positive and brave. As I thought ahead to 150 more days in the saddle I found it hard to be either of those things. Although the Ashes were approaching fast, I could not envisage the completion of my journey. I doubted whether I had the energy or inclination to keep on pedalling.

Becca's company, and particularly her positivity at the start

Pedalling the Thai–Burmese border.

of each day and during the long climbs, was all that had kept me going since Chiang Mai. I had come to rely on her, and that was not a healthy state to be in since she would be leaving me in Mae Sot. I tried to persuade myself that it was easier for Becca to be confident and upbeat in the mountains. In just a few days' time the pain she felt as she climbed would be long forgotten as she reminisced with friends over a few vodka and Diet Cokes in a London bar. She would be home.

As we rode the final miles into Mae Sot, huge refugee camps lined the road at intervals. Tuk-tuks whizzed past us and men in blue boiler suits waved laconically. Forty thousand people lived in the largest camp, a seemingly endless hotch-potch of bamboo huts and dusty lanes covering low hills in a narrow, lush valley on the Thai side of the river.

It felt great to arrive in Mae Sot, although the following morning I was sad to say goodbye to my latest cycling companion. Seeking comfort after her departure, I went to the only internet café in town and began my latest blog: *Big Ole Mountains Round Here*. That is when I heard the strangely familiar voice . . .

I racked my brain as to who it could be. Still nothing. The only left-arm spinner I knew with such impressive facial growth – and I only knew him off the telly – was the former New Zealand cricket captain Danny Vettori, and I considered that he was unlikely to be holed up in a town near the Burmese border.

'I still can't figure out how you know me, I'm sorry,' I explained to the beard.

'Sheffield . . . 2002?'

And then it struck me. Surely not?

'Baggers? Is that you under there? Really?'

'Sure is!'

And we rose from our respective seats and gave each other a warm, hearty bear hug. The last time we'd seen each other was seven years before when we had played together in the Durham University Combined Colleges team that won the British Universities Championships in Sheffield. Chris Bagley, or Baggers, was our secret weapon. He had been drafted into the Worcestershire Academy at the age of sixteen, managed a few second-team games and the occasional run-out for Herefordshire in the Minor Counties League before heading off to Durham where he was selected for the university's Centre of Excellence. After only a year he had been chucked out for not turning up enough; and when he had turned up he'd had 'the yips'.* After a year off, he had joined our team and it turned out he was far too good for most of our opponents, so he helped us win fairly often.

Baggers was also known for being able to talk himself out of tight corners, which turned out to be a blessing because, when I met him in Mae Sot, he had just talked his way out of

---

* 'The yips' is a common and sudden, unexplained, loss of a previous skill acquired, particularly in sport. In cricket it applies mostly to bowlers and seems predominantly to affect left-arm spinners. Bowlers have trouble releasing the ball at the end of their action.

being illegally inside one of the most repressive regimes in the world. He told me he had sneaked into Burma without the authorities finding out, explored for a few days, sneaked back into Thailand, and was heading to Bangkok later that evening.

Hearing about his adventures in Burma made me all the more angry at not having made it there myself. It felt so frustrating being so close, yet unable to go and take a look. I had been particularly keen to visit because I had not yet managed any cricket in South-East Asia and I knew that the country was – or at least once had been – a hotbed of cricketing activity. It was, after all, a British colony for more than sixty years at the height of Victorian cricketing expansionism.

In 1926–27, more than twenty years before Burma's long struggle for independence from Britain came to pass, MCC toured the country, playing two first-class matches against the Rangoon Gymkhana and an All Burma XI. But since the British were ousted in 1948, cricket has died a slow death in the country, as it has in other parts of South-East Asia. Between 1988 and 1995 there was no cricket there at all, and because of the country's well-documented political instability it may be some time before MCC makes the decision to tour again.

Still, who needs the world's most famous cricket club? Now, led by one of Burma's most famous movie stars – sixty-five-year-old Nyunt Win – cricket is enjoying something of a revival. Australian expats developed the country's first permanent grass wicket in 2003 and in 2006, after a visit from the International Cricket Council, the country was made an Affiliate Member of cricket's world governing body. By all accounts children in schools in Yangon and Mandalay are now being introduced to the game by enthusiastic expats and ever-keener locals. It struck me as a rare positive story about Burma, and one that I had been eager to explore.

Not so positive was Burma's first appearance in an ICC competition. Shortly after they were admitted as the body's ninety-seventh member, Burma's national team travelled to Kuala Lumpur to play in the Asian Cricket Council Trophy, where they suffered one of the heaviest defeats ever recorded on a cricket field: they were bowled out for ten runs (including five extras), before the opposition, low-lying – in cricketing terms – Nepal, took just two deliveries to reach their target. The Burmese opening bowler bowled five wide balls before his second legal delivery was hit for three to bring the mismatch to an abrupt end. The next day Burma did slightly better – they were bowled out for twenty against Hong Kong.

Baggers and I chatted cricket and travelling over a beer in town before he decided to cancel his plan to head to Bangkok that evening and continue drinking with me instead. We ended up in a bar with a former Burmese freedom fighter and student ally of Aung San Suu Kyi who had been released from a twenty-year stint in prison just a couple of months earlier and seemed to have since developed a penchant for Thai prostitutes. When he began trying to persuade us to join him we politely declined. On the way back to our respective hostels we rode three-on-a-motorbike and ended up crashing into the outdoor dining area of a packed restaurant. My leg was badly grazed, my hip bruised, and it delayed my departure from Mae Sot for two days. Still, Baggers was barely able to move either, so we enjoyed hanging out a little while longer.

HIGHWAYS, NOT HIGHLIGHTS

When I eventually managed to tackle it, the climb out of Mae Sot was horrendous. I wished I had Becca with me to spur me on, but I made it and, once it was over, the ride through Thailand was far less taxing. Out of the mountains I rode flat highways through endless paddy fields and a staggering number of building sites – in fact, the whole of central Thailand seemed to be one big building site. In an attempt to put on some much-needed weight, I ate huge amounts of food at clean roadside cafés where I was served quickly and without fuss. One bowl of pad thai was never enough. I ordered two, three, sometimes four, and got some funny looks. But eventually my tactic, combined with the fact that

I was no longer dragging myself up mountains on a bicycle, began to work. By the time I reached the highway town of Khlong Khlung I weighed seventy-two kilograms: still underweight, but not ridiculously so.

Riding became easier. I found myself able to spend longer days in the saddle and, somewhat perversely, my energy levels soared. Although I still did not feel quite myself – I had not felt so good since about halfway across India – I welcomed the change, taking on huge ninety-, one-hundred-, one-hundred-and-ten-mile days – sailing down perfectly maintained bitumen highways with wide hard shoulders. Days went by in a blur of 7 Elevens – my favourite places to stop for a blast of air-conditioned bliss although I rarely bought anything from them.

But eventually I got bored. Central Thailand, in particular, did not win me over. Cycle touring was not meant to be so easy. After three weeks in the country I found myself yearning to be elsewhere. Some days I wanted cold winds and snow that I could wrap up against. I was fed up with being hot and sweaty all the time. But on others I wanted to be back in India. I seemed to have forgotten the maddening times, the pain and suffering that the place had forced me to endure. I remembered only the good bits; the kindness, the fascinating, astonishing sights and sounds at every turn.

In the corner of one paddy field outside Nakhon Sawan I set up camp at the end of the day and took a call from Dan on *Test Match Sofa* (an alternative cricket commentary show) during an England versus Pakistan Test match. While the England team was busy wrapping up a 3-1 series victory – good preparation for the Ashes – I surprised myself by talking about how much I missed India. When I hung up I considered for the first time that I would like to return there to cycle again one day. After all I had been through, I could not fathom why.

Further south, Kanchanaburi was a rare highlight and I became a tourist for the day, visiting the bridge over the River Kwai and playing backgammon with backpackers on the South-East Asia tourist trail. Before I left town I bought a hundred new albums for $15, from a dodgy Thai man in a dark shed off the main street. The Smiths, Lou Reed, Josh Ritter, Chuck Berry, The Strokes, 12th Man, Johnny Cash, Devendra Banhart, King Creosote, Leonard Cohen, Neil Young, Manu Chao, Ryan Adams, Wolf Parade and the Royal Philharmonic Orchestra. They would provide the soundtrack to the rest of my ride. I was just pleased to have some music other than Elton John.

On and on I pedalled; 7 Elevens; highways; pad thai. Locals were all friendly enough, but utterly uninterested in saying more than hello. Even the weather was predictable: the sun shone until mid-afternoon, then storms rolled in every day at four o'clock and I made sure I was near shelter. In Hua Hin I stayed with the Scottish family of a man I had met in Bangladesh. I walked the main drag and was sickened by all the sex tourists, prostitutes and late-middle-aged Europeans with Thai girls on each arm.

I was pleased when I crossed the border into Malaysia, my twentieth country, and continued putting in huge days. Little inspired me enough to make me look up from my handlebars and take notice. The speed at which I tackled the highways of South-East Asia gave me a fighting chance of making it to Brisbane on time after the delays of the past few months, but I did not enjoy them. I was just pedalling furiously, desperate to run out of road in Singapore and determined to finish this last chunk of my Asian leg as quickly as possible.

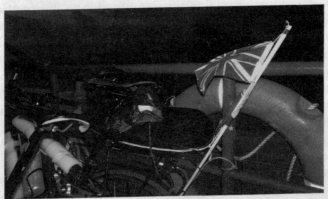

A Brit on the way to Malaysia. I caught the boat from Satun to Langkawi.

As I got within a few days of Johor Bahru, the gateway to Malaysia, I began to feel ill again. Camping out in a police station forecourt one night, I woke up in a cold sweat. The following day every bone in my body ached and however much water I drank my mouth remained parched. I thought I might have dengue fever again; but I could not afford to hang around to find out, so I pushed on.

I felt equally bad at the beginning of my last day in Malaysia, but towards the middle of the day adrenalin must have kicked in because, with a huge tailwind at my back, I tore through mile after mile. I managed 140 miles that day, not far off the personal record I had set into Kolkata. I arrived a wreck and slept for sixteen hours on the floor of an otherwise empty hostel dormitory because the mattress springs dug into my ribs. It had been tough getting there but I was a step closer to the Ashes and, besides, I had a cricketing date to keep.

A team from the Singapore Cricket Club was in town on a two-day tour, playing against a couple of local sides. I had been asked to take to the field the following day against Malacca. I staggered out of bed, grabbed my cricket bat and rode my bicycle to their hotel. The team were in blazers and chinos when they climbed on to the tour bus. I felt like a vagabond; looked like one, too. In the changing room before the game I was asked by the captain to give a short motivational speech. I felt uncomfortable doing so, and even more uncomfortable half an hour later when I returned from the crease after suffering my second golden duck of the tour. For my ineptitude, after the game I was made to drink beer out of a particularly sweaty and hairy team-member's box. I washed it down with a couple more from a pint glass.

During my few days in Singapore I enjoyed the city's botanical gardens (always a first stop for any self-respecting Englishman in a world city) and tasted Little India (which made me miss the real thing even more). On my last morning I cycled to the most southerly point of mainland Asia and stared out at the Strait of Malacca. I remembered the last

Post-match celebrations: first drink of the night, from a sweaty box.

line in Tim Slessor's book and felt proud that I, too, had run plumb outta road.

But Singapore was not my last stop in South-East Asia. Although I was ready to tackle Australia's remote outback, I had one more cricketing appointment to keep, and, on 6 September, I caught a boat out of Singapore harbour, bound for Jakarta.

BALDY'S OVAL

22 October 2009
Dear Oli

I am writing on behalf of the East Indies Cricket team. We are based in Bogor, 40 kilometres south of Jakarta in Java. This is our website.

www.eastindiescricket.blogspot.com

I have read about your epic journey and we are proud to offer you honorary membership of our club. We would be delighted to entertain you and arrange a friendly fixture next year to fit your schedule.

We are associated with Bogor cricket, which is training local players here to a good and improving standard, with recent on-site assistance from former international cricketers Chris Cairns and Graham Yallop. We would aim to involve some of these local Indonesian cricketers in the game.

We play at a ground in the Java mountains that was featured in Wisden Cricketer *in 2007. This ground is currently being expanded and developed ready for 2010.*

Please let me know if you are interested. With best wishes for your trek!

Will Symonds
Skipper – East Indies Cricket

The email arrived just twelve days after I had cycled out of Lord's at the beginning of my journey. At the time I was delighted, partly because it showed there was some enthusiasm for my cricketing odyssey, but also because the ground looked so incredibly beautiful. I wrote back to Will, promising to visit, and was pleased a year later when I was able to stick to my end of the bargain.

I arrived in Jakarta on 7 September 2010. One night in the city was enough to persuade me to head for the hills, specifically to the former Dutch and British colonial city of Bogor, forty miles south of Indonesia's capital. The ride only took me a day, though the staggering density of development and traffic meant that, despite the startling mountains, it was one of the most terrifying rides of my entire journey.

Still, I made it to a beautiful house in a leafy suburb of Bogor, where Will lived with his Indonesian wife and their two children. The game was due to take place a couple of days later so I spent the following day exploring the botanical gardens, which I considered to be the best I had seen anywhere in the world; better even than Singapore's.

On the morning of the cricket match the Muslim festival Idul Fitri, celebrated at the end of Ramadan, was in full swing. It seemed to bring everybody out on to the streets and the noise and colour were extraordinary, even as Will and I drove deeper into the Java mountains. After about an hour on the road it started raining. 'We'd better call Baldy, see what the track is like,' Will suggested.

Robert 'Baldy' Baldwin was the proprietor of the cricket oval we were due to play at. He had moved from his native New Zealand to Indonesia in the 1970s and, deciding that he missed cricket, had got involved in the burgeoning Indonesian scene. In 2006 he started developing cricket leagues for Bogor schoolchildren and now had more than twenty schools involved.

When he built a house in the hills south of Bogor, complete with a few hectares of land, he carved off the top of a mountain and, by all accounts, created one of the most attractive cricket grounds in the world. Each year he brought a former Test cricketer to Bogor to coach some of the more talented kids. In 2009 Graham Yallop, the former Australian Test captain, visited. He came again in May 2010 to formally open the ground, alongside former Test players Glenn McGrath, Robin Smith, Nantie Hayward and Chris Cairns. Baldy sounded like a great bloke and I could not wait to meet him.

'Baldy, it's raining. What's it like up in Pancawati?' Will asked.

Baldy said it was fine, but that rain was forecast, so we'd better hurry. The 'track' that Will was worried about was not the wicket, as I had thought, but the dirt road that led to the ground. Apparently it was impassable once rain got to it. When we reached the final section of road leading to the ground, I saw the problem. It was red clay and steep as hell. Although the government were due to pave it in the coming weeks, for now we had to tackle it as was. Even in a 4x4 in the dry it took us four attempts to reach the top; but what a reward we had when we did finally summit the hill.

The Pancawati Oval sat perched on top of a mountain, high above the almost sheer walls of a narrow, verdant gorge. In the distance, some of Java's highest volcanoes rose above a jungle plain. A two-storey wooden pavilion stood beyond the gorge fifty metres from the boundary edge. The walk from the pavilion to the ground took a good five minutes, although Will told me Baldy planned to recruit some local miracle-workers to build a bamboo bridge across the gorge one day, a task that would surely result in the most stunning, and terrifying, walk to any cricket outfield in the world. The whole site had to be seen to be believed.

The Pancawati Oval, the most beautiful cricket ground in the world?

When twenty-two players had arrived, the game got going. It was between a Jakarta side made up of a few expatriate businessmen and some local players, and a Pancawati XI made up of exactly the same, plus me. We batted first, and I was given the opportunity to open the innings. While I was batting I was joined at the crease by an Australian. 'Dick Slaney's the name, mate. Long way to ride a pushie to watch ya team get beat, but good on ya for givin' it a go. Your arse must be a bloody mess, mind you.' Dick's lazy drawl betrayed a life spent in the Australian outback; Charters Towers in Queensland I later learned. I liked him immediately, although I had to tell him that I had had no problems with my arse since leaving England.

We batted together for a while, chatting between overs about everything but the game we were playing. At the end of one over I happened to mention that I was still trying to figure out a way to get to Australia because I did not want to use another aeroplane. It turned out that Dick was the country head of one of Australia's largest exporters of livestock. He immediately promised to try to sort out a passage on one of their ships going back to Darwin.

'It's the least I can bloody do for a fucken crazy Pommie bastard,' he said as he wandered back to his crease. 'The ships always go back home bloody empty to give the crew a few days to clean up the shit of thousands'a filthy beasts. There's gotta be room for a Pom and a pushie.'

I thanked Dick, and said that if he could not manage to sort it, then no worries.

The rain held off until the final few overs of the game, with the Jakartans needing more than twenty runs an over to win. But the heavens unleashed hell on that cricket ground for more than an hour and when the sun eventually broke through again play was quite rightly deemed out of the question. Most of the players agreed that a rain-affected draw was a suitable end to a game that was arranged in honour of an Englishman.

Cricket has always attracted eccentrics and enthusiasts, more than any other sport, perhaps because it is such an acquired taste. To sit and watch a ball being thrown and hit about a field for hours on end – days on end, even – is not everyone's cup of tea. Cricket lovers like it that way; they are happy with their status. And Baldy, if not an eccentric himself, certainly had an eccentric vision. Eating barbecued steak in the pavilion after the game had been called off, I watched the black clouds roll off over the volcanoes and out of sight. It was my last game of cricket in Asia, and what a fitting end; I could not believe that there was a more unexpected or more beautiful cricket ground anywhere in the world.

A couple of days later Dick invited me for steak and Bundaberg rum at his house in Jakarta. He had managed to secure my free passage to Australia. I could not have been more grateful; there would be a pleasing symmetry to the end of my journey because, just as my first border crossing had been made by boat all those months earlier, so my final international border crossing would be over water, too.

FOURTH INNINGS

AUSTRALIA

'Aussies are big and empty, just like their country'
– Ian Botham

'It is the journey, not the arrival, which matters'
– Montaigne

> 'I'm a ringer from the Top End, where ya gotta muster
>   three thousand head in a day
> Move 'em to the yards and water them at end of day
> It's not the sort of job you'd take if you're looking for a
>   soft one
> But ya take a kinda pride in saying, 'I'm a ringer from the
>   Top End' – Slim Dusty, 'Ringer from the Top End'

FINOLA

I wake at dawn on 22 September to a disconcerting sight. As my eyes adjust to the bright light pouring through the porthole above my head, I see that my belongings, rather than being strewn across the room as they have been each morning for the past week, are organised as I left them last night. My two large panniers are still beside me, acting as a makeshift bedside table, with my phone and book on top; my cricket bat is still wedging the door shut and my clothes are neatly folded on the shelves above the desk, my laptop open below. There is no lurching, no pounding of twenty-foot waves against the ship's hull, but a gentle rolling motion more akin to a Thames river cruise. A muffled voice travels from the corridor, but it seems to be a one-sided conversation; is he on his mobile phone, I wonder? I reach for mine and see that eighty-two new emails and seven voicemail messages have arrived, all from the past week. I jump out of bed and peer out of the porthole to see an eerily calm sea, our steady motion the only thing causing the slightest ripple.

I smile, because there, in the distance, is a silvery sliver of land peeking above the horizon. It is my seventh day at sea and we have made it to Australia.

Finola is a Danish-owned ship that sails the oceans delivering live cattle from Australia to the rest of the world. As I was about to lug my bicycle up the gangway in Sumatra, the Indonesian customs officer, who had previously agreed with Dick to let me board her, suddenly refused. It took a $400 backhander to persuade him to let me on the boat. Eventually I boarded her as nineteen hundred beasts were being unloaded. It was the evening of 15 September.

Dick negotiating my passage to Australia as the crew prepare to unload *Finola* of nineteen hundred head of cattle.

That night I slept well in my tiny cabin, waking up only once in the night and noting how calm the sea was. When I woke up the following morning I saw that we had in fact not yet left the port in Sumatra; the cattle were still being unloaded and transported to a nearby feed-lot. It took twelve Filipinos and an Australian stockman fourteen hours to unload every one of them and it was only then that *Finola* was ready to begin the long voyage back to Australia.

There were nineteen of us on board: Danish captain, Danish first-mate, Finnish second-mate, Icelandic engineer, Filipino bosun, a twelve-strong Filipino crew, Filipino chef and me. The captain was a grumpy old seadog with tattoos (the last of which he had had inked on when he was fifteen), a bushy moustache and an omnipresent sock and sandals combination. He had been at sea since the age of fourteen and had been divorced three times. Still, he was the only officer I was able to get more than a few words out of for the entire journey. The Filipinos were friendlier and I was pleased to have been offered a room in their quarters.

The voyage was supposed to take four days. The sea was calm at first, the sun shone and while the crew got to work cleaning out the cattle yards deep in the ship's bowels, I took the opportunity to read, write and work on my cyclist's tan.

Things changed on the first night at sea when a twenty-foot swell appeared and did not relent for six days. At first sleep was impossible as electrical storms rolled in one after the other. During the day, reading was out of the question, writing, too. I just lay in bed trying not to vomit, jumping up to look out of the porthole whenever a particularly large wave smashed against the hull; it sounded like a gunshot every time.

I alternated eating my meals with the officers and crew, not because I wanted to, but because I was always invited to eat with the former. The crew's dining room was all boisterous energy and banter during their rest from hours of back-breaking labour. The officers' mess was wood-panelled, stale and near silent. They all moaned about life at sea, despite the fact that each had spent more than forty years living it.

The captain told me he had never experienced such rough water on this particular route. 'It's not a good boat for rough seas,' he explained, stroking his bushy moustache. 'The bridge and accommodation is at the bow; it feels the full force of every wave.'

By our third day at sea I was used to it. I had adopted the irresponsible habit of popping a couple of allergy pills just before bed and they seemed to knock me out. During the day I ventured out of my room into the crew's mess – nicknamed Manilla – where more than five thousand DVDs, mostly Asian martial-arts movies, lined the shelves. I got to know that room pretty well over the second half of the journey. When the bell rang I knew it was time for a feed, but other than that I learned to cope with the lurching and enjoyed resting up ready for the challenge awaiting me in Australia.

During the captain's shift on the bridge he would often call down to the mess on the intercom: 'Come up to the bridge, there are dolphins!' I would grab my camera, run outside and

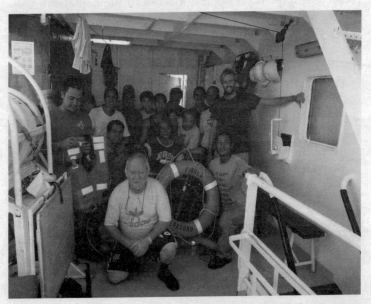

My bicycle and me with *Finola*'s Filipino crew and Danish first-mate.

clamber the various ladders that took me to the bridge, the only place on the ship from which there was a 360° view. But I never saw dolphins. 'Agh, that's a shame, they disappeared,' I would be told. I reckoned he just wanted some company; it must have been lonely up there during five-hour shifts.

As I watched the crew and officers go about their daily lives, I wondered how anyone could live at sea for months at a time. The Filipinos did six months on, two months off. At sea they worked every day from five in the morning for thirteen hours. Dinner was followed promptly by bed. All were devout Christians, honest and hard-working. The Icelandic engineer told me that, because the pay was so good for the Filipinos, when they got home they tended to treat friends and family to flat-screen televisions and new cars, so that the money normally ran out within a week. It was therefore rare for any of them to be on dry land for as long as a month.

I was not excited about arriving in Australia until the moment I saw that sliver of land at the beginning of our seventh day at sea. At that moment, I thought of the Ashes and the end of my journey and could barely believe I had made it through twenty-two countries already.

'Land Ahoy!' Darwin, my first sight of the Australian mainland.

The captain was forced to wait for an evening docking slot, so we spent the whole day anchored just outside the Port of Darwin a few miles north of the city. I offered to help with anything that needed doing, but was not allowed to, so, while I sat out in the sun, the Filipinos, having finished cleaning the ship's bowels of cow dung, painted the entire deck. Only then, they said, was *Finola* ready for her next journey.

By the time the pilot, in a small dingy with outboard motor, had guided *Finola* into her berth, I was ready for my next journey, too.

BASTARD ON A PUSHIE

Once docked at the Port of Darwin, I found myself face to face with an Australian customs officer who was, as befits the role, a pedantic bugger.

'You'll need to be getting all that dirt off them tyres before stepping down the gangway, mate,' he whined, inspecting their tread. I knew that Australia had some of the strictest quarantine and entry requirements in the world but, even so, I could see little trace of dirt on my bicycle tyres.

I was under the impression that it was the England cricket team who were the only ones due to come up against stern Australian opposition in the next few months, not me on my bike. I considered taking inspiration from the story of a cricket match between the Lord Harris XI and New South Wales, in 1879. When the crowd started chanting 'Not out, go back!' after the umpire had ruled against an Australian batsman, one of the Lord Harris XI retaliated by shouting, 'You are nothing but the sons of convicts'. While two thousand spectators stormed the pitch, Lord Harris himself remained steadfastly in position, believing that if he fled the game would have to be conceded. He received a number of kicks but no serious injury and after an hour-and-a-half-long riot the game had to be abandoned.

I thought better of calling the customs officer 'the son of

a convict', obeyed his orders and celebrated my arrival on Australian soil by microscopically inspecting every tread of my bicycle tyres for hints of dirt or pebbles. Eventually, just after dark, the officer was satisfied and I was allowed to wheel my bicycle down the gangway and on to the smooth tarmac of a deserted dual carriageway that took me into the heart of Darwin.

Darwin city was largely rebuilt in the 1970s and 1980s after Cyclone Tracy tore through it in 1974, wiping out 70 per cent of its buildings. As a result it lacks the frontier town charm it apparently once had but, on the plus side, it is a modern, well-planned city that's easy to navigate.

A friend of Dick's, Ashley from the North Australian Cattle Company, had kindly offered to sponsor my accommodation in Darwin. The hotel he had chosen was clean and functional, with a working lift, air-conditioning and wifi. As I watched the tap in the bathroom sink run, a thought occurred to me and I rushed downstairs to ask the girl on reception if I could drink the water from the tap. When I replied to her 'Yes' with a stunned 'Thank you, thank you Lord, I am a happy, happy man!' she looked at me like I was mad, but I ran back upstairs and filmed myself glugging from the tap for more than a minute anyway. It was the first time I had been able to do such a thing for over a year: a simple pleasure but one that felt significant, and *so* good.

In the city that evening I wandered around wide-eyed, marvelling at the familiarity of the world I was now in. There were ATM machines, clean streets, supermarkets with stocked shelves, people who looked like me everywhere, drinking in pubs with English names like Ducks Nuts Bar & Grill or Humpty Doo Tavern. It felt great having arrived by boat, a sort of natural extension of my journey, but I seemed to come across policemen around every corner and half expected to be cuffed and arrested for sneaking into the country on a cattle boat.

I squeezed past two burly bouncers outside the classiest looking establishment, Dolly O'Reillys, and ordered a schooner of Victoria Bitter – the worst beer I had ever had – quickly followed by a Carlton Cold – a little better. I propped up the bar to watch a brawl unfold between two heavily tattooed men in vests on the dance floor. The police were called and the men were escorted from the premises. Within a minute or two I felt a wave of depression wash over me as I wondered if my arrival in Australia represented the end of the exotic part of my journey and the beginning of a slow reacclimatisation to Western customs; the beginning of the end. Would the remaining 2,500 miles be a procession of familiarity, of ATM machines, bar brawls, bouncers and tattoos? I was in Australia after all, a modern, developed nation. I had pedalled plenty of those in Europe and had found them to offer little in the way of real adventure.

The following morning I bought various maps that linked up my route, and calculated that although I had just one country to cross, I actually needed to pedal further than I had across India to get to Brisbane and the Ashes.

I spent a few days preparing for the ride, replacing bits of kit that had either broken or been left behind and doing some local radio interviews. The night before I left Darwin I laid out all my kit on the bed in my hotel room. Although my bicycle would be the heaviest it had been on the entire journey thanks to the weight of water I would be carrying, my actual kit was at its lightest. It consisted of a tent, ground sheet, inflatable sleeping mat, thin cotton bed sheet, two five-litre water bags, water filter, tool kit, stove, two litres of fuel, travel documents, solar charger, maps, battery pack, mosquito repellent, laptop, two external hard drives, charging equipment, wash bag, medical kit, two hats, one T-shirt, one long-sleeved shirt, swimming trunks, one pair of shorts, one pair of boxer shorts, open sandals, a fleece, loo roll, two notepads, a book on the snakes of Australia, two more reading books, cable ties, peanut butter, bread, Vegemite, raisins, rice, garlic, sweet chilli sauce, Fisherman's Friends, pasta, two tins of tuna, my bicycle sign and, of course, a cricket bat and ball. The following morning I strapped and packed twenty one-and-a-half-litre water bottles to my bicycle and, with exactly fifty-seven days before the Ashes were due to begin, set off across the vast, arid land mass of Australia.

My kit laid out across the double bed in Darwin.

At a bicycle shop on the main street I stopped to get a couple of spare tyres and the shopkeeper, seeing my loaded bicycle, did not ask where I was heading, or wish me good luck. In fact, no one took much notice of me as I pedalled south out of town along the Stuart Highway, and I liked it that way. For a year I had been the centre of attention and the sudden anonymity felt liberating. As I reached the edge of town the flat-pack houses in well-tended neighbourhoods ended and there was nothing but red dirt and featureless scrub as far as the eye could see. I had forgotten that Darwin is so cut off from the rest of the world – so much so that Europeans only settled there properly in 1839. It is closer to the capital cities of East Timor, Papua New Guinea, Indonesia, Brunei and Palau than it is to Canberra. Its closest neighbour down under is Adelaide, 1,876 miles south across the red centre of Australia. I learned that 95 per cent of Australians live within thirty miles of the coast, and I did not doubt why.

I treated the first week out of Darwin as acclimatisation: to a hot, dry climate; to lazy flies and rampant mosquitoes; to more daylight hours; to taking a break in a 'servo' (Australian speak for 'service station'); to being back in the saddle riding stark plains . . . and to road trains. Whenever a friend emailed to ask how I was getting on, they would generally warn me against being bitten by one of Australia's many deadly spiders or snakes. I told them I wasn't worried about snakes, that there were far more perilous things lurking in the outback, and that they travelled at about sixty miles an hour.

Australia has the largest and heaviest road-legal vehicles in the world. Road trains, huge trucks that pull two or more trailers, weigh up to two hundred tonnes and generally measure between fifty and seventy metres in length (in one servo I saw a faded aerial photograph of a world-record-breaking road train that was pulling thirty-two trailers down the only street in an outback town).

Darwin is one of Australia's busiest ports and road trains with two or three trailers flew up and down the Stuart Highway at a frequency I had not been expecting. They normally carried cattle, but sometimes sheep. When they passed the drivers never veered from their paths so I had to take evasive action because, depending on the wind direction, they seemed either to suck me towards their wheels or push me away, off the edge of the road. Several times I fought my handlebars to remain upright, and my temper to remain calm.

Riding through towns like Berry Springs, Adelaide River and Hayes Creek (or at least places that called themselves towns because once upon a time they probably were. Now each was just a collection of dilapidated wooden buildings that usually included a campsite and, always, a pub) I told myself that I had not come to Australia to do battle with speeding seventy-metre juggernauts, but to experience its vast wilderness. Road trains were killing my journey through one of Australia's remotest corners; not literally yet, but if I stayed on the Stuart Highway I felt sure one of them would eventually. Although I had carefully mapped out my route across the continent, I became desperate to escape and to find a different path.

The enemy: road trains. I look minuscule sitting next to this one on the road outside Hayes Creek.

In the former gold-rush town of Pine Creek, four days' riding and 270 miles south of Darwin, I sat in the Lazy Lizard Bar and searched my map for viable alternatives to the Stuart Highway. I noticed a road marked Roper Highway. I followed its path eastwards with my finger until it arrived at a place called Roper Bar, where it was joined by a track from the south. That track was not labelled but it did look to exist and, sure enough, an internet search confirmed that it had been graded* a few weeks earlier, and was passable. Now all I needed to know was whether the Roper Highway was sealed (bitumen) or unsealed (dirt), and whether it was suitable for a bicycle. An old bloke with a Santa Claus beard and, disconcertingly, a sizeable carpet python around his neck, had just bought me a bottle of Coopers Pale Ale so I thought I'd ask him to put me straight:

'Excuse me, mate, but do you know if the Roper Highway is sealed or unsealed?'

'Aaarh she'll b'right, mate,' he whined, stroking his reptilian friend.

'Sorry, what was that?'

'You the bastard on the pushie, are ya?'

'Yes, I'm on my bike. Now, do you know if the Roper Highway is sealed or unsealed, and if it's unsealed, whether it's been graded recently?'

'Pushie'll be fine, mate, no worries. Course, there's a few 'ucken herds'a wild buffalo out that way.' It was my first encounter with the silent 'F' of the outback. 'Wouldn't get too close to those ugly beasts, but she'll b'right.'

'But you'd be happy riding a bike out that way, would you?'

'Only if she had a 'ucken engine,' came the old man's final retort as he swung around to celebrate his wit with his mates. Cue raucous laughter which, to my credit, I joined in with. I left that particular watering hole certain that Australians no longer spoke English, and no surer of my onward route. I decided I would wait until I reached the turn-off, in Mataranka, before I made my final decision.

It was three days' riding to Mataranka, but I took a day off in Katherine to escape the debilitating headwinds that at the time seemed unusually fierce, but that turned out to be a sign of things to come. In the Katherine Country Club that evening men played the slot machines (pokies), and kept half an eye on the cricket on television (Australia 230 for 5 against India, Shane

---

* Dirt tracks across Australia are maintained by an army of 'graders', huge bull-dozers that iron out the rutted surfaces that build up during the months between grading.

Watson 104 not out). I got chatting with a Kiwi who bought me a drink. When I told him what I was doing in Australia, he wished me good luck. 'I'm fed up of gloating Aussies; make sure your boys take those Ashes home.' I had to tell him that, so far, I had found frustratingly little evidence of gloating Aussies, as he put it; in fact, most seemed to be disappointingly down on their own team and thought England would win the forthcoming Ashes series. Outback Australians were growing on me. In my diary I described them as 'friendly but indifferent'; that is, if you crossed their path, they were friendly and interested, but if you didn't actively engage them they didn't really notice you were there at all. Although I never quite knew where I stood, I did enjoy their laid-back approach to making friends; it made a pleasant change from elsewhere around the world.

Two days out of Katherine I reached Mataranka, former

A typically nondescript stretch of road, north of Katherine.

home of the great Australian writer Jeannie Gunn, author of *We of the Never Never*. And it was there that I made the decision, based on the fact that the Roper Highway was real and not just marked on a map, to get off the Stuart Highway and begin to explore remote Australia. It was 7 October when the real adventure began.

BIG PADDOCK

Flies sit on my arms, ears, cheeks, lips and, occasionally, tongue. At first I swat them away constantly. But after a while I find myself studying their behaviour. I watch as one lands silently on my puny bicep. It rubs its front legs (are they legs, or are they arms – flies don't have arms, surely?) on my bare skin in a move that looks uncannily like a human spreading butter, or petting a dog. Then it lifts both its front legs and rubs them together, again much like we would warm up our hands in the cold. Finally the fly moves its front legs towards its face and wipes its eyes. I guess it is using my abundant sweat to cool itself and, if I am honest, I feel used. I put an end to the flies' fun by reaching for the head net I bought in Darwin. I feel, and probably look like, an idiot wearing it, but it does the trick, even if it does diminish the cooling effect of the breeze. From now on the flies have restricted access to my sweaty brow.

It took me two hours to negotiate the first twenty-five miles east out of Mataranka, dodging potholes and rotting kangaroo carcasses as I kept one eye firmly in my wing mirror in case a road train appeared. At least it was still bitumen. Eventually I managed fifty-three miles before setting up camp (mosquito net, no outer lining – it wasn't going to rain) in a clearing beside the road. An Aboriginal family pulled up at one point, opened their car bonnet and poured an entire jerry can of water over the bare engine; a novel tactic to cool it down. They drove off again without noticing me, which presumably meant that I was well hidden.

For two months, daytime meals were a lesson in fly-evasion, but my head-net helped.

The cool nights were far more enjoyable.

I was excited by the wild country. To my left was the southern boundary of Arnhem Land, an historically significant Aboriginal Reserve about the size of Scotland and Wales put together. I was reading a book called *Hell West and Crooked*, pages of which were falling out because the glue couldn't cope with the humidity, a bit like me. It is the Englishman Tom Cole's account of his life as a horse breaker, drover and buffalo and crocodile hunter in the Top End – the northernmost part of Australia's Northern Territory – in the 1920s and 1930s. He wrote the book fifty years later, and talked a lot about the places I was heading through. 'Arnhem Land,' he wrote, 'even today, is one of the most remote spots in the world.'

I could well believe it. But for the hiss of a million crickets there was complete silence. I could see nothing but a high moon and a sky full of stars, meaning that I didn't even need my head-torch to write my diary:

Diary entry: 6 October 2010, Mataranka towards Roper Bar (53 miles)

First day on Roper Highway. Huge, dense flocks of galahs, pink and grey cockatoos, flew in front of me all day as if, like me, they needed the track to guide them. Galahs were far from my only companions. Brumbies (wild horses), donkeys, kangaroos, wedge-tailed eagles, the odd buffalo and flocks of bright green parrots dropped in to see how I was getting on, and perhaps noted that I wasn't coping too badly.

Just worked out that if I manage fifty-five miles a day for forty days, with nine rest days, I'll get to Brisbane in time for the Ashes. But while there may only be one country to cross, it's Australia, and it's bloody big.

I say I camped next to a road, but the following day the Roper Highway proved itself to be undeserving of its name. At 7 a.m. I reached two signposts: GRAVEL ROAD – CAREFUL DRIVING TECHNIQUES ARE ADVISED and

The daily appearance of thousands of galahs was a
welcome distraction on the Roper Highway.

BEWARE, NO FUEL FOR 350 KILOMETRES. It suggested
things might get pretty wild from then on. At least the only
fuel I needed to worry about was water and I was carrying
twenty litres in bottles and bags strapped to every part of
my bicycle. No need to panic just yet.

The bitumen ended and the road became no more than
a rutted dirt track. It was like riding a corrugated tin roof
covered in two inches of sand. It made life pretty tricky, but
I had to get used to it.

I was going deeper into the bush, closing on Roper Bar
where I would take a right turn and continue south through
an area that would apparently soon be a national park, but
for now was wild, and then along the Barkly Tablelands. I
hoped to pop out back on to a bitumen road at the Barkly
Homestead in a couple of weeks.

Just before noon a ute heading in the opposite direction screeched to a halt, covering me in red dust. 'Looks like you could do with a cold Coke, mate!' the chirpy driver told me.

'You bastard,' I thought to myself, 'you're right, but where the hell am I going to get one of those out here?'

The man must have noted my reaction. 'Name's Bruce, mate,' he offered, jumping down from the ute and climbing on to the flatbed at the back. He reached into a fridge that was parked in one corner. 'She should sort you out, mate,' he said, throwing me a can of Coke and taking one for himself. As soon as the Coke touched my palm I wanted to hug Bruce.

'Do you always carry a fridge when you're on the road?' I asked, perplexed.

'Course, mate, Territory's a bloody big paddock. You'd look pretty stupid if you got caught short'a water, don't ya reckon?' I did reckon, but I told Bruce that it had never occurred to me that a fridge might ever form part of a car's make-up; I was English, after all. We had heaters.

I chatted with Bruce for a while, about the big-money buffalo hunting that still goes on in the area and about the plight of the Aboriginal population, especially in the Top End.

'Tough being a white fella in these parts,' he said, "Cos it's our bloody fault they're in the mess they are.' I got the gist of what Bruce was saying. In Katherine I had come across a group of fifteen or so Aboriginals gathered on the steps of the tourist information centre. They were drinking beer around a campfire at eight o'clock in the morning. When I asked the lady in the information centre if such behaviour was normal she gave me a look that suggested it was, before adding, 'It's terribly sad.' I had seen similar scenes in Adelaide River and Mataranka, too, blokes snoozing by the side of the road in the midday sun, beer cans strewn about them.

'Drink and unemployment, they're the big problems for those fellas 'round here,' Bruce said. 'They're bloody good bushmen, mind you; the best.' I would discover later on my journey through Australia that Bruce was certainly right about that.

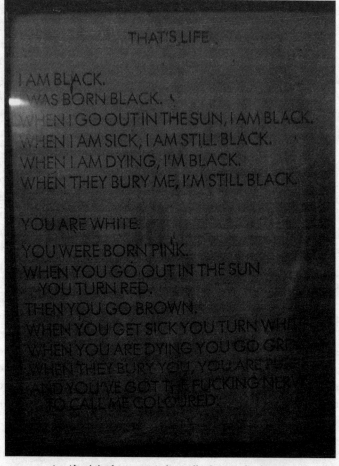

THAT'S LIFE

I AM BLACK.
I WAS BORN BLACK.
WHEN I GO OUT IN THE SUN, I AM BLACK.
WHEN I AM SICK, I AM STILL BLACK.
WHEN I AM DYING, I'M BLACK.
WHEN THEY BURY ME, I'M STILL BLACK.

YOU ARE WHITE.
YOU WERE BORN PINK.
WHEN YOU GO OUT IN THE SUN
   YOU TURN RED.
THEN YOU GO BROWN.
WHEN YOU GET SICK YOU TURN WHITE.
WHEN YOU ARE DYING YOU GO GREEN.
WHEN THEY BURY YOU, YOU ARE PURPLE.
AND YOU'VE GOT THE FUCKING NERVE
   TO CALL ME COLOURED.

An Aboriginal poem on the wall of an outback pub.

Cokes finished, Bruce got back in his ute, me on my bike and we headed our separate ways.

'You'll see Kris and Emma, my wife and daughter, on your way to Roper Bar. We always travel separately in case one of the trucks breaks down; bloody pain in the arse if you get stuck for a day or two out here. Anyway, they might give you another Coke if you're lucky.' And then Bruce was off, bound for his monthly shop in Katherine.

About an hour later another ute bounced its way towards me and I hailed it down. 'G'day, Kris, g'day, Emma,' I said, when I saw a mother and daughter in the front. The mother looked startled and, frankly, a little terrified (miles from anywhere in outback Australia, stranger, cricket bat: I guessed it equalled a worrying combination). 'Who the bloody hell are you?' she asked, before adding, 'Bruce has been at it again, has he, making mates on the track?'

Some hours later, as I sat eating a peanut butter sandwich under the shade of a tin roof in a lay-by, I read some more of *Hell West and Crooked* and came across the line: '. . . a billy can of tea and damper* and I was overflowing with the milk of human kindness.' I supposed that Bruce's gift of a can of Coke was the twenty-first-century equivalent, and one that was equally well received. Bruce and I have kept in touch ever since and I hope, when I return to the Northern Territory, to pay him and his family a visit.

By mid-afternoon I was down to five litres of water so I dropped into the Flying Fox cattle station and the friendly lady running the place let me fill up my remaining bottles from their bore hole in the yard. When I finally reached Roper Bar, just before sunset, I was shattered and collapsed on a bench outside the General Store. A smartly dressed Aboriginal man appeared out of the bush and I asked him where the rest of the town was.

'This is her, mate,' he said simply.

I looked at the basic two-storey wooden building to my right and chuckled to myself. If I had wanted outback Australia, I had found it.

I chatted with the man for a while and it turned out he

---

* Damper is a traditional outback bread favoured by bushmen and cattle workers, made from self-raising flour, almost any liquid, sugar and salt. It is cooked on coals.

lived in the same community as Bruce, on the Gulf of Carpentaria. He had come to Roper Bar to stock up on food. Inside the General Store, the young girl behind the counter told me about a camping ground next to the river and when I got there I found an empty field with a standalone toilet. I cooked rice and onions on my stove, sprinkled some of my luxury item, cheese, over it and refuelled at the end of another long day under the outback sun.

The next morning I turned off the Roper Highway, heading south on a dirt track that provided me with the wildest country yet.

ROPER BAR TO CAPE CRAWFORD

That night I took a pee outside the tent (I'd lost my water bottle a few days back) and, shining my head-torch across the earth, saw what must have been thousands of spiders glinting in the torchlight; a reminder to zip up my tent from the top, not the bottom. The next morning I watched the sunrise, bright red against an unusually dark blue sky, from beneath my mosquito net. I climbed a hill the girl in the General Store had called 'Telstra Hill', the only place in the area that got mobile phone reception. I texted a friend in England to wish her a happy day; it was her wedding day. I counted that I had missed seven good friends' weddings for the sake of my ride. I hit the road at 6.30 a.m.

Curious about the Roper River Bar, I pedalled a couple of miles in the wrong direction just to see what it was, and discovered a semi-submerged natural shelf that could almost have been mistaken for a man-made causeway. It crossed the river at a beautiful spot surrounded by eucalyptus trees, marking the place where the salty, tidal waters meet the fresh water upstream of the bar.

On a bike ride across Australia it is not often that you reach anywhere at all so when you do it is likely that the place is going to be of fairly significant historical importance. A sign next to the river told me that a German named Ludwig Leichardt was the first European to discover it during an expedition in 1845, and was therefore the first to cross the bar. During the 1870s the river was opened up for cargo, paddle steamers plying it to deliver supplies to the men working on the construction of the Overland Telegraph from Adelaide to Darwin. It's not used much these days, except by crocodiles that bask on the warm rock and by local people who, somewhat unwisely, swim in its waters. A local was taking a dip when I arrived and she called to me to join her.

'What about the saltwater crocs?' I asked.

'She'll be right,' was her reply (the standard Australian response to pretty much any question). 'Haven't seen a saltie here in days.'

Comforted by her seemingly relaxed approach, I got back on my bicycle, checked left and right for crocodiles, and went for it, racing across the fifty-metre-wide bar which lay under about a foot of rushing water. When I reached the safety of the northern bank I was on Arnhem Land and the lady let out a shriek of delight. 'That's it, boy, no worries!'

I couldn't continue my journey on the track that led north into Arnhem Land even if I had wanted to; a special permit is required even to set foot in the Aboriginal Reserve, so I was already breaking the law. Instead I jumped into a shallow pool that had been formed by the low water table, and chatted for a while with the lady. I wanted to know more about the crocodiles and supposed her people knew more than most.

'Shit there's plenty round here. The freshies [freshwater crocodiles] aren't worth worrying about but the salties bloody well are. They'll take you down pretty easy. Saw a big 'un just there a few days back, maybe six metres,' she said, pointing at a patch of bare rock no more than five metres from where we were bathing.

'Six metres long?' I asked. 'Just there?'

'Yep, that's her.'

'I thought you said you hadn't seen one here for days.'

'Aaah yeaaah that's right. She was sleepin'; doesn't count.'

And, with that, I inched my way out of the pool and on to my bicycle. The short ride back across the bar was significantly more terrifying than the one I'd made fifteen minutes earlier, but I got across and pedalled hard to get away from the river and the dangers lurking within.

'She'll be right!' Going for a dip in the Roper River.
I am leaning on the bar that I used to cross it.

Back in the Roper Bar General Store I stocked up on water and food and asked the girl there what supplies I might find in the next settlement, Cape Crawford, 235 miles south.

'Bugger all,' she said, 'it's just a motel. Next town you'll come across'll be Camooweal, in Queensland.' I inspected my map; Camooweal was more than a thousand miles away – further than John O'Groats to Land's End without a town or village. Fuck! Bruce was right. It was a big paddock, the Northern Territory.

The riding was tough all day in temperatures that reached 44°C. I was caked in sweat, sand and flies and beginning to wonder if I had made the right decision to leave the Stuart Highway. Then, respite. Two miles before Tomato Island I saw a large puddle by the side of the road. Except it wasn't a puddle, but a small billabong about the size of a king-size bed. I checked for running water nearby but found nothing, meaning no crocodiles – I was learning. I stumbled into the crystal-clear water, about a metre deep, washed myself for the first time in days, brushed my teeth, filled up my water bottles ready for filtering later; then continued the short distance to Tomato Island which, it turned out, was not an island at all, but a large patch of grass beside the river.

As I pitched my tent I hoped crocodiles didn't come too far out of the water at night.

A few days later I hadn't been on the road for twenty minutes when a truck and trailer pulled up, spraying me with dust. I guessed the driver could see I already had a coating and thought I needed a second. Inside were three men, one bald-headed, one in a truckers' cap and the driver in a white vest and wide-brimmed Acubra hat.

The driver took one look at me. 'You 'ucken stupid bastard. "Straaaya" looks small on a 'ucken map but it's a bloody big paddock once you get here, especially on that 'ucken thing.' He pointed at my bicycle. 'You gotta be a Pommie, right?'

I admitted that I was English, but before I had time to protest my sanity, the driver was out of the truck and delving around in his freezer. He grabbed a couple of bottles of frozen water and chucked them at me like a pitcher might throw a baseball.

'These'll keep ya from dyin' at least. We'll be drivin' back in a few days; should have more'a nature's fine wine for ya then if ya lucky. 'Ucken stupid bastard.'

With that and a spray of dust, he and his mining buddies were gone. I was getting used to the ways of the outback man: no formalities, quite a lot of straight-talking and a whole lot of camaraderie, if not respect, for fellow travellers.

It was another hot day, mid-forties I guessed, and the track got worse throughout the afternoon. I was told a grader had smoothed the path within the last few weeks, but evidence suggested it hadn't. It was bloody hard on metalwork, bum and wheels, although my record of no broken spokes on the whole journey remained.

I fell off twice in the afternoon, once cutting my foot deeply on a sharp stone, which meant I got to use my first aid kit for the first time since Africa. I was off the bicycle and pushing when the sand got deep, which was often, but never for more than half a mile or so. Even pushing was tough and I could barely keep the bike upright. Progress was painfully slow and bloody hard work. I couldn't open my right eye all day because it was so full of dust. The left wasn't much better. I was grateful for my mosquito head net. Flies stuck to it like glue but couldn't get on to my face and had to be content with my arms.

Finally I reached Towns River. It was just before sunset – not a good time to cross rivers in the Top End because crocodiles begin to slink back into the water about that time after a day basking in the sun. But my map told me there was a decent camping spot on the other side, set back from the river on a small escarpment out of reach for crocodiles. I really wanted to cross.

I left my bicycle at the top of a small incline and wandered to the water's edge where another submerged bar, a concrete one this time, offered a short route to safety. There was no sign of any crocodiles upstream. I turned downstream and there, with half its body in the water, was a huge saltie, maybe five metres long. That's the height of a two-storey building! Its eyes were shut, but it was still one of the most formidable, opportunistic predators the world has ever known; a prehistoric killing machine. It flicked its tail and that was enough to set my pulse racing. I sprinted to my bicycle, mounted it and pedalled like the wind for a mile. Only then did I notice that there were creeks everywhere, concealed behind thick foliage.

I could not bring myself to pedal further in the wrong

direction so I stopped to cook some pasta on my stove in the middle of the road, trying to be as quiet as I possibly could. I really hoped a car would come to take me safely across the bar, but it was unlikely. I hadn't seen one in hours. I would have to sweat it out until morning on my own.

The middle of the road – a good spot for a feed.

4.30 a.m. – still can't open my right eye; bloody sore. No cars came. I'm still in the same spot. I stuck up my mosquito net by the side of the road last night. Every splash and rustle is making me more and more agitated. I've barely slept at all. An infestation of thousands of flying maggot-type insects sneaked through a hole in my zip about an hour ago. I can't believe I left it open. I had to get up and that's why I'm ready and packed, waiting for a car to pass to take me across the river.

The nights and early mornings were getting increasingly cold and would continue to do so as I made my way southwards. I had to wear a fleece, woolly hat and long trousers while I waited. When the sun came up I debated pedalling across the creek, but it's one thing doing it when you haven't seen a crocodile there; it's quite another when you've seen one and it's big! I decided to sit it out. I was down to five litres of water. I had a feeling it was going to be a rough day.

I waited until midday for a vehicle to pass; two young boys in a flatbed ute. Being called a 'Fucking Pommie pussy' by a couple of eighteen-year-olds hurt a bit, but not too much, and I was happy to be across the bar, back on the bike and out of danger, at least for a bit.

The landscape was more varied than it had been in recent days, with red sandstone escarpments rising from plains high above the endless scrub and red dirt. The thick, low trees that had typified the ride since Mataranka were sparser and occasionally there were small hills with views across vast wilderness from the top.

There were more creek crossings, though, and I expected they would carry on for days to come. Only when I reached the northern edge of the Barkly would they disappear entirely. For now there were one or two every hour and, having come face to face with Australia's most potent killer the previous day, I knew I didn't want to see another one. There were plenty of hiding places, even for five-metre-long crocodiles, with vegetation abundant whenever I reached a riverbank. It was the dry season and the creeks and rivers were low so at least I had that in my favour. I tended just to fly across the bars, bridges and bare riverbeds. But no sooner had I conquered one creek, than another one would appear and I would have to do it all over again.

Eventually I made it to Butterfly Springs, well after dark. Under the light of the moon I swam in its clear waters beneath a cascading waterfall and had the place all to myself. I realised for the first time that that day was a significant one in the life of Cycling to the Ashes. It was 10 October, the anniversary of my departure from Lord's.

I had seen a lot in the last year and I wondered if people would see a change in me when I got home. I expected they would, although I hoped not for the worse. My mind was beginning to turn to the end now, but that could be dangerous. There were only forty-four days until I needed to be in Brisbane. I had to remain focused.

I lazed around the following morning, a deserved break spent swimming and reading. I had a feeling I had nothing in my legs, and I was right. Adrenalin must have taken it out of me. I only managed twenty miles along the worst surface yet, falling off regularly on to hot sand. I cut my knee quite badly. It wasn't my day. When I saw a sign marked 'The Southern Lost City' I took a detour and set up my tent under the shade of a eucalyptus tree, overlooking the impressive red sandstone rock formations of an ancient Lost City in the heart of the bush.

The following morning I had packed up and loaded the bike by five o'clock, but I noticed that the uneven surface of the past week had snapped my bicycle rack again: there was little chance I could make it the sixty miles to Cape Crawford along such a rutted road. Even if I did make it, I doubted I'd find a welder there. I hadn't seen a human being for eighteen hours. I was a long way from anywhere.

What to do? My map suggested Borroloola was a fair-sized settlement and I had heard some barramundi fishermen talking about it. It was in the wrong direction and would add another eighty miles to my journey, but I didn't really have any choice. I tied the rack tightly to the bicycle frame with five or six cable ties and again used an old sock to stop it rubbing and damaging the frame. I made it through the creeks and rivers, praying that I wouldn't see a crocodile and that my rack would hold. Then, as the road began to veer eastwards, it opened out on to a plain and the wind was at my back for the first time in days. I flew to Borroloola, nailing the eighty-three miles in just seven hours. How I wished the wind could be at my back every day.

I found a mechanic who said he'd have my bicycle ready by seven the next morning, so I treated myself to a campsite and cooked sausages and baked beans on the barbie.

I turned up at the welder's yard at 7.30 the next morning: 'Oh yeah, sorry, mate, don't have any gas, so couldn't weld your bike.'

As much as I wanted to punch him, the guy was huge, so instead I took the bike to another mechanic with a long grey beard threatening his belt buckle, legs like matchsticks and ball-buster denim shorts who did the job in under five minutes for $10, 'no worries', even throwing in a few cable ties for free.

By 9 a.m. I was on the road, bicycle fixed, tyres hydraulically inflated and, would you believe it, the wind at my back again; perhaps thirty- or forty-mile-an-hour winds at that. It was the easiest day's riding of the whole tour, made even better by a production line of kangaroos that bounded across the road in front of me all day long; no road trains to take them out round there.

I made it to Cape Crawford in just four hours, headed straight for the fridge in the small shop and buried my head inside it. I had pedalled at an average of about seventeen miles an hour. And thank God I had detoured via Borroloola. Cape Crawford was neither a village, nor a town, but consisted of one motel, its walls coated with peeling pink paint, called the Heartbreak Hotel. The irony of the name was not lost on me.

It seemed I was the only guest who was there on purpose. Five fishermen were stranded because their truck had broken down and they were waiting for a mechanic to arrive from Borroloola. The only other guests seemed to be a former Queensland police officer, called Bill, and his new girlfriend, Susanna, who had got a puncture earlier in the day and could make it no further before nightfall. We decided to have a 'feed' together in the bar.

Despite being the only male not wearing shiny rugby league shorts and a wife-beater vest, I was not made to feel left out and we had a great time, attacking the Heartbreak Hotel's stock of alcohol with a fair enthusiasm. I wasn't allowed to pay for a drink all night, which may explain the fact that when it started raining in the middle of the night I didn't wake up. When I finally woke at six o'clock in the morning my gear and I were soaked through. I should have used the tent's outer shell.

The bar at the Heartbreak Hotel.

I was on the road by 8.30 a.m., but only three miles out of town when I got a puncture to my front tyre; miraculously, this was my first in Australia. I stripped the wheel, repaired it with a patch and got going again in under fifteen minutes. Two miles later I got another puncture, this time to the rear tyre. They're like London buses and good-looking girls; you wait ages for one . . .

Rear punctures were always harder to deal with because they meant unloading the entire bicycle of several tens of kilograms of kit. I repaired it and carried on, but I must have done a shoddy job because two miles later it went again. While I was repairing my third puncture within an hour an army of giant ants made their way inside my shorts and nipped at me in a place where it hurt; little fuckers. I decided it wasn't my day, cut my losses and headed back to the Heartbreak Hotel, heartbroken.

That evening I got a text from Bill and Susanna, the policeman and his girlfriend: 'We've left you a bag of food and drink behind the water tank, two hundred miles from Cape Crawford. Good on ya, take care, Bill and Susanna – p.s. hope our boys thrash the Poms in the Ashes.' It was so kind, and what a fantastic gift for me to find in a few days' time.

The food from Bill and Susanna, with a note that read: 'Please do not touch. Essential for passing cyclist arriving Friday afternoon. Go Ollie!'

BRUNETTE DOWNS

Leaving Cape Crawford for the second time, I focused my mind on the task of reaching the mining centre of Mount Isa within a couple of weeks. My maps told me the journey would be about six hundred miles along a mixture of rutted dirt and bitumen, south along the single-track Tablelands

Highway, the Northern Territory's least populated neighbour-hood (six thousand people living in an area half the size of France) until the Barkly Homestead, and then east on the two-lane Barkly Highway.

There must be a collection of words that, if organised into the right order, would perfectly explain to the uninitiated the scale of the Australian outback. I struggled to find them when writing my diary each night, I struggled to find them when blogging during my journey and I struggle to find them now, as I write about it several months later. It is mind-bogglingly vast and arid, a place where some of the greatest European explorers of the nineteenth century perished, but where people have learned to respect the extreme climate, the croc-odiles and the loneliness, and to carve for themselves a way of life. It is a place where these days children schooled from home are taught via radio or satellite link, where a neighbour can be someone living a couple of hundred miles down a dirt track and where, if a traveller takes a wrong track and finds himself lost in the bush, he will surely die. It is not a place in which the casual cyclist feels remotely comfortable.

From Cape Crawford the land changed almost immediately, opening out into the famous grazing country of the southern Northern Territory. Huge paddocks were the size of English counties rich with robust, golden Mitchell and Flinders grasses, and the stockman's livelihood, cattle. I had never seen the curvature of the earth so clearly in all directions. Mirages were always up ahead, and I began to understand why so many early explorers died chasing the horizon for water that simply did not exist.

I had been riding for two and a half days through increas-ingly open and unforgiving country when, around lunchtime, a sign beside a cattle grid told me I was entering Brunette Downs, a cattle station managed by the Australian Agricultural Company, which I later discovered controls about 1 per cent of Australia's entire land area across Queensland and the Northern Territory. A fence stretched off into the distance on either side of the road until it merged with the horizon.

While I was eager to continue with progress towards Brisbane, I was equally keen to get a taste of real outback life. However many characters I met while I was in the saddle, I did not feel I would get a genuine grasp on what it took to live there unless I visited a cattle station. I was lucky that Ashley from the North Australian Cattle Company had put me in touch with a number of cattle station managers along my route, and although most stations were simply too far out of my way to visit, Brunette Downs seemed close enough to the road to pop in for a day or two. I was particularly pleased to have the opportunity to visit Brunette Downs, because I had read a little about it through Tom Cole's exploits as a stock camp cook there in the 1920s.

I had been told the entrance to the property itself was accessed via a track on the right-hand side of the road, so I pedalled on, eyes peeled for anything that suggested civilisation. But for miles and miles of grass, I did not see a single living organism. The heat, again, was staggering, the wind debilitating. It wasn't for another three hours that I eventually saw a swirl of dust approaching on the road to the south and twenty minutes later a ute with three working stockmen pulled up to ask me what the hell I was doing.

'Looking for Brunette Downs,' I replied, 'any ideas where she is?' I had taken to calling everything 'she' in an effort to appear normal.

'Sure, mate, that's where we work but we're headed up to the top paddock, so can't offer yers a lift. She's about another ten k's down the track,' the driver said, pointing behind him. 'Name's Woody by the way, we'll see yers for a cold one later.'

I thanked Woody and rode on. Sure enough, six miles further on I came across a severely rutted dirt track and turned off the highway. It was an hour shy of sunset and the entire plain, indeed my entire universe, was lent an incredible glow by the setting sun. It was a spectacular show and I had the best seat in the house.

I expected to see the station properties roll into view pretty quickly but it turned out to be another half-hour cycle before a large cluster of buildings came into sight, a mirage at first and then, for once, civilisation.

It was like arriving in a parallel universe; a splash of colour in a barren landscape. I pedalled the paths between white-painted washboard houses, dormitories, workshops, stables and kitchens that sat on stilts surrounded by emerald green lawns, neatly trimmed hedges, bougainvillea and mature trees. The odd kangaroo bounded across the gardens and back on to the plain. Two Cessna light aircraft sat in a small hangar and a bubble helicopter was parked outside it. Horses lazed in the shade of the eucalyptus trees. Grader drivers, gardeners, pilots and stockmen busied themselves at the end of another day on the station, heading for a well-earned beer in the station's social club. I got some funny looks, but then I must have looked pretty out of place in cycling shorts, sandals and a torn, filthy Hawaiian shirt.

Brunette Downs is the largest single-lease property in Australia and the second largest cattle station in the Northern Territory, covering 12,500 square kilometres, or 3.5 million acres, making it just under half the size of Belgium. I wondered how all this life could exist so far from anywhere and was given my answer by a couple of young stockmen over steak and chips in the station canteen.

Although much of the outback, including Brunette Downs, looks to the uninitiated to be incredibly infertile, it is, in fact, abundant in the one natural resource that is crucial: water. The Great Artesian Basin, covering 661,000 square miles and about a quarter of Australia's land mass, is the largest and deepest artesian basin in the world. In places it is as deep as 3,000 metres below the earth's surface and in much of Australia it is the only reliable source of fresh water. Before European occupation, the water from the basin was visible through the natural springs that supported the nomadic Aboriginal communities, but in the 1870s the Europeans discovered and named the Artesian Basin itself and were able to open up vast tracts of land, far from any other water sources, for use as cattle and livestock stations as well as other rural and farming activities.

It is the Great Artesian Basin that has enabled Australia to become one of the largest exporters of cattle in the world, the reason places like Brunette Downs exist in the first place. Brunette's first artesian bore was sunk in 1903 and now 180 bores pump water into 220 turkey nests (water storage ponds) and 400 troughs. There are around 100,000 head of cattle and they feed on fifty-three separate paddocks, at an average of 130 square miles each.

I was there during the 'on' season of mustering, so there were about fifty staff servicing the station. The social club was a good place to get an idea of how the group mingled, and I noticed a definite divide. While the experienced workers – grader drivers, bore-hole experts, gardeners and mechanics – drank at one end of the bar, at the other young, straight-out-of-high-school stockmen – or 'jackaroos' – flirted with their 'jillaroo' contemporaries. Obviously I fitted into neither camp, but was made to feel welcome by both.

Everyone I spoke to on the station agreed that Tony, the old Aboriginal fellow who had worked at Brunette since he was a young man, and who went about his business quietly and without fuss, was the finest stockman around. I was disappointed not to get a chance to go out mustering with him, but that is not to say I did not enjoy my time in the paddock.

During most of the dry season, from May to November, teams of stockmen and cooks go out mustering for several weeks at a time, setting up camp each night and guiding their particular mob of cattle to water each day. But I had arrived at the end of the season and the camps had been called in, so I went out with Woody and a team of stockmen for the day, to gather up a herd in a southern paddock forty miles south of the station buildings.

Whereas in the old days mustering was done only on horseback, many stations now use modern equipment. Brunette is rare in that horses are still valued for their versatile mustering skills, so they are used in partnership with motorbikes and helicopters or light aircraft.

I followed up at the rear of a herd of thirteen hundred beasts as Woody chased them on his motorbike. A couple of young stockmen rode alongside and thirty-five-knot winds buffeted the helicopter above. When the team had managed to get all the bulls into the holding pen, about seven hundred were yarded for drafting later in the month. While the best bulls would soon be given access to the heifers to breed, the rest would be culled and sold for beef.

I was not allowed in the chopper during mustering. It is a dangerous business and carrying passengers is illegal (later on during my ride across Australia I met several widows who had lost their husbands in helicopter or light aircraft accidents while out mustering). But when the job was done, I was offered a ride back to the station buildings, a half-hour journey that made me certain that while I normally prefer doing my travelling on solid ground, the best way to see the Barkly Tablelands is definitely from the air. It gave me a new perspective on the land I was pedalling across.

I would have liked to stay longer at Brunette Downs, but

Crossing the cattle grid on to Brunette Downs.

in the end I left having barely scratched the surface of a way of life that was so different from my own, and certainly from the one I was experiencing in the saddle.

At six o'clock on my third morning there I said my good-byes, rode the rough track back to the main road and turned right to continue my journey.

NOTHING

I see a ute on the horizon, white with chrome bumper, a motorbike strapped to its rear. The driver slows as he approaches; another friendly outback driver perhaps? Some water would be nice, but a soft drink, oh my God that would go down well.

But wait, hold up, he is accelerating again. Now he's swerving across the lanes; he's on my side of the road. What's he doing? Is that a middle finger he's holding up? It is! He signals his car's horn, hand sitting on it. He is close enough now that I can see his face and he looks crazed, drugged even, wild red hair kept at bay by a dirty pink baseball cap.

Whooosh! He misses my handlebars by inches. I would have been gone if he'd hit me. I still might be. I can't keep my bike upright and I veer off the bitumen, on to the copper-red dirt as he flies into the distance.

If I was expecting my few days off at Brunette Downs to have made life in the saddle any easier, I was wrong. I had learned long ago that I was cycling across Australia in the wrong direction for the time of year. From about September, south-easterly winds begin to whip up from Sydney and the New South Wales coast, travelling for thousands of miles before they reach the Northern Territory, then Darwin and off towards Indonesia. It was therefore unfortunate that my direction of travel was south-east. The wind caused me anguish for two whole months.

I had noticed since Borroloola that I was beginning to treat cycling more like a job, a task that had to be undertaken, than I had in any other country. Although Brisbane was still more than 1,300 miles away, I put my new approach down partly to the relative proximity of my final destination but also to conditions that were some of the toughest of my entire journey.

I slogged along at a tortoise pace for days; three, four, five miles per hour into heart-breaking headwinds. Every pedal stroke sapped an inordinate amount of energy out of my legs, not to mention my brain, and sweat poured down my face in buckets. It was like cycling in soup. Winds like that do not exist where I come from. Occasionally I peered over my shoulder, staring at a water tower, or the burnt-out wreckage of a car I had passed several minutes earlier, and wondered how it was still within sight. Neil Young's *Greatest Hits* did their best to keep me sane.

When I reached a signpost that said 'CC 350 KMS' I leaned my bicycle against it and took a photo. I had made it 350 kilometres from Cape Crawford and the photo I took is one of my favourites from my time in the outback; the image itself tells only half the story. The headwind was so strong that I could barely stand while taking the photo and although my

The immense Australian outback. Shortly after taking the photo,
the wind knocked my bicycle over.

bicycle weighed in excess of seventy kilograms, the wind blew it over as if it was a piece of cardboard.

Infrequently (although I may be a glutton for punishment, I am not stupid), when the wind whipped particularly fiercely into my face, blowing dust into my eyes, I turned my wheels to face downwind and let nature do the rest, freewheeling with ease back in the direction I had come from, cursing the hand nature had dealt me. Then I turned back to face Brisbane and the raging wind, and decided that Perth would have been a far more preferable location for the first Ashes Test.

Two days' hard pedalling took me 150 miles from Brunette to the junction with the Barkly Highway. There I found the Barkly Homestead, a servo where I treated myself to a shower, chicken kiev and a camping spot in the garden out the back. The next morning, instead of turning left downwind towards Alice Springs and the 'red centre', I continued east, stopping on the second night at Avon Downs cattle station, also owned by the Australian Agricultural Company, before crossing the border from the Northern Territory into Queensland. Apart from a huge signpost welcoming me to the sunshine state, nothing changed. Grassland stretched on and on in all directions, not so much as a tree in sight. Not even the wind considered dying down a little.

Queensland's proud heritage was displayed on road signs across the state. I never found out what the Tambo Teddies were.

I camped most nights, pitching my tent a couple of hundred yards from the road in a spot I felt was safe enough. Before I got cooking I stomped around my campsite to ensure that I had not stepped into a snake's territory (most species have very sensitive vibratory sensors and if they feel movement, will go away from it rather than towards it). Nights were cool and pleasant. Stars were my constant companion and although I usually set up camp well after dark, I was rarely forced to use my head-torch because it was so light.

There was not a hint of variety to the weather pattern all the way from Cape Crawford more than one thousand miles south-east to the Queensland town of Longreach. I knew what to expect every hour of the day. At least that meant that, unlike in India, I could slip into something of a routine. Most mornings I spent half an hour filtering the water I had picked up the previous day from tanks along my route, ate a breakfast of bread and jam and was on the road well before sunrise. I enjoyed the cool of the early mornings, wrapped up in a fleece and woolly hat as eagles silently stalked the plains and the wind was at its least violent. By eight o'clock the sun was intense and by eleven the wind was too much to bear. The sun and wind combined not only to dehydrate me, but to dry the sweat on my face, creating my own little salt pan. I enjoyed licking it off, and it did me good.

Whereas in Sudan the desert offered no shade at all, in the outback I was at least blessed with roadside shelters erected specifically for the benefit of travellers. I ate pasta or a few peanut butter and jam sandwiches most days for lunch, always wearing a mosquito head net to keep the flies at bay and shovelling food up through the hole at the bottom. Often I would be watched while I ate by huntsman spiders, one of Australia's deadliest, clinging to the eaves of the shelters. After refuelling I would sleep through the middle of the day until the light began to soften and the climate and wind became bearable. Then I would pedal until sunset, often well beyond if the moon was bright.

I pedalled through Camooweal, Queensland's most

westerly town, and was within a couple of days' ride of Mount Isa, the region's mining centre. Because Camooweal is officially part of the Mount Isa Shire, the section of highway that links the two towns is known locally as the longest 'main street' in the world, at 116 miles. It might have been the longest, but it was also the quietest; I barely saw a person, let alone a bakery or butcher's.

When the chimneys of Mount Isa's famous copper, lead, silver and zinc mine (the largest single producing mine of such minerals in the world) appeared on the horizon, I got my video camera out and screamed at the top of my voice 'I'VE MADE IT TO CIVILISATION'. With 22,500 inhabitants it was the first proper town I had seen in just under a month, since Darwin. I headed straight for an ice-cream parlour and ordered three tubs of Cookies and Cream.

It was on the Matilda Highway a couple of days out of Mount Isa that the crazed ginger in the white ute did his best to run me off the road. After the couple of weeks I had endured, I felt I did not deserve such treatment. But, as ever, cycling alone it was easy to take random acts of lunacy to heart. As a wave, a smile or a cheer could brighten up a morning, so an idiot trying to mow me down could dampen my mood.

Thankfully, on this occasion, my sombre reflection did not last long. Shortly after the man's vehicle had merged with the horizon, I was faced with something that took my mind off him as well as the wind, the heat and the flies. It was something that made me grin from ear to ear; a simple signpost that read:

BRISBANE   1,695

It was the most beautiful signpost I had ever seen. Make that the *only* beautiful signpost I had ever seen: small white letters on an Australian green background. I doubt the person who commissioned the sign ever considered the joy it could bring to a lonely cyclist. I repeated out loud: '1,695 kilometres . . . 1,695 kilometres.' It did not sound far when I considered I had already covered more than 21,000 kilometres.

Arriving at the first road sign to Brisbane was a big moment.

Unlike the moment when I had seen the sign to Kolkata, I was awash with positive thoughts: only 1,695 kilometres until I could forget about cycling for a while; only 1,695 kilometres until I could hang out with friends; only 1,695 kilometres until I would reach Brisbane and the end of my road.

When I was easing into life in the saddle in Western Europe and sweating my way across Sudan and the subcontinent, Brisbane had seemed like an impossibly distant city; a nirvana that I was unlikely to reach. When I made it to Darwin I started to dream of Brisbane, but whenever I told people in the Top End that I was nearly there, they scoffed and said 'bloody big paddock, Straaaya'. So I tried not to think of Brisbane too often in case my mind jumped ahead and I forgot about the task in hand.

But when I saw that first signpost to Brisbane I pictured the road ahead, winding across plains of endless grassland, through Queensland's cattle towns, up and over the Great

Dividing Range and the Glasshouse Mountains and down to the Gold Coast and Brisbane. It all seemed so achievable. The England cricket team had arrived on Australian soil the day before to begin their preparations for the Ashes. I really did not have far to go now; I was nearly there.

I sat down beside the signpost and ate a banana, wondering how many little targets I had set myself in my quest to achieve 'The Big One'. I marvelled at the result; at how lots of little targets had almost brought me to my final destination.

Unsurprisingly, I cried as I ate the banana, not because I thought I could not cope, but because I knew I could. I remembered the pain in my knee all those months ago and how sure I was, after the first couple of weeks through Europe, that I would never make it to Africa, let alone Australia and Brisbane. I cast my mind back to the headache, both literal and metaphorical, of the Indian subcontinent, and the weeks in bed in Thailand, when I wondered again if I would be able to complete the journey. I recalled days shielding myself from the rain of Europe and the snow of Turkey and Syria, I remembered Vladimir, Saif, Kapil, Amit, James Bond, Will, Baldy and all the other cricketing friends I had made. I thanked them, silently, because I knew now that I was going to make it to Brisbane, whether in time for the Ashes or not; and I knew they had helped me.

'1,695 kilometres,' I repeated; seventeen good days on the bike.

But I was still in the middle of the outback; vast and majestic, of course, but also unforgiving and inhospitable. I loved it; I hated it; I still had to conquer it.

STENCH

It had not occurred to me before I arrived in Australia just how much my ride across the country would be defined by wildlife. It had not been anywhere else, and I suppose I imagined Australia as a stark landscape where it was such an effort for living things to survive, that there just wouldn't be that many of them. I could not have been more wrong.

It was not just the flies and the mosquitoes. Spiders surrounded my tent each night, making my peeing ritual slightly more perilous than I would have liked; snakes, sometimes as long as three metres, lined every highway I rode, the victims of speeding motorists; I found live ones occasionally, too: a brown snake, a couple of baby taipans, but they never threatened me; huge swarms of locusts, hiding in the tall Mitchell grass along the edge of the road, jumped up when I passed so that I could barely see where I was going for mile after mile and had to wear my mosquito head net to protect myself from their sharp, cardboard-like wings.

It was never nice to see a dead animal by the roadside,
and this two-metre-long taipan snake was no exception.

One unexpected animal intruder was the cane toad. They are not native to Australia, having been introduced in 1935 in an attempt to control the native cane beetle, which was damaging sugar cane crops across Queensland and the Northern Territory in particular. One hundred and two toads were originally introduced; now their numbers are out of control, at more than two hundred million. They are huge, measuring up to twenty-five centimetres in length, and they are everywhere. Not only have they had a negligible effect on the cane beetle population, but they also spread disease that affects local biodiversity and, more worrying for the outback camper, pack a mean poison secreted in glands behind the ear that, although rarely responsible for human death, is apparently exceptionally painful. I was told by folk in every town to kill cane toads whenever I saw them, and was pleased to add another skill to my cricket bat's growing armoury.

My cricket bat came in handy for killing a cane toad that seemed keen to join me for a night in the tent.

But it was not only live animals that troubled me. In the sanitised world of a four-door saloon it is, I imagine, impossible to get a grasp on how much life, and by extension death, exists in the outback. I will never forget the stench of decay that clung to my nostrils almost constantly for more than two thousand miles in the saddle. I would be pedalling along quite happily when a fractional shift in wind direction brought the stink of some rotting animal or another. Cows, wild boars, sheep, snakes, eagles, rabbits, dingoes, wallabies, brumbies, camels (who knew there were camels in Australia?); none is immune to starvation or vehicle wheels. But by far the biggest cause of the incessant smell were dead kangaroos.

Carcasses of Australia's famous marsupials, in varying states of decay, line the highways of the outback in quite staggering numbers; ten, twenty, thirty, up to a hundred every mile. At the end of some days I had to camp close to a dead kangaroo because my legs were shot, I could not pedal any further, and there was simply no way to escape them.

A recently run-over kangaroo, one of thousands that lined my route.

Most cars that frequent isolated roads are fitted with 'roo bars' to minimise damage caused by a collision. But it is not cars that cause most kangaroo deaths in the outback. It's my old friend, the road train. Men of the bush will tell you it is a great modern technique for controlling the swelling population of kangaroos. 'They're vermin, mate; we'd be better off without 'em.' The road-train drivers stick on cruise control and if a poor kangaroo chooses to bounce across its path at the wrong moment, tough luck. Whereas the kangaroo feels the force of 150 tonnes of metal, the driver might not even notice he has hit one. The nostrels of the outback cyclist certainly do.

THE OUTBACK PUB

On the 330-mile stretch from Cloncurry to Longreach I came across a road-train driver fixing a puncture. We chatted for a while about the heat, the wind and cricket before he informed me that the Tattersalls Hotel, a couple of hundred miles down the road, was a 'bloody good spot for a decent feed, mate'.

So when I arrived in Winton three days later I pitched my tent next to a hair salon, asked the hairdresser (who had a wet-perm) to keep an eye on my kit, and headed for that very pub.

Winton is not short on history. The Combo Waterhole, a peaceful billabong lined by paperbark gums a few miles out of town, is the birthplace of Australia's unofficial national anthem, 'Waltzing Matilda', written by Banjo Patterson. The North Gregory Hotel, just down the road from the Tattersalls, is where the song was first performed live and there is now a fascinating Waltzing Matilda Museum in Winton, too: 'The only museum in the world dedicated solely to a song', I was informed by the proud elderly lady on reception.

The Tattersalls Hotel stood on a corner of the wide main street, wooden and imposing, lit by Victorian street lamps. A wide first-floor balcony ran around three sides of the building, with rooms running off it. It was an archetypal outback pub.

I walked into the main bar and a dozen pairs of eyes fixed on me. Winton was the sort of place where a stranger is big, but not necessarily good, news. An Australia vs Sri Lanka One Day International was showing on all of the five televisions in the bar.

''Ucken useless bastards, we got no hope against the Poms in the Ashes this time round,' the publican bemoaned.

'I've got to agree with you there,' I commented, before introducing myself.

In most countries I never liked to talk about my journey unnecessarily, but in Australia I quite enjoyed telling people that an Englishman cared so much about his country's cricketing fortunes that he had cycled all the way around the world to watch them triumph. And I often got a good reaction; Australians are nothing if not good sports. By the time I had told my story to the publican, Paul, and the few locals propping up the bar, I seemed to have won them round.

'You're mad as a cut snake, mate, I'll give you that. You won't pay for another drink in my pub that's for sure, and hats off to yers if you make it out of town tomorrow after the nectar we're gonna get down ya throat tonight.' I did not doubt his intentions.

Over the course of the next few hours we chatted freely at the bar, mainly about cricket, agreeing that the Australian team was indeed on an awful run of results and that the English were quickly becoming heavy favourites to retain the upcoming Ashes, despite having not won in Australia since 1987. Locals came and went, each propping up the bar for an hour or two before staggering off home again, and each as friendly and open as the next. To each one the publican introduced me as the 'mad Pommie bastard on a pushie'. I took it in the endearing, typically Australian way in which it was meant.

Once we had talked enough cricket, the locals turned to subjects ranging from Australia's lack of ancient architecture, party-line telephones in the bush and the key role 'Remittance Men' played in the pioneering days of the early twentieth century (often the black sheep of an English family, so-called 'Remittance Men' were sent abroad and paid to stay there). I was pleased to be able to show off my knowledge of one particular Remittance Man, Tom Cole, author of *Hell West and Crooked*.

Later on, as slurring replaced chatting, the Australian government came in for a hiding: 'Dunno why we gotta have a bloody sheila running the country anyways; it's a bloody embarrassment.' The weather was next, and each and every one at the bar agreed that I should not ride out of town the next morning because 'She'll be a bloody hot one tomorrow'. I felt like telling them every day since I'd landed in Darwin had been a 'bloody hot one'.

Near closing I was forced to resign my status as the only foreigner in the bar. An attractive French girl walked in and got chatting straight away, introducing herself to me as 'Wind Flame', an unusual name apparently born from a spiritual experience her mother had had on the east coast of Australia in the 1960s. When I asked her what she was doing so far from anywhere particularly civilised, she told me she was a masseuse for the crew of the French version of the reality television show *Survivor*. They were filming about an hour off into the bush. It was a reminder just how desolate and remote the country was round there.

After closing time I staggered down the deserted main street to my tent and decided that Australian outback pubs were possibly my favourite drinking establishments in the world. I counted tens of them that I had already sampled: the Heartbreak Hotel in Cape Crawford, where I had met the police officer who left me a bag of food down the track; the Blue Heeler Hotel in Kynuna, where I drank and sung with the staff of a local cattle station, all in their glad rags on a day out enjoying the Melbourne Cup; the Walkabout Creek Hotel in McKinlay (population officially twenty, although the policeman and his family had left the week before I arrived, so it was down to fifteen), made famous by the film *Crocodile Dundee*, where I had got chatting to a couple of telecoms technicians who paid me $300 for a day's work and told me if I didn't come and visit them on the east coast when I was done pedalling then I was a 'bloody bastard'.

The pubs all seemed to cherish their heritage as refuges where the tough early settlers could get together and have a beer; they exemplified the traits of 'mate-ship', toughness and giving people a fair go that gave the outback its reputation in the days when journeying across the rugged centre of Australia was far tougher than it is these days. In England most old-fashioned pubs have succumbed to the march of time. I reckon it will be a while before Australian outback pubs do the same.

The following morning, burdened with the worst hangover I had had since a night on cocktails in Singapore, I cycled my unloaded bicycle down the main street and, seeing Paul the publican, stopped to say hello.

'Feeling a bit groggy this morning this end, mate, how about you?' I asked him as he wiped off last night's mess from the tables on the veranda.

'Aaah, not feelin' too bad as it goes,' he replied. 'You a visitor in town are yers?'

I was slightly perplexed. We had, after all, spent several hours chatting at the bar the previous night. 'Yeh, I'm visiting. I'm cycling through on my way to the Ashes. We had a couple of beers at the bar last night.'

Paul looked at me, embarrassed, before slinking inside with a simple, 'Good on ya, good luck, mate.' He did not have a clue who I was, and it occurred to me that perhaps he was a publican for good reason.

Just as he ducked inside, I jumped back on the bike and rode it to the town's Greyhound bus stop. I had spent forty-seven of the past fifty-three weeks cycling alone, making progress at my own steady pace towards what I consider to be sport's greatest rivalry. As I sat waiting for the bus to arrive I realised that I had not given much thought to the fact that from a few moments' time, my adventure as I knew it would come to an end.

When the bus did eventually roll in, half an hour behind schedule, I was just pleased to see my new companion's face. It was strange; we had met briefly in Budapest, then again in Belgrade, but ever since had only got to know each other on Skype and by email. Although I knew he enjoyed cycling and was slowly warming to the gentle charms of a game called cricket, I knew little else about him.

LEASE OF LIFE

Since we had met all those months earlier, on a bitter Budapest morning pedalling towards the Serbian border, László had promised that he would try his best to join me for the final leg of my ride. Having invested so much time and effort, not to mention money, into getting the film off the ground, he was desperate to document my final few weeks on film himself.

I encouraged him, partly because he had been so good to me, and partly because I wanted it to happen; but I never thought it would. I suppose I thought his plans would be dashed by his new family life, or work responsibilities, or funding; or just a diminishing enthusiasm for my ride. I would not have blamed him.

But I should have known better. László had already proved himself to be a man who made things happen by finding tens of film-makers around the world to document my journey. Once he got involved in Cycling to the Ashes, he was not about to let go.

When he did finally send me an email saying he had booked a flight to Brisbane and was taking a twenty-four-hour bus journey to join me, I could not have been happier. The only proviso, he said, was that when we reached Brisbane I would not force him to watch too much cricket, and that after a couple of days at The Gabba he could take Bori down the east coast of Australia for a well-deserved, belated honeymoon. I had no arguments.

Within a couple of hours of his arrival in Winton we were out on the open road, pedalling alongside each other, getting to know each other and catching up on all that had happened since Budapest. It was the first of twenty days we would spend together in outback Queensland.

Me and László riding out of Winton.

On a cattle grid a few miles south of town we rested our bicycles against the railing, sat down and planned out our route and a rough schedule. We had 850 miles to cover in just under three weeks. Fifty-two miles a day, with four rest days, would get us to Brisbane in time for the Ashes. We would ride the exact same route through outback Queensland that László had taken on the bus, but in the other direction. We agreed, therefore, that it was lucky he had slept all the way to Winton.

I knew fifty-two miles a day would be far harder than it sounded, but for now I just relished having company once again. From the off, I found László's enthusiasm for the outback infectious. He had never been anywhere even similar; had not even begun to imagine the scale of such a prodigious back country. The wispy, straw-coloured Mitchell grass that is prevalent in so much of the outback, and that stretched for hundreds of miles in all directions on the ride out of Winton, enthralled him. The road trains terrified him. The flies, snakes and spiders worried him; most of the wildlife astounded him. 'MAN, THIS PLACE IS LIKE JURASSIC PARK . . .!' he screamed as hundreds of kangaroos bounded alongside us for mile after mile; he stopped to film when a huge herd of wild camels trundled past and again when emus stood peering at us from the shade of a rare bush. He posted the films online and all his friends back in Hungary seemed amazed by what he was seeing and doing.

Since leaving Brunette Downs the outback had ceased to charm me. I had grown cynical, tired of riding endless stretches of bitumen, tired of road trains and flies, cooking for myself and eating on my own, exhausted by unrelenting headwinds and a landscape that seemed not to change from day to day. All I saw was a road that would eventually spit me out into a cricket stadium in Brisbane. I had ridden for so long, and was so close to the end, that I had lost sight of the fact that in just a few weeks I would not be cycling to the Ashes any more, that life would return to normal again and that all I would have would be memories.

László's arrival reminded me that I was lucky to be doing what I was doing, and that the outback, far from being a stark, empty wilderness, was a rich land packed with endless diversity.

I wished László had been with me in India; perhaps he would have helped me cope better.

QUEENSLAND HOSPITALITY

About seventy miles before Longreach we camped under our mosquito nets, in fleeces to protect ourselves from the cold night air, staring up at a sky that was the equal of the one I had seen in Sudan's Nubian Desert. As then, I struggled to imagine friends back home under the same sky. Most of them would have trudged to and from the same railway station, in and out of the same office every day since I had been in Sudan; since I had left home even. That lifestyle and that place seemed so far away now. Over the past thirteen months I had seen and done so much, learned more about the world than I could possibly have done staring at a computer screen at my desk. I knew that that life was not for me and I felt lucky to have made the break, cut my ties and pedalled off in search of skies like the ones in Sudan and the outback.

At sunrise we were back on the road again, bound for Longreach, one of Australia's most famous cattle and sheep centres. Nature bestowed on the area some of the most prodigious grazing country in Australia, and it has been the basis of the town's livelihood since it was founded in 1887. We were excited to see what it was like.

Warm hospitality from strangers was a feature of my ride across all four continents. It tended to be unconditional, especially in Islamic countries; I do not mean to belittle such kindness when I say that, in many countries, I got the sense that it was offered out of a sense of duty rather than a desire to meet a new person.

In Australia it was slightly different. I felt I had to earn my right to decent hospitality by showing I was a reasonable, or 'fair dinkum', bloke. It felt more normal; more like it would have been at home, albeit far easier. I had taken on the challenge and succeeded a few times, generally in bars across the outback. But my greatest piece of luck in this regard came when I met a lady called Joy McClymont back at the bar of the Heartbreak Hotel in Cape Crawford. She had offered me a bed and a feed if and when I made it to Longreach. She and her husband, she said, lived 'just outside of town'.

Five weeks later, it was dark when László and I arrived at a petrol station on the outskirts of Longreach. I called Joy and, to my relief, she picked up. I reminded her who I was.

'I've got a Hungarian mate cycling with me now, but we'd still love to take you up on that offer of a bed for the night if you'll have us,' I told her over a crackling line.

Joy laughed. 'Course I remember you, well done for making it! But I'm afraid you'll have to wait until tomorrow. I'm in town, and besides, I live on a station a couple of hundred miles down a dirt track; takes a few hours to get there even by car.'

It turned out that Joy, like all outback Australians, considered living in the middle of precisely nowhere to be 'just outside of town'. Still on the phone, my mind turned towards finding a decent place to pitch our tents.

'But I'm sure my mates wouldn't mind if you came along to a barbie they're hosting tonight, and we can find you a place to sleep no worries,' Joy offered. 'I'll get Macca to come and pick you up.'

Ten minutes later László and I had introduced ourselves to Macca, or Mary-Ann Ringrose, and were following her Holden through the wide, deserted streets of Longreach to the edge of town where we stopped at a beautiful white washboard property surrounded by open fields of high Mitchell grass. A couple of dozen horses grazed beyond a low wooden fence. We pitched our tents in the garden beneath a wide veranda, killed a couple of cane toads that were lurking nearby and headed with Macca to the barbecue.

It was always a shock reaching a town after days in the bush, and arriving at a barbecue where there were a couple of hundred guests was particularly daunting. But it was a welcome change. Most of the guests seemed to have driven (some had even flown) in from across Queensland. There were stockmen, flying doctors, station managers, rodeo clowns, station owners, accountants, lawyers; we seemed to have lucked upon Queensland's society set. Most were dressed in the outback uniform of checked shirt, Wrangler jeans and cowboy boots, while László and I wore the only clothes we had; filthy rags more suited to hot, dusty days in the saddle. We may have looked out of place, but we were made to feel more than welcome. After a few beers some of the men got into some fairly incessant Pommie-bashing, but I enjoyed the banter, particularly as most of it was cricket-based and I was confident our boys would beat the Australians in a few weeks' time anyway.

Joy McClymont (centre) outside the Heartbreak Hotel in
Cape Crawford, where I met her.

By the end of the night we had several phone numbers and email addresses for people who lived in towns along the length of our route through Queensland; we were told if we didn't take them up we were stupid, so we agreed to. It was a barbecue that we were both delighted to have attended because it changed our ride across Queensland.

László and I spent a couple of nights in the home of Mary-Ann and Bill Ringrose. I spoke at the school their kids went to, about my ride and about the Australian outback in particular; László and I were interviewed live on ABC Longreach, the local radio station (apparently László was the first Hungarian ever to appear), and I got called a cricket tragic again; we played my only game of cricket in outback Australia, a hit on the Ringrose lawn while their dog ran about trying to avoid cane toads. When we left, we were sad to say goodbye, but promised to keep in touch.

On the way out of town a journalist from the *Courier Mail* joined us to get some information on my ride. The piece appeared in the paper the next day.

Yesterday he left Longreach in western Queensland for the final 750 miles of his journey through Roma, Toowoomba and the Glass House Mountains to Brisbane. To many people that journey alone is a ride to the moon. To him it will be like scooting off to the corner shop for a loaf of bread.

It was not like scooting off to the corner shop, but it was made easier by the hospitality we received over the final two weeks of our journey, all thanks to Joy, Bill, Macca and their generous friends. While days were long, and made longer by our desire to get as much of my final few days filmed as possible, most nights we were provided somewhere safe to sleep.

On the first day out of Longreach we were stopped by Hutch, a rodeo clown we had met at the barbecue a few days earlier. He told us that although his place wasn't 'much cop', we were welcome to stay. 'I won't be there, but the place is open; help yourselves. If you hear a plane in the morning, that's me. I'll be off mustering.'

He sped off, having left directions to his place, and when we arrived well after dark a few hours later, we slept on the floor of his sitting room and discovered that it really wasn't much cop after all. A dead bird, a dead mouse and several huge, dead grasshoppers were strewn across the room when we woke the next morning. Neither of us had any idea what had killed them. Still, we were grateful to Hutch for putting us up.

Towards Tambo we noticed slight changes in the land. There were more trees, more kangaroos (live ones) and the grass in the plains was higher. Horses, rather than cattle, roamed vast paddocks. It was lovely country to ride through, but progress was still slow because of the headwinds.

A big sign marked our arrival in the town.

WELCOME TO TAMBO
THE OLDEST TOWN IN CENTRAL WESTERN
QUEENSLAND
SETTLED 1863
SHIRE POPULATION: 710
TOWN POPULATION: 400
SIZE OF SHIRE: 10,308 SQ KMS
CLIMATE: COLD WINTERS, HOT SUMMERS

It summed up outback Queensland quite nicely. Big place, few people, extreme climate. From beneath the sign we called another of Bill and Macca's friends, Susie Swanson. She had no idea we were passing through. 'No worries, I'm not home but the house is open. Help yourselves and I'll see ya tonight.' Like Hutch and so many other Queenslanders, Susie never locked her house. In fact, there were not even any locks on the doors; no windows either, just mosquito nets. I guessed the communities were so tight-knit, and the distances between them so vast, that a thief would struggle to go unnoticed and would most likely be caught before he made it to the next town.

Queensland hospitality was like nowhere I had ever been before. For a Londoner who had never spoken to his neighbour in the three years we had lived next to each other, it was all very strange and I got a real sense of a community that extends not just from one neighbour to the next, but across hundreds of miles of remote bush. But while we might have been treated to some tremendous outback hospitality, Queensland's status as 'The Sunshine State' was seriously threatened. The last couple of weeks were characterised by heavy rains and storms that simply refused to abate. I had bought a full set of waterproofs in Longreach because I had been warned the rains were on the way, but they were non-breathable and made me sweat too much so I had to be happy getting wet.

The rain slowed our progress; that, our desire to film as much as we could and the increasing press coverage. The reach of the *Courier Mail* article was astonishing. At times it felt like almost every driver who passed stopped to offer some sort of encouragement or refreshment after reading about us in the paper. A few other local papers picked up on the story, too. In most towns the local ABC reporter got in touch to ask for the Ashes prediction of an 'English cricket tragic'. I always said it would be 3-1 in favour of the English, and, far from being booted out of each studio, my predictions were met with approval. Not even the Australians were backing their team on recent form. International stations and media outlets got in touch, too. The *Sun* ran a piece calling me a 'Barmy Englishman', the *Daily Express*, the *Telegraph*, London's *Metro*, TalkSport and Radio 5 Live all seemed interested to hear how I was getting on.

One evening I received a call from the *Today* programme, Australia's biggest television breakfast show. They wanted to interview me in a studio in Dalby. When I told them that was impossible because I was in the back of beyond, they sent an early morning limousine to pick us up, drove us two hours to Dalby and, when the interview was done, drove us back again.

All the media attention might have been fun but I was getting increasingly worried about reaching Brisbane in time. We put in huge days, pedalling frantically into ferocious headwinds and rainstorms. Often we pedalled until nine or ten o'clock at night and set up camp in the pouring rain, soaked through.

László and I had grown as close as brothers in a short space of time on the road together and, most of the time, I was pleased to have him with me; to share the misery when a headwind stopped us dead in our tracks, or the elation when a new view unfolded. But occasionally we got cross and impatient with each other. I blamed myself; I was so used to being on my own that I often ignored László when he was tired, or had a go at him when he wanted to stop and film. 'I just want to make it to Brisbane!' I would say, and it was unfair. It might have made good film footage, but he had given so much to my ride that I should have shown more gratitude.

About a week from Brisbane, as we cycled out of Miles and away from our latest host, we were confronted with a different type of outback hospitality. From behind us we heard a car and, turning around, noticed that it was some girls we'd tried to stop the day before. We began riding in the middle of the road to get them to stop, and this time it worked. Carly and Naomi had been visiting friends in Roma and were on their way back to the Gold Coast. László asked if he could do some filming from their car boot and the girls agreed so, for a few miles, I rode along behind their car, talking about what I thought of cycling in the outback, and about cycling with László.

When we were done, I thanked the girls and waited by the side of the road while they gave László a lift back to his bicycle. When the car reached me again a few minutes later, Naomi jumped up through the sun roof, pulled off her top and bra and screamed 'WE LOVE YOU GUYS . . . YOU MADE OUR DAY!'

Needless to say, Naomi made my day, too. She befriended us both on Facebook and followed the remainder of our progress towards Brisbane.

With Carly and Naomi.

ARRIVAL

László is up early making tea. I can hear him getting his bags packed and camera kit ready. I just stare at the roof of my tent, watching a large ant make its way from one corner of the mosquito net to the other. That's a long journey for an ant. I know how he feels.

I had spent my penultimate day on the road cycling alone. I asked László if he minded and he said he did not. I wanted one last full day to myself, to feel how I had felt most days since leaving home thirteen and a half months earlier; to feel alone. Despite the prospect of renewed contact with friends, family and the real world, I knew I would miss it.

I spent the whole day on the verge of tears. As I descended the Great Dividing Range out of Toowoomba with ninety miles to go and stared out at the coastal plain that would deliver me to my final destination, I cast my mind back over the past year and the path I had cycled across four continents. Although my status as a traveller meant that I was not able to delve deep into a culture like someone who visited for an extended period, I had been given glimpses of life in all its myriad guises.

I recalled Frank, the young Belgian who gave me some apples and a rogue cabbage on my only morning in France; Rasmus, who set me a treasure hunt on my way out of Frankfurt; my first evening in Turkey, cycling into the former capital, Edirne, to the sound of the sunset call to prayer; four weeks of getting naked to dry my clothes in countless Anatolian petrol stations; dusk encounters with wild dogs and the night-time howls of wolves beside the River Jordan; cycling out of Damascus in the snow; sleeping under the Milky Way in the Nubian Desert; the Eritrean refugees we stayed with in Khartoum; dancing with a TV star and her bodyguard in a Khartoum record store; pedalling into Dhaka among 300,000 cycle rickshaws; my first view of the Bay of Bengal; sleeping in army barracks, police stations, mosques, churches and shops; tasting countless national dishes; practising my Laughter Club moves with a bunch of ousted communists; Ramadan in Malaysia; sailing into Darwin harbour after seven days at sea. Finally, I remembered the past seven weeks cycling across the vast expanse of Australia.

I could still remember almost every day, although I could barely believe that it was me who had lived each one. During my final peanut butter sandwich lunch for a while, I received an email from one of the members of the Go Green Initiative who had cycled out of Hyderabad with me.

23 November 2010
Hello Mr Oli Broom,

*Please excuse the grammatical errors in my writing. Let me
introduce myself. My name is Girish and want to Thank You
for all the Inspiration.*

*I'm proud to have cycled along with you, Krishna, Richie
and others for some distance while you were on your way from
Hyderabad to Vijayawada. It was one of the hottest scorching
Sundays when the temperature was hovering around 53
degrees C.*

*I was so excited to have cycled with you on my cycle
that the heat really did not matter and I thoroughly enjoyed
the experience and will cherish it throughout my lifetime.
Thank You Oli for the inspiration, here is how you changed
my life.*

*After I met you and read your blogs, following you
through your journey, I was getting inspired every day and I
could not wait to read your blogs and see the pictures. Over
the time as I followed you through your journey I decided to
make a decision and enjoy life and do things I would love to
do. This inspiration lead me to quit my boring job as a
Legal Advisor in a Financial Services company and made
me to attempt some things that I always cherished to do
besides cycling. I'm enjoying my life and learning to do
some new stuff which I love to do every day. Life is
beautiful.*

*You are one of the inspirations and a major one at
attempting to do things which is not very common in India;
we like to live life in a safe zone. You are the man Oli who
lives life to the fullest and taking life as it comes one step at
a time enjoying the moment.*

Thank You Oli and wish you all the best.

*PS: I would like to personally have one copy of your
autographed book please. If you make any documentaries
of your journey 'Cycling to the Ashes' please do remember*

to send us the details of the same and we would love
to show it to the members of Hyderabad Cycling Club.
  May God bless you.
  Wish you all the success, happiness, peace &
Nirvana in life.

Girish

I had set off from London for largely personal reasons. I wanted to escape a stale office environment, I wanted an adventure, I wanted to see places I had never seen before, cities like Istanbul and Damascus, deserts like the Sahara and the outback. I wanted to learn about cricket in strange places around the world, to meet the people who made those places what they were, and to test myself on a bicycle journey of magnitude. I wanted a lot, and I had been given a lot.

Although my ride had turned into one that was characterised by incredible kindness and hospitality from strangers, I rarely considered that what I was doing might have a lasting effect on other people; that they might take more than an ounce of inspiration from it and change something in their lives. I felt proud to have touched Girish's life, and humbled that he had felt inclined to let me know. That ride, on my penultimate day of the journey, was one of the most emotional days of my life and I was grateful to László for letting me enjoy it alone.

Now, on the morning of my last day, I felt positive and excited about finishing my journey; a journey that had defined my existence since I had come up with the idea almost two years earlier. It was 24 November 2010; 412 days since I left Lord's on my bicycle. The Ashes were to begin in Brisbane the next day and, perhaps to celebrate the arrival of the English, it was raining.

Pouring, in fact. The rain was pounding the roof of my tent, which was pitched in a field next to a warehouse in Plainland, thirty miles west of Brisbane; an undistinguished place to spend the last of so many nights under canvas.

One more day, I told myself; then life would return to normal and I could forget about cycling for a while.

László and I rode our bicycles to a nearby café where we ate pies and met a car full of friends: George, an old colleague who was out to follow the Ashes; Sampson, who had joined me in Istanbul and was now out in Australia as part of the Ashes media pack; and Bori, László's wife. It was great to see them and it brought a premature taste of what normality might feel like.

Back on the road, riding alone, the rain continued to lash down and it mixed with sweat to pour down my face and sting my eyes. Despite riding down off the Great Dividing Range the previous day, the hills continued but, for once, I did not mind. The roads were smooth tarmac, of course, but now they meandered through densely populated suburban Brisbane. Roundabouts, traffic lights and buildings combined to create a civilised scene as I rode past, adrenalin kicking in.

Drivers slowed as they passed and, seeing the sign on the back of my bicycle, encouraged me to complete my journey, just like their counterparts had in every other country; the difference now was that I knew I was going to make it. Through Chuwar, Anstead, Kenmore I pedalled, stopping briefly for a short ferry ride across a wooded tributary of the Brisbane River. I had never been to Brisbane before and it looked like a beautiful city. Not for the first time, it struck me that it was my destination by default because the first Ashes Test match was taking place there. But now, because of that twist of fate, whenever I thought of Brisbane in the months and years to come, my mind would go on a journey of its own, through Europe, Turkey, Sudan, India and the rest. I liked that thought.

László continued to follow in the car with the camera trained on me, waiting for some final tears. But they did not come. Adrenalin carried me now and I felt nothing but relief and excitement that I was about to achieve what I had set out to do fourteen months before.

The sun showed its face for the first time that day when I reached the Brisbane River and began weaving through the city's skyscrapers. Maybe they weren't skyscrapers, but they seemed like it after where I had been. László and the others drove ahead. I was on my own again, left to enjoy my final few minutes in the saddle. I stopped on a steep incline for a slug of water and a convertible pulled up alongside me.

'You the crazy Pommie bloke I saw on the *Today* programme?' the young man in the driver's seat asked.

'Yeah, possibly,' I replied, not knowing if there had been more than one of us interviewed recently.

'Good on ya,' he congratulated me.

I climbed the rest of my last hill and thought to myself that I was not crazy at all. Crazy would have been conceiving of the idea to cycle all the way to Australia and not giving it a go in the first place.

When the floodlights came into view there was nothing but a short downhill stretch to complete. 'Don't get run over now,' I thought, as a truck hurtled by.

Freewheeling, I leaned down over my handlebars for the last time, took a deep breath and looked back up again to see the smiling faces of László, Sampson, George, Bori, Bill Ringrose from Longreach, Phil Spray – my old school cricket coach – and, lurking behind them in a pair of dark glasses, Naomi, my own personal outback flasher.

And there in the mêlée, arms aloft and jumping up and down, were Mum and Dad, who had left England thirty-six hours earlier and were now standing outside Gate 6 of the Brisbane Cricket Ground, where I had wanted to be for so long.

'You've made it!' Mum said.

She was right. I had, and it felt very good indeed.

The Gabba – I made it.

EPILOGUE

Things did not start well for England. Andrew Strauss was caught for a third-ball duck and memories of the 2006–07 series, when England had got trounced 5-0, seeped uncomfortably into the consciousness of every English supporter inside the ground. Even Billy Cooper, the Barmy Army's resilient trumpeter, was silent. Australia bowled England out for 260, and by the end of the day they were in a commanding position.

On the second and third days Australia built themselves a first-innings lead of 221 runs. They looked like going 1-0 up in the series. But then the fight-back began. In England's second innings Strauss and Alastair Cook put on 188 for the first wicket. Strauss made his nineteenth Test hundred and Cook went on to score an unbeaten 235; Jonathan Trott 135. England eventually declared on 517–1 and the match was drawn.

England won the second Test in Adelaide, thanks largely to another hundred from Cook and a double from Kevin Pietersen. The third Test was in Perth, three thousand miles away. I caught the Indian Pacific railway from Adelaide, a forty-two-hour journey across the Nullabor Plain. England played poorly and lost. The series stood at 1-1. I found a bloke from Nottingham who was driving back to Melbourne for the fourth Test. On Boxing Day the magnificent Melbourne Cricket Ground was bursting with just shy of 100,000 cricket fans, most cheering vehemently for the home team. But England, and particularly James Anderson and Chris Tremlett, bowled superbly, restricting Australia to 98 in their first innings. They never recovered. Within four days England had gone 2-1 up in the series with one match to play, meaning they were unable to lose and had therefore retained the Ashes.

On the day after the fourth Test had finished I represented Marylebone Cricket Club against Melbourne Cricket Club at the Melbourne Cricket Ground. Before I had got the chance to have a bowl, I found myself running in from deep square leg and diving to attempt a catch off the bowling of the former England off-spinner, John Emburey. My finger caught the turf and snapped, resulting in three weeks in a cast. So it was with one arm that I headed to Sydney, where England went one better, thrashing Australia again to win the series 3-1.

Both my bicycle ride and the Ashes had turned out just the way I had hoped but that did not stop the sense of anti-climax that I felt when they were over. Cycling to the Ashes had been the extent of my world for so long that I felt like I had lost a good friend. Even as I celebrated England's victory with friends in a Sydney bar, I longed to be on the open road in Turkey or Sudan or India or Australia, arms outstretched, hands leaning on a couple of dirty socks wrapped around handlebars, bum planted firmly in saddle, legs turning gently and wheels taking me onwards, towards another night's sleep in an unfamiliar place. I yearned to feel the bite of a cold headwind or the thrill of a winding descent. But it was all over and it was time to go home; time for the next adventure to begin.

ACKNOWLEDGEMENTS

Not long after I began to plan my journey, in early 2009, I realised it was going to be far from a solo and unsupported adventure. Writing this book has been much the same.

Firstly, thanks to all those who worked on the book: my agent, Jon Elek at AP Watt, Matt Phillips, Rowan Yapp, Louise Court and others at Yellow Jersey Press. A special thanks to my editor, Caroline McArthur. You have calmly guided me through the writing process, and I am exceptionally grateful.

I would also like to extend sincere thanks to the following people and organisations for all sorts of help, advice and support before, during and after my trip (grovelling apologies to those I have missed out):

Will Brown at Betfair, without whom the journey would never have begun; Marcus Codrington Fernandez at Mongoose Cricket, for helping to keep me on the road and stocked with cricket bats; Hugh Morris, Maria O'Donoghue, Andrew Walpole and Rob Johnson at the England and Wales Cricket Board; Marylebone Cricket Club; James and Katherine Taylor; Sam Collins; Andrew Strauss; Bear Grylls; Rachael Heyhoe-Flint; David Gower; Peter Hayter; Alison Mitchell; Claire Taylor; Michael Vaughan; Adam Mountford; Jonathan Agnew; the late Christopher Martin-Jenkins and all at *Test Match Special*; Daniel Norcross and the *Test Match Sofa* team; Simon Hughes; Tim Brooke-Taylor; Andrew Miller; James Gillson, Shona Langridge and Tom Rigby at The Lord's Taverners; Paul Dimond and Geoff Raisman at the British Neurological Research Trust; Craghoppers; Eric and Pam Michel at ClipTaxi; Nick Chapallaz at ESRI UK; Santos Bikes;

Alasdair Scadding at MSG Bikes; David Roberts Physiotherapy; the *Wisden Cricketer*; Sanoodi, Buff Wear; the Royal Over-Seas League; Merril; Dazer; Everyday Hero; Solar Technology International; Garage Tek UK; Capitalize; Tilley; Rob Clegg at Carderoo; The Tamarind Group; the North Australian Cattle Company; Dick Slaney at Elders; Melanie Chevalier at Creative Culture; Jock Mullard at the Radleian Society; Knight Frank LLP; Tom Wharton at Barrington Ayre Shirtmaker & Tailor; Cricket Australia; Queensland Cricket; The Bangladesh Cricket Board; The Cricket Club of India; The Head Partnership; Ben Southall and everyone at Tourism Queensland; Henry Kelly at BBC Radio Berkshire; Philip Brown; Mike and Tessa Padfield; Michael Asberry; Nick Hoyle; Chris Austin and family; Hannah Durden; Helen Bryer; Snehit Vemulapati; Ed Clark; Harry and Francesca Bowman; Peggy Hoyle; Alex Bradley; Clare Skinner; Cath Brazier; Rob Hillman; Marine Casalis; Jonathan Norman; Sameer Panchangam; Gus Williamson; Margaret Price; Chris and Liz Leakey; Joy McClymont; Danny Kennedy; Dan Martin; Natalia Higgins; Rory Allan; Sanjana Sarkar; Bjørn Heidenstrøm; Abbie MacAndrew; Gemma Francis; Jules and Alex Fuller; Jill Dean; Anthony and Katie Campbell; Hannah Marsland; Ayşegül Albe Özdemir; Tanya Dickson; Guy and Tracey Coleman; Isabel Parker; Prue Button; Samantha Whitaker; Gareth Walsh; Chris Padfield; Syd Daftary; Dave Strachan; Rachel Fitzgerald; Camilla Skov Larsen; Haris Brasidas Deutsch; Vladimir Ninković and the Serbian cricket fraternity; Saif Rehman and his band of Bulgarian cricketing brothers; Lucy Howkins; Rob Lean; Olly Barratt; Deniz Tapkan; Gozde Efe; Di Mackey; Michael Dalton-Smith; Batian Craig; Becky Hooley; Krissie Ducker; Alan & Lynsey Mann; Alastair Humphreys; Alex & Lou Eventon; Claire Leon; Kaye Cousins; the Hollingsworth family; Anne Karine Thorbjørnsen; Max and Marthe Southall; Angus Bell; Ben Schofield; Brian Fell; Charlie Goldsmith; David Wilson; the Butler family; Ed Craig; Gabriella Romano for the song; Georgie Lloyd Parry; Tom Kevill-Davies (AKA The Hungry Cyclist); Jamie and

Caroline Thomas; Jill Maxwell; Elizabeth Ammon; Martin O'Connor; the Reynaert family; Peter Buscall; Vinodini Carapyen; Uday Raj; Avinash Raj; Keith Adderley and all at Temple Golf Club; Laura Borthwick; Baldy; Will Symonds and family; Taco; Mark Singleton; Simon Doggart; Andy Baker; Chris Masterman and the staff and pupils at Caldicott School; Turkeys for Life; Mike Bellhouse; Neo Khama; the Broom family; Nicky Gilmour; Ollie Brett; Bori Jozsa; George Calvocoressi; Philip Spray; the Ringrose family; Ral Gilmour; Richard Holdsworth; Rod Gilmour; Roger and Sarah Mawle; Ross Colson; Ross Williams; Alex and Shelley Vlassopulos; Noel and Laura Gallagher; A-Rod; J-Rod; Ebony Dee Cheyne; the Macwhirter family; Katy Darlow; the Emerson family; Aman and Kate Sharma; Tim Abraham; Mary Graham; Nikki and Edo Shale; Rupert Henson; Serena Tommasino; Jarrod Kimber; the Cripps family; Stuart Fraser; Sunil Malkani; Mike Van der Gucht; Natalia and Jojo Schrader; Tiffany Broome; Tim Mitzman; Tim Pitman; Tom van Poucke; the Blewett family; the Moore family; Will Little; Will Luke and Olive Jenkins.

Although I was alone on the road for 358 days, a few kind souls did keep me company in the saddle. Thank you to James, Serpil, John, Duncan, Dicky, Lindsey, Becca, Syd, Paddy Robinson, Sammy and Kate Jenkins, Charlie Van der Gucht, Kate Hudson, Alex Traill, Alex Thom, David Edmed, Katie Rigby, John Corby, Jimbob Lewis, Lizzie Hollick, Dan Coulson and Krishna Prasad Mandava.

One person not only joined me for three weeks at the end of my journey, but poured his heart and soul into finding film-makers around the world to record my ride. László, your determination, both with a camera and on the road, was an inspiration. I am grateful that, because of you, I have an archive of footage to rekindle the memories in old age. I hope we can watch it in 50 years' time, over a batch of home-made Hungarian cider.

On the road I met thousands of people, some for a few seconds, others for much longer. From the old ladies who gave me fruit on the side of the road in Serbia, to Muhammad, my rifle-toting friend in Atbara, I was constantly amazed by the kindness shown to me by strangers. You kept me smiling all the way to Australia and have continued to sustain me through the long, often painfully drawn-out process of writing this book. My heartfelt thanks goes to you all.

I would like to thank Clemmie. Your patience, optimism and sense of humour are the reasons I got this book finished. Your thesaurus brain wasn't half useful either. Thank you.

Finally, Mum, Dad and Annabel, thank you for everything. This book is for you, and for Peggy.

Readers are welcome to get in touch with me on oli@olibroom.com or via my website www.olibroom.com